THE FACTORS RESPONSIBLE FOR LOW EDUCATIONAL ACHIEVEMENT AMONG AFRICAN-CARIBBEAN YOUTHS

Cajetan Iwunze

authorHOUSE®

AuthorHouse™ UK Ltd.
500 Avebury Boulevard
Central Milton Keynes, MK9 2BE
www.authorhouse.co.uk
Phone: 08001974150

First published by AuthorHouse 10/13/2009

ISBN: 978-1-4490-2710-0 (sc)

This book is printed on acid-free paper.

CONTENTS

Abstract

YEAR AFTER YEAR, at the end of every annual period of study many black children will leave school without any qualifications. Different professionals put it down to one factor or another based on their own perspectives. Restricting it to one particular thing is a narrow way of identifying the problem. There is no one factor responsible for low academic achievement among young African-Caribbean people. In other words, there is no universal definition for this intellectual calamity among these young people. Some historians' believe the problem is associated to their history which forms the grid by which African-Caribbean are seen as service users, good for nothing who cannot become service providers. Some Social Scientists put it down to family composition and low income. Some perceive it or see the problem of these young men as "Unemployment" and lack of access to the labour market while to some, the problem occurs and persists due to lack of education, discrimination and political culture. All these factors identified, form the nucleus of low educational achievement levels among young people of African-Caribbean origin. The reason why so many African-Caribbean people are service users and not service providers is due to long time suppression beyond human imagination. They have the notion that the state uses repression as a means of social control because black colour is seen as highly infectious and is viewed as a disease British society does not want to catch. For that reason whenever a black person is seen walking on the street the some people in the society seem to become offended, the only way out of it becomes repression and exclusion from partaking in the freedom African-Caribbeans helped to fight and won. Institutional racism becomes embedded into the British way of life and educational system, as an instrument to achieve a permanent exclusion of African-Caribbean people from the economy. Because of economic exclusion and systematic oppression directed against African-Caribbean people, they find it difficult to give their children decent education and because they do not have adequate education themselves, they are not able to provide for their off springs with the necessities of life and consequently, the lives of these young children turn out to be a life of misery. In this Book, **chapter one** will look at the impact of Economic Lynching on African-Caribbean people. **Chapter two** will demonstrate how Repression contributed to low educational achievement among black youths. **In Chapter three** we shall illustrate how Unemployment helped to aid low educational achievement among African-Caribbean youths. **Chapter four** will show how educational system has contributed to low educational attainment. **Chapter Five** will explain how political culture has contributed to the problem by atomizing the black families into modern individualism. **Chapter six** will look at the new set of unwritten rules (moral code) concerning the acceptable standard of behavior from African-Caribbean people and how it has impoverished the black communities. **Chapter seven** will be the conclusion chapter focusing more on the consequences of British Political culture and it contribution to the low educational achievement among the African-Caribbean children.

Chapter One
Economic Lynching

Introduction

ONE OF THE factors responsible for low educational achievement among African-Caribbean youths is "economic lynching". Having said that, the phrase "economic lynching", sounds ambiguous without further explanation. For it to make sense to a lay person without any background of Political Economy, the term must be clarified further. The question now is what is lynching? Lynching here has two dimensions, (1) killing someone without the use of physical force such as through starvation, (2) killing someone with force by using an instrument. The former could be achieved through discrimination and the later through suppression, which we shall expand further in Chapter Two. In a simple definition, "economic lynching" is discrimination on the basis of skin colour, denying a certain group of people the right to earn a living because of their skin colour. Economic Lynching could be defined as treating someone differently when seeking employment because he or she is ascribed to a particular racial category. This could, in another sense, be defined as employing hostility which is biologically determined due to differences in physical appearance. Economic lynching is when someone is denied promotion to certain jobs or positions on the basis of his or her skin colour; Let us assume, for example, that Mr. A, is a brilliant lawyer and one of the most senior judges in the land. He is in line for promotion to the top job, Chief Justice of that Country, because the current Chief Justice is about to retire in 6months time. According to the rule of the game, Mr. A. is a natural successor to that position but Mr. A. happens to be African-Caribbean. When that 6months are up, Mr. B is appointed the Chief Justice instead of Mr. A the reason being that Mr. B. is White and due to the differences in physical appearance they think it is more appropriate for Mr. B. to become the next chief justice. Here the natural rule has been broken, Mr. A. has been denied this top job because he is ascribed to a particular racial category; this is economic lynching. Again, let us assume there is an economic down-turn and a lot of people are now claiming unemployment benefit and contributing nothing to the society. As the economy begins to improve and businesses start to create jobs, people are employed to fill the vacancies. Let us assume that the total vacancies created by these businesses so far are 300 jobs; however, out of these 300, only White people are employed. The African-Caribbean people who applied for the jobs were not taken on thereby forcing them to remain jobless even when they want to work; this is economic lynching. From this definition the picture of what "Economic Lynching" means has emerged. In a very simple term "it is a kind of behaviour in which a person is treated differently because he is attributed to a specific social group[1].

Justification of Economic Lynching

The question we have to ask then is "why is it that some people economically lynch others? To begin with, it is convenient to consider the reasons people advanced for behaving as they did. They may not always have been fully aware of what caused them to practise economic lynching, but in many cases they gave reasons which can serve as starting points. According to Barton, there are three kinds of response on the part of people he interviewed. He discovered that there is a wholesale rejection of African-Caribbean people with no attempt of justification[2]. This he called "emotional antipathy" which means strong hostility or opposition towards African-Caribbeans because some people in the society believe they are annoying and disgusting. These feelings degenerate to agitation against the community. However, "emotional antipathy" appears to be the least common motive for Economic lynching on the part of the people he questioned, although it may be more common than his surveys suggested because people influenced by this attitude may have concealed it during that research. Many white people, in defence of their actions, argued that they could not behave as they wished to "other people" (such as Eastern Europeans, Indians and Pakistanis) but would not accept African-Caribbean people in such capacities. Some maintained that economic lynching was justified because African-Caribbean people are uneducated. As a result of this they are higher risk than Whites and Asians, and more prone to accidents than the rest of British society[3].

Recently, John Snow made a programme about Immigration which was broadcast on channel 4 on the 26th September 2007 at 8pm. The shocking news was that among these immigrants from outside the EU, and when you categorize them according to countries Nigerians came on top, as the most educated when compared with other new members of EU. Yet Nigerians are the least likely to be employed which disproved the negative thinking that African-Caribbeans are uneducated and this is the cause of their economic lynching. Nonetheless, some went further to justify their actions by arguing that most African-Caribbean drivers are higher risk than Spanish motorists, although both had been driving in Britain for eight years. On that note, Barton imposed the question, "had there been any evidence that the African-Caribbean's are worse drivers (e.g. that they had been involved in more accidents?) Barton's research showed that, not to be the case. If there is evidence to prove that African-Caribbean people are worse drivers than their White counterparts, their analogy would not have been regarded as Economic Lynching. In this case however it is Economic Lynching because there is no official data to prove that African-Caribbean people are worse drivers than the White people, but rather what statistics has shown was that youths under 25's are more likely to have accidents than the older people. There is no place in the official figures that shows that African-Caribbean people have more accidents than their White counterparts. We are now beginning to see how economic lynching occurs when a person is treated

1   Stewart, R., (2001) Collin English Dictionary, Glasgow: Omnia Books Limited.
2   Berton, M., (1967) Race Relations, London: Tavistock.
3   Ghose, A., (1971) Editor, Tricontinental Outpost, Voice Of The Grassroots. Newsletter Issues 12 And 15, London 30" October.

differently when seeking employment or other social amenities such as housing services because he is ascribed to a particular racial category[4].

Judging from Barton's research, economic lynching is wide-spread in every part of British institutions including employment and housing as mentioned above. For example, in the early sixties, some white people do not want to work alongside African-Caribbean people, that does not mean that in the 21st Century something has changed but instead, the statistics are going down rather than up in other words some people do not want to work alongside African-Caribbean people and that is why there is a lot of hostility against them in British inner-cities[5]. So, when some politicians talk about crime, what they are saying is that they want African-Caribbean people removed from the street and the one of way to stop them working alongside British people is by imprisoning them[6] . Even though a proportion of British people claim they would accept non-white persons as workmates the percentage that would accept a Pakistani or an Indian as a workmate is higher than the proportion who would accept an African-Caribbean person as a workmate. The proportion of White people who would accept Asians as neighbours were again higher than those that would accept an African-Caribbean person, which suggests that the social relationships based on working close together with Asians is more acceptable than that of African-Caribbean people, which may be due to the reason that they have a lighter colour.

Figure1

Working along-side African-Caribbean People

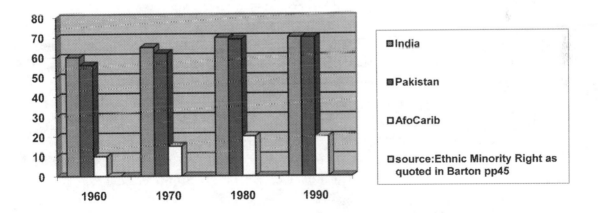

However, that is changing because of the Eastern Europeans coming into UK. The position of the Asians and their acceptability has been reassessed. As a result they are fighting back to maintain their economic

---

4   Narayan, R., (1976) GRASSROOTS Newspaper Volume 4. No. 8 SeptemberOct0ber, Cricklewood To Leeds -The Cross-Country Legal Conspiracy, London.

5   Angus, M., (2005) Exclusion and discrimination against the Minority: Metro newspaper

6   Etom, H., (2002) Racism: the New currency, Oxford: Oxford University Press.

position in the social hierarchy. They do not want the Eastern Europeans take away the privilege they have enjoyed for so long and they are prepared to do anything to secure it.

In housing, African-Caribbean people were not given places because of restrictions imposed on them. What that implies is that the justifications advanced by practitioners in housing goes far beyond what is rationally defensible. Many ethnic minority people (in the case of Africans, nearly three- quarters) have never applied for a flat to the council. Because the councils are inclined to regard African people as falling short of English standards of decorum and hygiene, but the recently arrived immigrant of whom this might be true are the ones least likely to be seeking houses from these councils. But Barton's critics argued that African-Caribbean peoples' inability to apply for housing to the council is cultural because they are 'closed up' communities who do not want other people to know what they are doing. Besides, it is only within their community that they learn the secret of home ownership even when they are not qualified to have them. In order to prove their point that there is no such thing as Economic Lynching, they impose the question "why is that ¾ of the housing in London, Birmingham, Bradford and Blackburn are owned by the Indians? Despite the criticism, it does seems stereotype ideas about unwelcome characteristics are extended to all ethnic minority people whatever their history, occupation, income and personality[7]. Some of the councils who practice economic lynching are determined to exclude African-Caribbean people from the economy by using colour as the sole criterion for evaluating their applications. Africans came out worse because they were economically lynched both in personal applications by their names, it is obvious where they come from. For a European or Asian it was the other way round[8]. The emotional significance of a strange skin colour could have be a major factor in explaining why the African-Caribbean people experienced twice as much economic lynching in housing as than a European and more when seeking low level employment. The main reasons advanced for economic lynching of the Indians could be cultural; whereas for African-Caribbean's, they were physical. Some critics argue that ethnic minority people in Britain cry out, "economic lynching" whenever they fail to get what they seek, whatever their qualifications[9]. This leads some writers to believe that accusations of economic lynching are unfounded: by stating that most British Businesses are run by Asians who also control most of the shops in Britain. They imposed the question, "if there is Economic Lynching how come Whites are relegated to the background when it comes to allocation of business premises[10]?" They may have got a point, but that does not wholly prove that Economic Lynching does not exist. For example, I went to apply for accommodation with the Haringey Council because my daughter decided to come and live with me after I have separated with her mother. They council told me to bring prove of parental responsibility, my passport, prove of address in the last five year, my pay slips, my bank statement, my daughter birth certificate, letter from her school showing attendance etc. I gave them all the information they requested for. One of the managers rang me on my phone on the 5th of October 2007, saying that the parental responsibility which I have handed in was not good enough that what they required from me was "full custody order" from the court. I went out and spoke to legal practitioners concerning the full custody order. They asked me why? I told them that I was living with my daughter in one room in a shared accommodation with other 6 other adults. They asked me where my ex-partner was and I told them "Coventry". And you were staying in London with your daughter? And I said "yes". Was she in school? "Yes", I replied. If you were living with your daughter and she was already in school what was the "full custody order" for? I then realise that the demand was

7   Race (1974) Towards Racial Justice, London Today Magazine. Volume 6 pp. 167-173
8   Berkin, C., (1980) Women War and Revolution, New York: Holmes and Meier,
9   Daniel, W., (1968) Race Discrimination and Prejudice, Harmonds: Penguin.
10   Daniel, W., (1969) Education and bigotry, Harmonds: penguin

a means to eliminate me because I am African-Caribbean. What the council was doing, was indirectly, urging me to declare a legal battle that would destroy my daughter including myself. It was then that I realise how the government policies may socially engineer the destruction of African-Caribbean people. This exclusionary measure is economic Lynching. Because they believe that I have come to take away their flats which are meant for Europeans.

This shows that economic lynching still exists. On that note, Daniel went on to investigate this economic lynching which some authors believe is unfounded. His findings pointed towards Barton's conclusion and hypothesized that there is, in reality, more economic lynching than would have been expected from calculations based upon the experience reported by the African-Caribbean people who were interviewed. He went on to suggest that sometimes economic lynching could exist even where the African-Caribbean person does not suspect it[11].

From a political standpoint, his two other findings evoked concern. Firstly, he pointed out that better educated African-Caribbean people experienced more economic lynching than when they were uneducated. He went further to elaborate on that by suggesting, that "as African-Caribbeans and their children acquired better qualifications and higher expectations they may experience not greater acceptance but more rebuffs[12]". He went on to argue, that awareness of economic lynching reinforced the tendency on the part of minorities to withdraw into their own communities and make integration progressively more difficult.

As a result of that, Daniel concluded that economic lynching was a problem in our society that needed to be tackled and for the British people to ascertain the level of this problem we needed to ask ourselves "how serious is this level of economic lynching in our society today?" Many might not believe it is very great if they compare it with the difficulties African-Caribbean immigrants often meet in Britain. If they rephrase it and put it this way "what significance has economic lynching been in this 21st century?" they may find the answer less comforting. If they ask what difference the prejudice of British people would make to their personal lives if their skin turned brown, they may like to reflect on the case of a Welshman, an ex – commando and former Services boxing champion, who used to live in a Dorset town. He suffered from a kidney disease which meant that he had to seek lighter work. The disease also darkened his skin so that he was mistaken for a black man. As a result he had experienced economic lynching[13]. Sometimes, he had been stopped on the street by strangers, who said something like: "You bloody wog, why do not you go back to the palm trees?", On another occasion when he applied for work as a sales representative in an insurance company the employer refused to interview him because he looked like a black man and was told that he looked like a monkey and could not get a job[14]. This treatment given to a British citizen would give one an insight into why economic lynching of African-Caribbean people is rampart.

Eventually, when Mr Welshman's incident was reported in the Observer. Mr Welshman was told that he was no longer to lose his home even though he could no longer keep up his mortgage repayments due to economic lynching he had experienced for looking black. As a result of this his local council bought

11   Daniel, W., (1970) Race discrimination and exclusion, London: Institute for Race Relation.

12   Humphrey, D., (1971) Because they are Black, Harmondsworth: Penguin.

13   Ray, W., (1970) Poverty and Exclusion of Young Caribbean's: Guardian,24 July

14   Brown, A., (2001) The road to development, detection and learning: Developmental Psychology, pp26, 429-38

his house and rented it back to him at a rate he could afford. His local lions club then bought him a refrigerator, and paid for a course of driving lessons to help him get a job as a driver. He was allowed to fall behind with his rents and electricity bills[15]. People only became aware of this economic lynching when it was reported by the media and probably, no-one would have believed its existence until they saw it in a newspaper.

Let us not forget that the media carried the news because the victim was White. If not it would have gone unnoticed, unspoken and when such cases are unspoken we assume it does not exist[16].

Three Outlooks and the Explanation of Economic Lynching.

There are three outlooks and explanation for economic lynching and Daniel's Report provides a snapshot of the incidence of economic lynching in this 21st century. How would this evidence be interpreted? Some people would regard the evidence of emotional resistance to intimacy with African-Caribbean people as readily comprehensible and perhaps beneficent[17]. While the tendency of employers to stereotype African-Caribbean people as indecorous and unhygienic, irrespective of their social background, may seem illogical from a psychological standpoint, while to some it is by no means accidental. The tendency is present because it has a function. It furthers biological evolution by keeping genetically different groups separate. Perhaps, it furthers social evolution by helping nations maintain a sense of identity[18]. Those who adopt this standpoint might regret individual cases of injustice and victimization but argue that they are best avoided by keeping nations homogeneous. Their critics insist that there is no evidence to support the notion that humans inherit such hostile dispositions and as such have many things to learn. Because members of the same family often have different dispositions and individuals change their behaviours[19]. Social changes such as competition for employment, explain variations more convincingly. As recent research has demonstrated, for example, that when people become blind they are likely to abandon the colour prejudices that they may earlier have expressed[20]. The hypothesis of biologically determined hostility could be employed to argue that, the greater the difference in physical appearance, the more resistance there will be to contact, and the more intimate the relationship, the greater the resistance. The disposition to hostility is the independent variable; social and economic factors are dependent variables influencing its expression[21].

---

15   Besson, G., and Brereton, B., (1992) (eds.), The Book of Trinida for Trinidad: Paila Publishing.

16   Stroude, L., (1986) Profile: Courtney Laws. 'SELF-HELP NEWS' No 10. Pages. Published by The National Federation Of Self-Kelp Organisations (UK), London

17   Herman, B., (1970), Secretary. General Letter Addressed to 'Dear Brothers And Sisters' on BLACK HOUSE, Racial Adjustment Action Society Headed Paper, pages 1,2 and 3.95-101 Holloway Road, London N7 2lst May

18   Hines, V., (1970) Conversation With Michael Abdual Malik (Michael X) Recording At The Black House 27 July.

19   Wood, W., (1994) Keep the Faith Baby, pages 10-16. published by The Bible Reading Fellowship, 1994

20   Wertsch, J., (2002) Culture, communication and cognition: Burton Perspective, Cambridge: Cambridge university Press.

21   Hines, V., (1972) Britain, The Black Man And The Future, Mangrove Court Report, London: Published by Zulu Publications, London

However, there are several independent causes of hostility. From watching the behaviour of given individuals over a series of actions it is possible to infer that they are motivated by particular attitudes. It is also possible to find out whether individuals hold attitudes (or dispositions to behaviour) by asking them questions, but it is not certain that their attitudes will necessarily be translated into behaviour. There is also evidence that if people are induced to behave in a certain way, they will start to express attitudes which make sense of their behaviour. There is a two way relationship here.

Daniel used university female students who often deprecate racial discrimination and seek to demonstrate to African-Caribbean men that not all White people are intolerant. So at a university dance in the late 1950s when there were more students from the colonies, a girl might show that she was not unwilling to dance with an African-Caribbean partner. Other African-Caribbean students might notice this and concluded that here was one girl who was not biased. Some of them, who had asked English girls to dance with them and had been turned down, might have found the experience a little humiliating; they would therefore be more inclined to seek from a girl they defined as open-minded. So, the girl initially wished to show only goodwill might find she was receiving a whole series of invitations to dance from African-Caribbean students. She might well find it more difficult to say no to African-Caribbean men than to White boys. If the White students saw her dancing with one African-Caribbean student after another they might inferred that she did so from choice, and refrained from asking her to dance with them. The African-Caribbean students might interpret her behaviour as showing a desire for greater intimacy than she actually wished[22]. A whole series of predictable consequences which were no part of the girl's original intention might come from her initial willingness to dance with an African-Caribbean man. Therefore Economic Lynching may be caused by the psychological disposition, usually labelled prejudice which makes people discriminate and exclude, it also may be caused by social factors[23]. Therefore he concluded that Social behaviour is patterned and it cannot be understood simply in terms of people's states of mind[24]. So, one's attitude might not necessarily explain his or her behaviour.

In other words, one might argue that the leading process cannot be fully understood on the psychological social levels, and that there is an underlying biological programme for it[25]. According to some scholars, the tension and the intention to exclude African-Caribbean people could have been the tensions of a monopoly capitalist society, the tensions of a racist society. It could be true in the case of Stephen Lawrence which will be elaborated more in chapter 7. However, the views of African-Caribbean Academicians are that racial attitudes are learnt, but not just any attitudes[26]. Some people or groups have the power to influence the expression of opinion. Consciously or unconsciously, they see to it that the television, radio, newspapers, universities and schools propagate ideas about the nature of society congenial to the

---

22   Dashiki Annual Report 1972/73. Published by The Dashiki Council, London. March, 1993.

23   Blake, J., (1961) Family Structure in Jamaica: The Social Context of Reproduction, New York: Free Press of Olendoe.

24   Conference Report by The High Commissions of Jamaica, Trinidad And Tobago, Guyana, Barbados, Commissioners For The Eastern Caribbean Government And Central Committee of Police Federation of England And Wales, 28ᵗʰ November, 1970. Held At The Commonwealth Institute, London. Published by Laurence London, Jamaican High Commissioner, 48 Grosvenor Street, London W1X OBJ

25   Race, (1976) Today Magazine Volume 8. No. 10. Pages 195-207. October 1976. Published by Race Today Collective, London.

26   BLACK VOICE, (1970) Issue August-September 1970. Page 4. BUFP Manifesto 26tb July, 1970. Popular Paper Of Black Unity And Freedom Party, London

rulers. Attitudes about strangers are boosted if they suit the interests of the ruling class[27]. Sociologists who accept this approach object to the implication that British behaviour can adequately be analysed by using concepts like economic lynching which in one sense take for granted the prevailing social order instead of assessing present troubles against the standard of the more harmonious social order that could be established by adopting correct policies. It is therefore important to uncover the mechanisms of exploitation rooted in the relationship between British government and African-Caribbean people, for it is within this relationship that the so called 'race problem' had risen.

If we put events into a historical sequence, it could show how national policies have been tailored to suit the interests of the ruling class. In the old days of the Empire, the policy of extending British citizenship to overseas subjects of the Crown was a cheap way of keeping the colonials quiet, with an appealing echo of Roman grandeur. Few of Her Majesty's African-Caribbean subjects came to Britain then and fewer stayed. In the early 1950s immigration from the African-Caribbean countries was not discouraged because there were vacant jobs for unskilled workers. It suited the employers to recruit undemanding African-carribbean labour rather than reorganize backward industries. After the 1958 disturbances and rise in South East Asia, mainly India, immigration in the 70s, the press raised the alarm and right-wing politicians began to manufacture a racial issue[28]. The mass of the working class was deluded into believing that the threat to their living standards from the 'unhygienic' Asian competitors was greater than the threat from the employers. The ideology of racial difference was used to make White workers feel they were no longer at the bottom of the "status hierarchy" and that therefore they had an interest in maintaining that hierarchy. An alien wedge was driven into the potential political unity of the working class. For that same reason, hostility towards African-Caribbean people will continue so long as the ruling class is able to utilize it for their political ends[29].

Many social scientists have accepted the propositions such as 'people learn the attitudes disseminated by power elites' and agree that it is legitimate and worth re-examination. They can be put to the test, and, if upheld, incorporated into existing theories of social structure. But the proposition is not falsifiable. Its adherents assume that a ruling class always acts in accordance with its long-run interests and represent the social order as operating in a more systematic and coherent fashion than is usually the case. John Rex's writings on race relations attempt to synthesize elements of these assumption. It seems to suggest that 'an individual's position in the housing market is a more important determinant of his attitude towards African-Caribbean people than his psychological predisposition or subjective orientation to the situation'. But what Richmond report finds was that there is a conflict with such a hypothesis, Rex replies to that was that 'it was never his intention to suggest a one-to-one correlation between housing, class position and racial attitudes'[30]. Because of that it became impossible to build bridges between the assumptions[31].

27   Blake,J., Family Structure in Jamaica: The Social Context of Reproduction, New York: Free Press of Olencoe, 1961

28   Rex, J., (1971) Race, Community and conflict: a study of Sparkbrook, London: Oxford University Press.

29   Fanon, F., (1997) the Wretched of the Earth, Harmondsworth: Penguin Books.

30   Rex, J., (2000) Discrimination a scar in our conscience, London: zenith Books.

31   Dupuch, E., (1982) A Salute to Friend and Foe Nassau, Bahamas: Tnbune.

Four Elements in Economic Lynching

Nevertheless, Rex's study concluded that some economic lynching behaviour sprang from an 'emotional antipathy', whereas other kinds were to be explained by what the people in question thought about African-Caribbean people to be like (i.e. less well qualified), or believed others to expect. 'Emotional antipathy' is an explanation stressing motive. The other kinds of economic lynching behaviour are explained as the outcome of a social situation in which people's ideas about others are apt to be distorted by the position they themselves occupy in a structure of social relations, which prevents them from knowing how well qualified the African-Caribbean persons really are or what others actually think about them. An understanding of the motives of individuals does not explain the way in which the structure of social relations has a distorting effect[32].

Most explanations of the motives behind economic lynching behaviour utilize the concept of intolerance which has been defined as a negative, unfavourable attitude towards a group or its individual members; it is characterized by stereotyped beliefs; the attitude results from processes within the bearer of the attitude rather than from reality-testing of the attributes of the group in question. Therefore some social scientists would add the qualification that an attitude could be intolerant only if it violates the norms of the society to which the bearer belongs[33]., but this then poses problems about how to define the society, for in matters of opinion and attitude there are minorities within majorities, from Rex's view point it is useless to seek a single definition of economic lynching, for it has many dimensions. The economic lynching which the Romans displayed towards the Celts in the days when Britain was a colony lacked some of the features of economic lynching as it has been known in recent generations. Economic lynching against Jews and against Catholics has points of similarity and of difference. Economic lynching against blacks in England is not the same as in the United States[34]. Economic Lynching itself is strictly speaking a concept which isolates just a few of the many features which an individual's attitudes display[35]. Hostile attitudes towards African-Caribbean people can usefully be divided into two general kinds, the economic lynching which results 'from processes within the bearer of the attitude' as an isolated individual, and the shared prejudice which results from processes within all members of his society or sub-society. The former can be described as rooted in some personality weakness; the latter will here be called ethnocentrism. Different labels are sometimes used but there are two important points to note. the former kind of economic lynching is resistant to 'reality-testing'. For example, someone who believes that all African-Caribbeans are more 'highly sexed' is unlikely to abandon his belief if assured that it is groundless[36]. He just finds new excuses for what he needs to believe. There must be some weakness in the personality makeup of someone who cannot respond rationally to evidence. The latter kind of attitude is less rigid. Secondly, ethnocentrism should be seen as a generalized attitude which many members of a society acquire during their upbringing rather than as an individual characteristic. Ethnocentrism can be defined as a tendency to prefer people belonging to the subject's own nation, to see things from the standpoint of that nation, and to set a lower value on other nations.

---

32   Jahoda, K., (1964) How long should this go on?London: Cambridge University Press.

33   Bousquet, B., and Douglas, C., (1991) West Indian Women at War: British Race in World War 2. London: Lawrence and Wishart.

34   Braud, A., (1985) No Magic Bullet: A Social Histo'y of Venereal Disease in the United States since 1880, New York and Oxford: Oxford University Press.

35   Brereton, B., (1979) Race Rations in Colonial Trinidad, 7870-7900, London and New York: Cambridge University Press, 1979.

36   Etittan, A., and Maynard, M., (1989) Sexism, Racism and Oppression, Oxford: Basil Blackwell

Ethnocentrism resembles a series of concentric circles: the man in the middle places other groups at varying distances from him according to what he knows about them[37]. Ethnocentric attitudes can be modified by contrary experience but they may be underpinned by the other kind of economic lynching. Everyone has certain personality weaknesses which may find outlet in a tendency to make a scapegoat of someone or others, so that ethnocentrism is likely to attract to it emotions that have other origins[38].

Economic lynching behaviour may be motivated by something other than skin colour. One obvious cause of economic lynching is opportunism, the utilization of ethnic distinctions in order to advance an economic policy or a political career (**as is the case with Morel, which will be expanded on in the next chapter**). Take for example, in 1988 general election in America; George Bush senior saw he was behind his Democratic contender in opinion poll by 17 points. What he did was to launch a blitz of television advisements featuring a black convict, Willy Horton, who raped again when he was out on parole. Bush accused the Massachusetts parole laws of being too soft on African-Caribbean people. As a result of this campaign, the 17 point lead of the Democratic Presidential nominee, Mike Dukakis collapsed and Bush the senior won the election. An unscrupulous man may be willing to appeal to the intolerance of others though he is without bias himself. William Hague did so during the 2001 general election when he made his famous speech on Britain turning into a foreign land if Labour was elected for the second term because of their open door policy on immigration. The essence of that speech was to appeal to the intolerance of the British people because he knew it works; even though it did not work for him because he got scared when criticised for it and apologized. Had it been that he stood his ground he would have made an in-road in that election but he did not. In 2005 general election Michael Howard the conservative leader saw that William Hague failed because he was scared; secondly, because he apologized meant he was not being sincere to the British people. Howard decided to stand his ground, campaigning on no other issue but immigration. On the last week of the election he decided to switch to a different subject. After the election he did very well; better than he had hoped for, and he said during an interview with Sir David Frost, "If I had known I would have stuck with immigration throughout". Why did he say that? Because he knew that race card works and it did work for him but his only regret was he would have appealed to the intolerance of the British people more. When the opinion leaders are under sharp attack, they would result to race card in order to extricate themselves. Such behaviour is not motivated by the chauvinism of the subject, but it can be successful because of the intolerance of others[39].

Another kind of economic lynching behaviour may be called role-determined. A man may have been appointed to a post in which he is expected to discriminate and will lose the post if he fails to do so. He may be frightened of what 'other people may think' and of what they might do if they disapproved of his behaviour. People may conform to a general norm because they think it is expected of them. Or everyone in a certain position, such as seeking work in a competitive market, may be subject to similar pressures, so that a uniformity of behaviour results[40].

---

37   Bryophyte, J., and Smart, C., (1990) (eds.), Women in Law: Expiration's in Law, Family and Sexuality, London and Boston: Rutledge and Kegan Paul.

38   Brown-miller, S., (1995) Against Our Will: Men, Women and Rape, London: Secker and Warburg, 1975

39   Bryan, P., (1991) the Jamaica Peopl6 1880-1902 London and Basingstoke: Macmillan, 1991.

40   Buckley, N., (1999) Slaves in Red Coats: The Relish West India Reagents, 1795—1815, London and New Haven: Yale University Press.

Discrimination is an attitude. Economic lynching is a kind of behaviour, in which a person is treated differently because he is ascribed to a particular social category and excluded economically[41]. Discrimination often results in economic lynching. A general tendency to exclude others economically breeds discrimination because it heightens ethnocentrism and attracts to the stranger group emotions springing from personality weakness. The pattern of economic lynching is linked to a society's power structure, for many important roles are defined by the government and by employers. For an example, a black Jew who came from Eastern Nigeria (Ibo), in 2005 was refused employment because he was black and the job was given to Asian person because the company, a law firm had a blanket ban on the recruitment of black people and had not recruited any Afro-Caribbean person for 15 years.[42]. Sometimes a publican can turn away black customers in the belief that other customers did not like their presence; the publican's role was determined to some degree by this belief.

Furthermore, the policies of governments and of powerful elites affect majority-minority behaviour by offering rewards for some kinds of behaviour, by imposing penalties upon others, or by majority refraining from taking action. Sometimes, governments encourage a majority to take action through protest and demonstrations so as to enable them to change or introduce policies that are discriminatory by nature so as to advance their own political careers. In this way they influence the definition and performance of roles[43].

Economic lynching has many causes and they differ in their relative importance from one set of circumstances to another. In theory, it might be possible to construct an index of economic lynching, like a cost-of-living index. Certain circumstances could be selected, like application for employment as an accountant and as a bus driver; application for a house mortgage, application for social housing, motor insurance and holiday accommodation. The incidence of economic lynching in each instance could be analyzed and the causes parcelled out in terms of the four kinds of cause listed above. The incidence of economic lynching in Manchester could then be compared with that in Johannesburg and London. The relative importance of the causes could be ascertained. It would be exceedingly difficult to conduct such an analysis because the element of economic lynching in the decision to employ someone cannot be measured like the price of bread, but the attempt to make such comparisons would bring out the complexity of the phenomenon. Having said that, there is no single or ultimate cause of economic lynching; it is part of the very structure of any conceivable society[44]. People are everywhere treated differently because they are ascribed to social categories, male and female, young and old, nobles and commoners, high status and low members and non-members. Some of these kinds of economic lynching are not considered objectionable. However, economic lynching base on race is widely regarded as very objectionable indeed[45]. The question now is how important to the British scene are these four elements in economic lynching?

41   Mamuwa, T., (2001) the effect of prejudice on Ethinic Minorities. New York: Sage

42   Campbell, M., (1990) the Maroons of Jamaica, New Jersey: Africa World Press.

43   Camegie, J., (1973) Some Aspects of Jamaica & liticr, 7918—1938jamaica: Institute of Jamaica, 1973.

44   Chambers, T.,(1992) New migrants, London: Churchill.

45   Chapman, R., and Rutherford, J., (1988), Male Order: Unwrapping Masculinity, London: Lawrence and Wishart.

Personality weakness

The best source of evidence about white attitudes is derived from a survey conducted by Dr Mark Abram for the research programme reported in African-Caribbean's and Citizenship[46]. In this survey, people's tendency to economically lynch was measured by their responses to four key questions. Their responses to ten supplementary questions were also analysed, but less weight was attached to these. In the four key questions people were asked

1. (i) Would you avoid having African-Caribbean people as neighbours even if they were professional people?

2. (ii) Do you think African-Caribbean people are inherently inferior?

3. (iii) Should African-Caribbean people be given council houses?

4. (iv) Should the landlords refuse to let to African-Caribbean people[47] even if they were other acceptable? A hostile answer to any of these questions scored 15. Hostile answers to the supplementary questions scored I each; from these scores a scale was constructed.

- 17 per cent, tolerant inclined
- 30 per cent tolerant
- 43 per cent not tolerant.

In the core designs of the Abram's questionnaire, his hypotheses have shown that the greatest intolerance was expressed by individuals with low social potency and by individuals with high authoritarianism.[48]. Social potency was defined as a willingness to give active support to a local movement concerned with community problems and a belief that the authorities would pay heed to such a movement. Forty three per cent of respondents were classified as being of low social potency because they said they would not involve themselves in community movements and that these would be unavailing[49]. The essence of authoritarianism is a belief that social problems are created by people whose activities should be curbed by more authoritarian social control. People of authoritarian personality tend to be conventional, submissive towards those above them, aggressive towards outsiders, concerned with power relations, critical of sexual permissiveness[50], etc.

Twenty one per cent of respondents were classified as authoritarian on account of their responses to six of Abram's related statements in the survey questionnaire. The percentage of respondents who were both low on social potency and high on authoritarianism is not given but what we deduct from it is that both

46   Christopher, J., (1988). The British empire at Zenith, London: Croon Helm.

47   Cipriani, A., (1993) Twenty-Five Years After: The British West Indies Regiment in the Great War, London: Caviar Press

48   Clothier, N., (1987) Block Valour: The South African Native Labour Contingent and the sinking of the "Mend?, Pieterniariizburg: University of Nagal Press.

49   Cobley, k., (1990) Class and Consciousness: The Black Eet Bourgeoisie in South Africa, New York: Greenwood Press,

50   Clayton, A., (1988) France, Soldiers and Africa. London: Brassey's, 1988.

are in extreme. This shows that there was a tendency for people of low social potency to give more hostile answers, and for high authoritarians to do likewise[51].

Figure 2

A simple test is to add together the rows for 'none' and 'one' and to add the rows for 'two' and 'three and four' and then apply the chi-squared test of statistical significance.

Prejudice and personality features Attitude Scores of Respondents (percentages)

Number of hostile answers to key questions	High Social potency	Low Social Potency	Low Authoritarianism	High Authoritarianism
None	36	33	39	30
One	40	34	41	34
Two	18	22	13	21
Three or Four	6	11	7	15
Number of Subjects	380	241	282	527

Source: Rose, 1968: 564-5 or Deakin, 1970: 324-5

51   Cowry, A., and Thompson, A., (1990) eds, The African—Caribbean Connection: Historical and Cultural Perspectives; Bridgetown: Dept. of History, UWI and the NCI.

This demonstrates that the association between low social potency and hostile answers could have occurred less frequently than once in every hundred times according to the laws of chance[52]. This is a high level of statistical significance, while the association with authoritarianism is even stronger. The 10 per cent registering extreme hostility were spread throughout all sections of the population, men and women, young and old, middle-class and working-class, Conservative and Labour supporters, council tenants and private tenants. Only marginally were they distinguished by such social attributes. Much more striking was the tendency for the extremely hostile people to be psychologically distinctive, chiefly in their authoritarianism[53]. Their hostilities are described as 'irrational "solutions" to personality inadequacies' by Rose. At the same time it is important to note that 64 per cent of the high authoritarians and 67 per cent of the people low in social potency gave one hostile answer or none at all. This result must qualify any inclination to try to explain hostility purely in terms of psychological variables[54].

However, Abram's survey has been subjected to criticism, and it is clear that it would be unwise to utilize its division of the population into three categories as a measure of how 'good' or 'bad' the situation is in the country. In a small Manchester survey of people in housing estates, utilizing the first three key questions of the Abram's survey only 6 per cent gave answers corresponding to the intolerant and intolerant-inclined categories, Ward argued.[55]. He went further to demonstrate that there is evidence to suggest that the methods of analysis used in the Abram's survey understate the extent of hostility expressed in his interviews, because the key questions appear to have been answered in a less hostile way than the supplementary, and the key questions were arbitrarily scored as fifteen times more important. Lawrence argue to defer that the failure to find stronger associations between hostility and other variables may also be due, in part, to technical deficiencies stemming from a low response rate in parts of the sample and too crude a measure of authoritarianism, partially agreeing with Abram's hypothesis.[56]

Since Abram's hypothesis has been causing controversy, Bagley, decided to carry out further research on the Abram's data. He selected six items from the questionnaire most in deceptive of hostility, finding that 14 per cent of respondents gave hostile answers on no items; 19 per cent on 1; 20 per cent on 2; 18 per cent on 3; 14 per cent on 4; 10 per cent on 5; and in all 6. Those hostile on all six seemed to constitute a special group but he, too, did not find extreme hostility concentrated very strongly in any particular social category[57].

Ethnocentrism

Nevertheless, much of the hostility expressed in the survey can be attributed to a generalized ethnocentrism observable throughout the population. Sixty four per cent of respondents in the five boroughs selected by Abram for special study believed that the British were superior to the African-Caribbean people, 61 per

52   Cockjacklyn, N., (1992) Women and War in South Africa, London: Open Letters, 1992.

53   Cohen, S., (1990) The Indian Army: its Contribution to the Development of a Nation, Delhi Oxford University Press.

54   Rose, E., (1969) Colour and Citizenship: a report on British Race Relations, London: Oxford University Press.

55   Ward, R., (1971) Exclusion in the means of plenty, London: Pluto Press.

56   Lawrence, D., (1969) How prejudiced are we?, Race Today, October, 174-5

57   Bagley, C., (1970) Social structure and prejudice in five English Boroughs, London: Institute of Race Relations.

cent superior to the peoples of Asia, 36 per cent superior to the peoples of Europe and 3 per cent superior to the peoples of America.

Figure 3

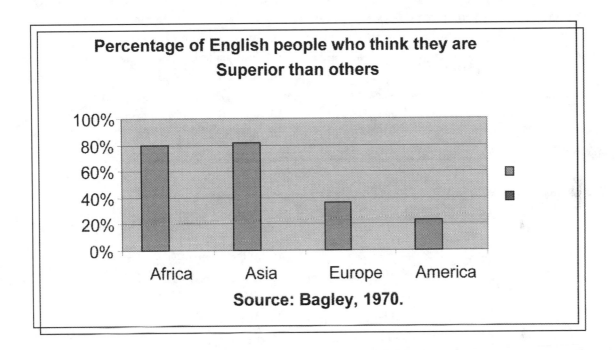

These figures jumble together with those who interpreted superiority as a matter of fact (as in a superior standard of living) and those who believed in racial superiority. From the information given, it is impossible to separate those two very different categories. However, it does seem that a lot of this feeling can be attributed to a general preference for 'our own sort' and a loyalty to the group with which a person identifies himself[58].

People who show ethnocentrism to a weak or moderate degree are likely to modify their judgement of other groups in the light of factual evidence. Thus 30 per cent of the sample said they felt less sympathy for disadvantaged African-Caribbean people than they did for white people in similar trouble. But when asked how they felt about African-Caribbean people who had been born in Britain the proportion saying they felt less sympathy for black people fell to 10 per cent. Very crudely speaking it could be said that 30 per cent expressed an ethnocentric attitude; two-thirds of them did not hold to it rigidly, but one-third expressed it because they had an emotional need to feel this way and would cling to this attitude[59].

---

58   Who is Educating who (1997)? "The black educational movement and struggle for power", Race Today magazine, Volume 7. No 8. pp. 182
59   Constantine, S., (1990) (ed), Emirates and Empire: British Settlement in the DDminio,,s between the Wars, Manchester and New York: Manchester University Press.

Evidence from Abram's survey suggests that the incidence of economic lynching found in the Barton's study is greater than might be predicted on the basis of individual opinions. One survey question asked: 'Suppose there were two workers, one white and one black, who exactly the same work. If one, and only one, had to be made redundant should it be the white or the African-Caribbean worker?' 42 per cent replied that the decision should be based on merit and length of service; 2 per cent thought the white worker should go, while 56 per cent would dismiss the African-Caribbean worker, usually on grounds that whites were entitled to preference[60]. When asked about housing, 49 per cent expressed no objection to African-Caribbean people obtaining council houses as long as he is not in employment that pays better than a white person. More than half of those questioned agreed to houses being offered to Asian immigrant families that had been on the waiting list for the full qualifying period, so that only 20 per cent expressed unconditional objection. Sixty per cent thought it wrong for private landlords to refuse accommodation to African-Caribbeans and Asians applicants. Half of those who initially sympathized with economic lynching institutions said they thought economic lynching would be wrong if the applicants were people who would take care of the property. Once more there was a residue of 10 per cent who were unconditionally hostile towards African-Caribbean people[61].

One of the best ways of explaining figures of this kind is usually to look for variations within them. Considering intense intolerance and ethnocentrism together, the question should be,

- Was economic lynching higher in localities of immigrant settlement?
- Did those who knew African-Caribbean people express less chauvinism?

However, variations of this kind could be weaker than might be expected, because psychological factors are still far from adequately understood. In the five boroughs selected for special study, more people in the London boroughs of Lambeth and Ealing favoured the exclusion of black people from council housing, sympathized with economic lynching employers and landlords, than did respondents in Wolverhampton or Nottingham where the housing shortage is less acute. People in Bradford had least sympathy for economic lynching in housing but this is probably related to the much higher proportion of Asians there who own their own houses[62].

In other respects, the variations from one locality to another do not help much to explain the general pattern. Women were slightly less inclined to display economic lynching attitude than men. Most economic lynching attitude was expressed by people aged 45-54 and the lowest levels of intense economic lynching were recorded in the age categories under 35 and over 65. The lower middle class and skilled manual workers most frequently showed extreme intolerance while the professional, managerial and the unskilled and semi-skilled workers showed much less[63]. People who at the time of the survey would have voted Conservative expressed more chauvinism than Labour supporters and still more than Liberals. But the Labour employers and Liberals are more likely to lynch African-Caribbean people than the Conservatives employers; the reason being that Conservatives are looking for cheap labour and could

60   Costello, J., (2000)Love, Exclusion and ethnic minority position, London: Pan Books.
61   Cross, M., and Hanuman, D., (1999) Labour in the Caribbean, London: Oxford university press
62   Cundall, F., (1998) Political and Social Disturbances in the West Indies: A Brief Account and Bibliography
Kingston, Jamaica: Institute of Jamaica.
63   Cundall, F., (1995) Jamaica's Part in the Great War 7914- 7918, London: Institute of Jamaica.

sometime employ African-Caribbean people to those jobs that their own citizens cannot do. However, none of these correlations was strong and, contrary to many American findings, there was little association between social mobility and economic lynching. Those who had moved upwards were more likely to practice economic lynching than those who had fallen in the social scale. But as nearly all the people in question were lower middle class or skilled workers, and these categories express more intolerance in any event, the finding is not one of significance[64].

When it comes to studies of how attitudes are related to a variety of social attributes it is necessary to allow for the way variables may be confounded. Given that the highest incidence of extreme economic lynching is amongst skilled manual employers aged between 35 and 54 who left school at 14 or 15 years of age, it would not be proper to compare the attitudes on any racial issue of people in, say, Wolverhampton and Lambeth, without allowing for figures that show Wolverhampton to have an unusually high proportion (48 compared with Lambeth's 34 per cent) of men who are skilled manual employers. In multi-variety analysis the contributions of the different variables to the total have to be 'partially out' if the total is to be compared with any other[65].

In Bagley analysis of the same material, he found that the least economic lynching social category was that of white collar workers below 45 years of age who have undergone further or higher education; which does not seem to follow, because in this 21st century it is the elite that are flying the banner of economic lynching of African-Caribbean people. Although, he reported a significant tendency for economic lynching to be slightly lower among those living close to African-Caribbean neighbours. This fits with Ward's finding of low economic lynching in his Manchester survey, in which almost all the whites employers interviewed were people with African-Caribbean neighbours. Those who had African-Caribbean neighbours on both sides were much less likely to give intolerant replies than those whites who had a African-Caribbean neighbour on one side only[66].

Going back to the evidence from the Abram's survey about the influence of contact was interesting; because nearly half the people questioned as we have seen previously in the five-borough sample said that they have African-Caribbean people living within a 5 minute walk of their houses, but 50 per cent of them said they have not spoken with these African-Caribbean people. While thirty- seven per cent claim to have met African-Caribbean people, that is only at work. From those who had encountered African-Caribbean people, 13 per cent reported friction with them at work; 8 per cent of those who had spoken with them in the neighbourhood claimed not to have got on well with them[67]. When answering the question about making a worker redundant, those least prepared to dismiss the black and Asian worker were younger people, upper middle-class respondents, those who received a longer full-time education, and (to a slight extent) trades union members. What seems to be missing is why those who received longer full-time education were less interested about making the African-Caribbean people redundant was because majority of these African-Caribbean's were uneducated and unskilled labourers, and as such the educated white people do not consider them as a threat job wise. Yet those people who had personal

64   Ward, R., (1971) Coloured families in council houses: progress and prospect in Manchester. Council for community relations.

65   Curtin, P., (1985) The Role of Idols in a Tropical Colony 183 0-1865, Cambridge, Mass: Harvard University Press.

66   Eisner, G., (1961) Jamica: A Study in Economic Growth1830— 7930, London: University of Manchester Press.

67   Estain, P., (1987) Women and War, New York: Basic Books.

experience of African-Caribbean people, or had worked with them, were much less inclined to support their dismissal. (This does not mean necessarily that contact leads to more favourable attitudes because people who are economic lynches may avoid contact.)[68]

The problem of deciding whether or not contact causes a reduction in economic lynching was complicated by Rose findings. When he asked them whether contact had made them more favourably disposed towards African-Caribbean people, both middle-class and working- class respondents (but especially the former) replied in the affirmative. But that is not the case when it come to employment or working with them because the respondents feel threatened; they feel their jobs are in trouble because they have the notion that African-Caribbean workers can accept any amount of pay just to stay alive. Therefore, having them around means that employers could one day come up with a wage cut and if they do not accept it they would be sacked. So in order not to weaken their solidarity, African-Caribbean workers among them are not acceptable[69].

Opportunism

We can argue that white attitudes and behaviour towards African-Caribbean people have been made more hostile by individuals who sought political or economic advantage from their actions? As we have seen with George Bush Senior in 1988 American Election. Some intellectuals believe that the activities of the politicians have not merely mirrored, but have been the primary cause of, the grave inflammation of economic lynching attitudes that has taken place in this decade'[70]. Dimmitt diverged by saying that we could not understand at all the character of what had happened to this country in the last eight or nine years if we fail to grasp the absolutely crucial, and almost uniformly disastrous, affects which the behaviour of both major parties, in and out of office, has had. He was criticised by his opponents for being economical with words, in the sense that when a politician is out of power his influence or ability to modify people's behaviour diminishes. Rex took a different view, by criticising the politicians of having failed to propagate the facts and yielding to extremist clamour to suit their own purposes. Because the debate about immigration, e.g., will never take place in Britain except when local or general election is approaching. Both Labour and Conservative starts positioning themselves as the toughest on immigration; a party that will stop the aliens coming into Britain or a party that will send back all African-Caribbean to unknown Island and leave Britain purely white and some Muslim communities . When you turn to the media the kind of massage you be getting is how Britain has been invaded by foreign criminals and how the system has collapsed by the weight of African-Caribbean crusaders. The two parties will be saying to the British people, look the government was sleeping when these crusaders invaded our land we are now wide awake and we are the only party that can and will wrestle our father land from the invaders. The moment the election is over, you will not hear anything about immigration until the next round of voting. That is why these intellectuals believe that, for historical reasons, the majority of the white population are influenced by an outlook that can be designated 'crypto-racialist'[71].

---

68   Emmanuel, P., (1978) Crown Colony Politics in Grenada 7917-7957, Barbados: ISEI1 (Occasional papers no. 7.)

69   Reshuffle, M., (1989) Ethnic minority children in British Schools, Brighton: Harvester Press.

70   Dimmitt, M., (1970) Experience of Black children in our Society, Oxford: Oxford University Press.

71   Mole, O., (1996) Untold hardship of Vulnerable black Children, London: Cambridge University press.

The British government's sentiments were assumed to combine deeply-rooted economic lynching traces which in a sense is very shameful. Therefore it is imperative that they disguise the issue from themselves so as not to have to make a choice between contradictory values, both of which are important to them. By hammering away at immigration control, economic lynching politicians were able to exploit their ambivalence. Initially, the major politicians did not understand that this was a conflict they would, sooner or later, have to face openly. But every time they put it off, they weakened their own position: 'if, in 1965, for example, the government had stood firmly on the principle of racial equality, it is true that a deep division would have appeared in the nation in 1965 instead of 2006; when a very strict immigration policies were put in place because African-Caribbeans are no longer wanted due to some of these Eastern European joining EU. Nonetheless it would have been a division in which the opponents of economic lynching would have been far more numerous[72].

Having said that, Dumsnett examined the historical evidence concerning changes in the attitudes of white people towards African-Caribbean and Asian immigrants and concluded that it was too patchy to support a confident conclusion. He also acknowledges that the situation had deteriorated since the 1980s and still getting worse. In his opinion, he thought the research into economic lynching did not go far enough, because of that many intellectuals regarded him as a left wing professional. His views on this field, and his research made him to see other peoples work as opinion polls rather than academic researches. He reason being that they have not probed into people's verbal statements in the attempt properly to understand how important what they say is to their individual lives, or how far their views are resistant to change; and become a bed rock for economic lynching of African-Caribbean people.

Nevertheless, what had been missed from the entire debate was the question of how African-Caribbean people should be treated which has been confused in popular discussion with the question of whether African-Caribbean and Asian immigrants should be welcomed[73]. Those who campaigned for the restriction, cessation, or reversal of the migrant flow were successful in concentrating attention on the second question, which makes it more difficult to judge popular attitudes to the first.

As a result, it does look as if there was an increase in hostility and many people involved in majority-minority relations believe this. The survey evidence suggests that over the period 1956-68 and 1980-2006 there was (i) an increase in resistance to African-Caribbean immigration. In 1956 a sample of the public was asked 'Provided there is plenty of work about, do you think that African-Caribbean people should be allowed to go on coming to this country?' and 37 per cent replied unequivocally 'yes'. On subsequent occasions the question was differently phrased, but in surveys conducted by the Gallup Poll the percentage supporting free entry fell from 21 in 1958 to 19 in 1963, 10 in 1964 and then even further in the following year. There was a sharp rise in the proportion of people asserting that if African-Caribbean people came to live next door they would move increases from 9 to 19, 1958-68 or would consider moving (from 21 to 43 per cent). That feed in an increase from 26 to 55 per cent between 1964 and 1968 in the proportion of people believing that the immigration and race relations situation was getting worse[74].

---

72   Fanon, F., (2000) Black Skin White Masks, London: Mac Gibbon and Kee.
73   Rose, J., (1972) Colour and Race: a report on British Race Relations, London: Oxford University Press.
74   New Society, 27 May 1971

Another survey compared the attitudes of over 1,500 grammar- school sixth-formers aged 17-19 in the years 1963 and 1970. In 1963, 74 per cent of the boys thought a colour bar is 'always wrong' while 24 per cent believed it is 'never wrong'.

While the proportion that were undecided had doubled the number of boys who never saw anything wrong with African-Caribbean people rose from 36 to 77 per cent and girls from 27 to 57 per cent). Derek Wright, who carried out the study, concluded from the pupils' comments that the change was part of a general trend away from the uncompromising condemnation of any kind of behaviour and towards more qualified and permissive positions[75].

Having said that, to debate whether Economic lynching as a whole has increased or decreased is to assume that economic lynching, as it existed in 1950, was the same phenomenon as could be studied in 1970, 1980 or this 2006. In 1950 there were English people who wondered if African-Caribbeans really had tails, who were astonished that they spoke English and could entertain remarkable. When African-Caribbean's were first employed as bus conductors there were passengers who grabbed them and then shouted to the rest of the bus that their hands were warm, some passengers tried to see if their blackness would rub off and others put their hands on the black man's hair for good luck. As ever, lack of knowledge and economic lynching were intertwined, but some ignorance has been banished and the mode in which economic lynching is now expressed is different. The social scientist can measure only changes in the amount of economic lynching on how African-Caribbean people are integrating and changes in the way it is being carried out[76].

On that bases we can say that Rex's attack on the Labour government's policies is more restricted than Dimmitt's' because he concentrates upon the government's failure to force local authorities to allocate housing in a non-economic lynching manner and the urgency of action to prevent the formation of ghettoes. Dimmitt went further in his criticisms that the policies intended to promote integration had had a harmful effect because they have avoided confrontations with racialism and tried instead to get the African-Caribbean people to adjust to the inferior status that was being offered to them. Dimmitt asserted that Britain had now become a racialist society[77]. It was in this finding that it began to emerge why some intellectuals in the academic world regarded him as a left wing intellectual because he stood for the truth and did not like any form of oppression on the basis of skin colour.
In other words, if you say the truth in favour of the African-Caribbean people you will be regarded as a left wing; which does not seem to be logical.

However, If Dimmitt's assertion means that the majority of the population believe that people are to be classified into groups based on supposed racial origin and then accorded rights appropriate to their classification, there is no evidence to support that assertion. Everyday experience would suggest that there are now many white people in England who are ready to make disparaging remarks about African-Caribbean people or to keep silent when others make such remarks but they do not necessarily have any personal contact with black people or act out such sentiments when they do. There is often a big gap

---

75   Emmanuel, P., (1978) Crown Colony Politics in Grenada 7917-7957, Barbados: ISEI1 (Occasional papers no. 7.)

76   Oliver, E., (2001) Social Change in Twentieth Century Europe, Milton Keynes and Philadelphia: Open University Press

77   Dopey, R., (1990) The Encyclopaedia of Military History, London and Sydney: Jane's Publishing

between talk and action. Moreover, many people regard racial differences as relevant to behaviour in some situations but not others. Few would seriously maintain that African-Caribbean people do not have an equal right to work in the bank or in the Houses of Parliament[78].

At the far end of the scale attitudes towards marriage show a high level of rejection of African-Caribbean people. It seems probable that during the 1960s there were some areas in which race relations become more harmonious as whites got used to African-Caribbean's in certain contexts. But in so far as this meant getting used to them as people who occupy inferior positions and are regarded as scapegoats. There are many questions here which need to be studied individually. Generalizations about British society are unhelpful when there are so many relevant divisions within it[79].

The allegation that politicians have exploited popular racial prejudice in order to draw attention to them has been applied to the speeches of Mr Duncan Sandy about the migration of Kenyan Asians to Britain. He supported the Kenyan Asians coming to Britain but campaign against the black Kenyans coming to Britain. His reason for keeping all Africans out of Britain was because the Asian were the new British ally in the fight against the Cold War and since Africa was not a strategic place against the new war; their presents would not be tolerated. On that bases he campaigned to stop African-Caribbean's coming to Britain as well as to tighten the immigration laws and for the government to incorporate suppression as a means of eliminating those already here. There is a question that needs to be answered. How did all Asian that went to Africa come to hold British passports? What was the reason for given all of them British passports? What year did these Asian arrive in Africa and what was the primary motive for it? These are questions nobody has answered. For the purpose of this book we shall not pursue this line of inquiry any further but it could be another line of inquiry in the near future.

That notwithstanding, Mr. Sandy's critics maintained that, the problem could have been handled better, had it been kept out of the headlines[80]" because the numbers involved were nothing like as great as the vociferously represented. The Asians were skilled workers who would not attract prejudice. But the publicity in Britain made other Asians in East Africa afraid that if they did not hurry they would not be able to gain entry. So the number of would-be immigrants rocketed and this added strength to the political shift in East African countries that favoured the self expulsion of Asians who had opted for British nationality[81]

Sandy's' theme was taken up by Mr Enoch Powell who had made no speech about the threat of ethnic minority immigrants before the autumn of 1967. For over ten years he had been in parliament, from about 1954 to 1966, he then claimed, Commonwealth immigration was the principal, and at times the only, political issue in his constituency[82]. During this period he had made no speeches on this subject though in 1964 he had maintained that he would always set his face like flint against melding any difference between one citizen of this country and another on grounds of his origin. He started to deliver

78   Dow, C., (1992) Record Service of members of the Trinidad Merchant and Planters' Contingent, 1915— 1918, Trinidad: Government publication.

79   Today Magazine, Vol. 11 No. 4. pages 104-105, November December, 1979, London.

80   Eisner, G., (1961) Jamaica, 1830   7930: A Study in Economic Growth, London: University of Manchester Press.

81   Black People's News Service, page 8, Issue February, 1970 and page 4 Issue September, 1970. Published by The Black Panther Movement, London.

82   Powell, E., (1968) Freedom And Reality, London: Arrow Books.

speeches about immigration at the moment when this issue was most useful to his political career and he had refused to lend his name to schemes designed to promote integration organized by the Community Relations Council (CRC) in his own constituency. This, and other evidence of a similar kind, had led his critics to the conclusion that his use of the racial issue was motivated by political opportunism. It could not necessarily be opportunism because his argument was, according to his supporters that the previous government who issued British passport to 20million Asians almost equivalent to entire population of Scotland, without thinking about the consequences, was making the future fearful. Knowing full well that majority did not have the intention of staying in Africa or going back to Asia. They were not interested in accomplishing the task by which they were sent to Africa, rather, their intentions were to enter Britain with that opportunity. On arrival, Blackburn, Bedford, Southall, Newham, Oldham, Bradford and Birmingham were taken; leaving White people in minorities in these towns and cities. His adherents stressed that Enoch Powell was trying to prevent trouble between English people and the new Asian arrivals from Africa because if the trend continued, it could come to such a time English people would have to move abroad[83]. Even though that could be an exaggeration, they were not saying it would certainly happen. The Powellnites accused people like Tony Ben, whose father was responsible for this error of judgment for using the media to make Enoch Powell look like a racist tort, from their view point, what seemed to be a genuine argument to build a sustainable race relation, was squeezed out from the political window[84].

Having said that, at a pettier, local level, instances had been reported of what appeared to be economic opportunism. The workers particularly African-Caribbean people were concern how bus companies in some cities had denied jobs to African-Caribbean workers to improve their own bargaining position. Appeals to white solidarity have utilized feelings of skin differences that showed there were employers who had played on their workers fears of Asian invasions of factories. This meant that the possibilities of economic opportunism are widespread but usually they were found at the margins of industrial policies and could not explain the overall pattern of economic lynching[85].

Role determined discrimination

In any social structure people's behaviour is to some extent determined by the roles they are expected to play and the strength of the sanctions others wield to keep them in line. At the same time, most people will on occasion go against others' expectations, while in some areas of social life what people do is not influenced to any very great extent by the roles they are recognized as playing. In this sense it can be said that if a man is economically lynched, that does not express the personal attitudes of the employer, but because the employer believes this is expected of him, his behaviour is determined by his role.[86].

83   Lunzer, M., (1975) International Political Economy, in D.Gowons (ed.) journal of Political pp254-60

84   Foot, P., (1969) The rise of Enoch Powell, Harmondsworth: Penguin. 84—128

85   Dixon, N., (1976) On the school of Military Incompetence, London: Jonathan Cape.

86   African Liberation Day, (1996) pages 13-15. Published by The All African Peoples Revolutionary Party, London.

According to Dixon's findings, some employers lynch African-Caribbean people economically because other people expect it, or because African-Caribbean people are less qualified. As we go further into this research the issue of qualification will be ruled out because education has not ameliorated economic lynching among African-Caribbean people. They suffer more economic lynching than those who were uneducated. The second justification is the less complex and will be considered first and **in more detail in chapter Three**. Following a convention in sociology the Latin word ego (meaning 'I') will be used to denote the person in a position of authority (employer or service provider), and the word alter ('the other') to denote the person towards whom economic lynching behaviour is directed to (African-Caribbean)[87]. Insurance company sees African-Caribbean as applying for something, in the vein of motor insurance, which the company can grant or withhold. In practice this is sometimes an application for insurance at a particular rate. The insurance company may decline to offer it at £45 for example, but believe that it is worth offering at £58 and African-Caribbean may either accept or reject the offer. If the insurance firm makes an offer which African-Caribbean accepts, they enter into the relationship of insurer and insured, which is legally defined by a contract which imposes obligations on both parties[88]. However, the insurance company may regard a African-Caribbean as a greater risk for motor insurance than a Spanish, but in another relationship, such as a request for a loan to enable an amateur dance band to turn professional, bank might consider the African-Caribbean as a better risk[89].

That shows that economic lynching occurs because of what 'others may think' involves a third party. One possibility is that employer might engage into economic lynching because he believes that others will not admit employee into a relationship which is important to the work that has to be done. An Employer may wish to employ an African-Caribbean as a plumber but fear that some housewives may not like to have an African-Caribbean man coming into their houses to do the plumbing and electricity. He may believe that they will accept a pale-skinned Indian but not African-Caribbean. Some may feel that their attitude are justifiable, while others might think it crazy that they should be worried to be treated by Pakistani doctors and nurses in hospital then worry about the plumber. The employer may be mistaken in believing that they would object. However, we must judge his behaviour, if we are concerned to explain it, that his ideas about others reactions may be among the causes of economic lynching, not necessarily because the employer is a racist, he is looking at it from a business point of view[90].

Having said that, It may be fair to his business, what about the African-Caribbeans that are lynched in this way, how are they going to survive? Since they are not given the opportunity to become wealth creators and cannot walk into the bank to ask for loans without being seen as a fraud star.

87   Daniel, C. (1978) 'S...' A Report On The Vagrancy Act 1824 Published by Runnymede Trust

88   DeWitt, E., (1978) India and World War 11, New Delhi: Manohar Publications.

89   Colby, K., 2001) Class and Consciousness: The Black Bourgeoisie in South Africa, 1924—7950, New York: Greenwood Press, 1990.

90   Daniel, B., (1968) Racial Minorities, Cambridge: Cambridge University Press. Pp. 107 also see Abbott, 1971:173—93 or Race, 1970, 9: 397—417.

Social status

Another possibility that may lead employers to lynch economically is for reasons of social status. For example, a landlady with three lodgers, one African-Caribbean and two whites, might be unwilling to take in a second black lodger if one of the white leaves, for fear that the neighbours may come to regard hers as Afro-Caribbean house. Her standing in the neighbourhood may suffer[91]. People may conclude that she takes in African-Caribbean tenants only because she cannot get a white one, because her lodgings were of poor quality. Or she may turn away African-Caribbean person for fear that with two black tenants she could have difficulty getting another white person if the third one leaves, and therefore she will be at a disadvantage economically because she is being forced to cater for a smaller market[92]. This is another variety of economic lynching explainable in terms of beliefs about other people's reactions. To use the terminology of the psychologist, it springs from unwillingness to be identified with the African-Caribbean people rather than from unwillingness to be exposed to having dealings with them[93].

The Daniel's report gives instances of people, such as financial institutions, treating African-Caribbean people differently because they think, their jobs require them to do so. It presents evidence that before deciding whether or not to employ an African-Caribbean person to a particular role many will consider first, what sort of black person they are dealing with and secondly, what the resulting relationship would expose them to[94]. Daniel also believed that there were general agreement among employers that educated Indians were much more acceptable than African-Caribbean in senior and staff positions when an investigation was carried out it shows deeper economic lynching against African-Caribbean people than Asian applicants for white-collar posts[95]. For example, in the Home Office, majority of the managers are from Muslim communities of sub-Indian continent. In the financial sector, 59 per cent of the management are from India, Pakistan, Bangladesh, sire-lanker etc. When it comes to business, they are literally running most of the British businesses because they have been accepted into the system.

It is worth noting that the tendency for African-Caribbean people to be less acceptable has no direct relation to criminal activity, personal characteristics or incompetence, its causes must be largely due to emotion and skin differences. However, sometimes working-class white people often consider unskilled African-Caribbeans socially more acceptable than unskilled Asian workers who are seen as foreign because of the linguistic, religious and cultural differences. But as unskilled Asian immigrants often obtain work through their compatriots and lodge in Asian houses, they do not expose themselves so much to economic lynching[96].

There is more economic lynching in some kinds of employment, and the hypothesis that the more it is greater, the more African-Caribbean people become employed[97]. Does not seems to follow, because what we are seeing in this 21st century is that any job or position that is left for ethnic minorities is likely

91   Race Today Collective. New Perspective On The Asian Struggle, Part 2. Race Grassroots Black Community News: Volume 4 No.3, page3 - 'What Is the BLF', 29 September, 1975. Published by The Black Liberation Front.

92   Abbot, S.,(1971) "The Prevention of Racial Discrimination in Britian", London: Oxford University Press.

93   Bagley, C., (1970) "Social Structure and Prejudice in Five English Boroughs", London: Institute of Race Relations.

94   Dhaya, B., (1999) "Arab Migrant Community", Oxford: Oxford University Press.

95   Daniel, W., (1968) Racial Discrimination in England, Harmondsworth: Penguin.

96   Calley, M., (2000) God's People: West Indian Pentecostal Sects in England, London: Oxford University Press.

97   Daniel, W., (2001) Racial Discrimination in England, Harmondsworth: Penguin.

to be filed by Muslims from sub-Indian continent rather than African-Caribbean because they were more accepted than African-Caribbean people. Take for example, it is widely agreed that in office work women staff are particularly resistant to the idea of African-Caribbean colleagues. The observation may be mistaken. If true, it cannot be explained by saying that English women are responsible for economic lynching of African-Caribbean people than their men folk this theory will be disproved **when we get to chapter two**, for the evidence does not support this claim. It may be a fragment of the problem because some white males do not want see African-Caribbean persons go out with white women.

The reason they were resistance could possibly be that women office workers were less career-minded and more intimate with one another than men. It would be interesting to learn whether this resistance was greater amongst older than younger women office workers, unmarried rather than married women, and office workers rather than garment workers. What most people agreed with Daniel findings was that there was more resistance to having African-Caribbean person play the superior role in an unequal relationship: 'The more senior an African-Caribbean person was to the white person in employment, the less acceptable was the African-Caribbean person[98].

His critics, the neoclassical Sociologist who did not want any policy implementation to address the issue of economic lynching came up with a counter argument that economic lynching was more likely to stem from fears that African-Caribbean people could be unable to fulfil the obligations that were their part of the relationship, than from fears of being identified with white.

Even though a man's reputation is known in part from the company he keeps, but at work he usually cannot choose whom he will associate with and therefore he is not judged by this. They went further to argue that people will generally hesitate before entering into relations with those whom they class as strangers, people who do not "know the ropes" and therefore cannot be depended on. They gave example with people from a different class background or way of life such as (vagrants, hippies) may be considered as strangers and inappropriate candidates for admission to a club. Therefore they seem to conclude that it is not just a matter of being African-Caribbean[99].

If you look at the counter argument to Daniel's statement, there was no doubt that it was logical, however, they fall sort in providing any evidence to support their claim that skin colour was not the issue but ability was the main reason why economic lynching was endemic in the employment? Abbot, in his own contribution to the debate concluded that it was about belief that black skin suggests a lower status, than a white or brown[100] Even to be identified with African-Caribbean people sometimes (e.g. by having them as neighbours) may therefore imply a loss of status[101].

The sentences in the preceding paragraph suggests a series of testable propositions about the determinants of distance indirect relationships (ideas about indirect relationships, such as resistance to admitting strangers to common citizenship, are less role determined and may be either emotional or, for example, rationally related to ideas about over population)[102]. Taking first direct relationships governed by the factor of exposure:

---

98   Deakin, N., (2000) Colour, Citizenship and British Society, London: Panther.

99   Deakin, N., (2001) "Ethnic Minorities in Britain", Cambridge: Cambridge University Press.

100   Abbot, C., (1998) Education and culture, Oxford: Oxford University Press.

101   Abbot, M., (1999) "Race Relations", London: Tavistock.

102   Mohammad, A., (1998) "The Role of Government in Britain's Racial Crisis", London: Sheed and Ward.

- Employer may (a) Economically Lynch African-Caribbean people because he understands them to be less accustomed to the job requirements;
- (b) when qualifications can be proved by certificates or by taking a test;
- (c) he will economically lynch them if it would be difficult to discharge an unsuitable appointee, or if he cannot easily check upon his reference[103].
- (d) If African-Caribbean people are believed not to share the off-the-job social interests of the white workers the latter will be more opposed to the recruitment of African-Caribbean workers in less formally organized groups (e.g. female office workers compared to school teachers)[104].
- (e) There may be informal segregation in the canteen though not at the workbench. People may readily enter into the relationship expressed in gossip over a cup of tea with someone who has information about the conversational topics that interest them, but avoidance of stranger groups in the canteen may equally well be due to fears of identification. Clubs are the more likely to refuse membership to people assigned to stranger categories,
- (f) The relationship between members should be informal in social setting rather than uniting members in a shared pursuit (which is one reason for expecting golf clubs to discriminate more readily against West Indians than cricket clubs)[105].

The identification factor will usually be stronger in the neighbour than the club mate relations but may vary,

- (g) according to the kind of housing or
- (h) According to employer's occupation some roles require people to lead a seemly and decorous private life lest suspicion attach to the way they discharge their work responsibilities (bank employees, for example) those who follow occupations such as (artist or entertainment) are less vulnerable to the judgements of onlookers[106]. Certain roles (e.g. clergyman) license association with the most disreputable people provided they are acted in such a way as to suggest that the association is entered upon only to discharge role-obligations[107]. The relationship of friend will be more affected by considerations of identification,
- (i) when it is a friend of opposite

---

103   Egbuna, O., (1979) "The Contradictions of Black Power", Race Today, August and September, pp.266-8, 298-9.

104   Evans, P., (1999) "Attitudes of young Immigrants", London: Runny-made Trust.

105   Mason, P., (2002) "A Role for the Institution?", London: Oxford University Press.

106   David, B., (1966) "The Problem of Slavery in Western Culture", Harmondsworth: Penguin.

107   Lawrence, D., (1990) How Prejudiced are we? Race Today, October: 174-5

Figure 4

The social Distance reported by English women teacher trainee in 1952 as a reflection of attitudes (Source: Barton, 1972:120)

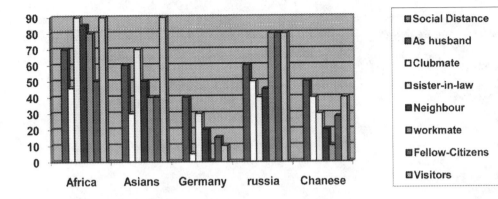

sex;

- (j) People who are closely involved with kinsfolk of their own will more strongly resist the idea of intermarriage than people who are on their own in life. This list can easily be extended. The reader should ask why economic lynching should be expected more in certain relationships than in others, and then see whether this can be attributed to the roles that have to play.

One way to test theories about tendencies to economically lynch is to employ the Bogardus social distance test. This has weaknesses as a test, but it can be used to explore some of the social factors involved in economic lynching. Different classes of students were chosen to try this theory for themselves[108]. They were asked to choose, say, twelve relationships and eight social categories and write out for each, 'I would have an Italian for a friend'; 'I would accept a Pakistani as a neighbour', 'a gypsy as a relative-by-marriage', etc., so that all ninety-six possibilities are listed in random order. Members of another class could then be asked to indicate which statements they would accept. From their response, can be constructed a table like the one below. This can be represented diagrammatically to emphasize either the dimension of distance stemming from ideas about the stranger group (African-Caribbean people) or that which reflects feelings about the relationship to which the strangers might be admitted[109].

From such an analysis it may transpire (a) that the order of distance varies for different relationships; (b) that answers vary according to the circumstances of the respondent, e.g. people living in an owner-occupier housing estate might be more worried about the identity of their neighbours than people living in council flats; (c) that two attributes of a group are confounded, e.g. respondents may associate Jews with middle-class incomes, making it difficult to isolate the response to the element of ethnic difference[110].

---

108   Field, F., (1991) Black Britons, London: Oxford University Press.

109   Haykin, P., (2000) Black Minority in Britain, London: Oxford University Press.

110   Jordan, W., (2001) Black Over White: British Attitudes towards the Negro, Harmondsworth: Penguin.

Figure 5

The social distance of five stranger nationalities

	I would marry one	I would allow my brother to marry one	I would allow into my club	I would let live in my street	I would like to be employed in my occupation in my country	I would allow to become citizens of my country	I would allow as visitors to my country
Germans	69	77	91	94	95	98	98
Asian	12	29	72	82	91	98	99
Africans	11	27	70	80	90	99	100
Chinese	5	21	58	76	83	97	99
Russians	16	27	42	50	52	75	97

Subject: 204 students at a woman's college of education tested by Mrs Sheila Kitzinger in 1952. It should be remembered that at that time attitude towards Germans were still influenced by the second world war and that the cold war with the Soviet Union affected attitude towards Russians. Responds has been express as percentage. Source: (Barton 1972:123)

Whatever the case, the element of role determinism in economic lynching cannot always be separated from other components. An employer who is motivated by opportunism may direct his employee to behave in a particular fashion. For example, the principal British shipping line to West Africa refused, until the late 1950s, to accept belongings from Europeans for third-class passages on its liners, and its staff were apparently under instruction to state that third-class accommodation was 'considered unsuitable for Europeans', Africans could travel either first class or third class[111]. The company thus utilized racialist sentiment to keep the demand for the more profitable first-class passages at an artificially high level. It was assumed that the passage fees of Europeans would be paid by their employers and that they would accept such measures to reinforce European social status[112].

When someone participates in customary economic lynching this is likely to affect his personal attitudes. A suggestion of this can be detected in a conversation dating from 1952. Barton travelled to West Africa and, on entering the ship's dining room was met by the chief steward who was allocating passengers to places at table[113].

---

111   Barton, M., (20002) Race Relation, London: Tavistock
112   Humphrey, D., (20000) Because They are Black, Harmondsworth: Penguin
113   Greeley, A., (1998) Why Can't they be like us?, New York: Harvard University Press.

Barton: 'What about putting us at a table with some Africans?'

CS: 'Well, that is an unusual request!'

Barton: 'Is it?'

CS: 'We usually put all the Africans together.'

Barton: 'Why, do you get any complaints if you mix people up?'

CS: 'No, I don't give 'them the chance!'

Barton: 'We're going to be with Africans for quite a time so I suppose we might start getting used to them.'

CS: 'Well, if you're going to be there for a long time why do you have to bother about it now? . . . 'Here, let me put you with Dr Robertson' (who was a European missionary).

If nothing else, this conversation may convey some of the flavour of the period. That does not mean it was in the olden days therefore does not apply in this 21st century; in fact it is even worse now after so many years of African-Caribbean's living in Britain.

When it is to their advantage to do so, some people may well try to define their roles as requiring them to economically lynch African-Caribbean people[114]. They may not succeed, for the nature of a role depends upon other people's expectations and sanctions. But the question of financial advantage does introduce an important factor in the analysis of economic lynching. Many people are prepared to forget their 'narrow-mindedness' if they are compensated for doing so. What price do people put upon their bigotry? This is a crucial line of investigation but it is difficult to pursue in a first-generation situation when so many other social differences are identified with differences in race[115].

This chapter has, inevitably, moved away from the analysis of (CAEL) Campaign against Economic lynching and the three outlooks upon majority, minority relations and it has demonstrated the argument. So, to understand majority attitudes and behaviour it is necessary to ask ever more detailed questions about their causes, seeing attitudes and behaviour towards minorities as explicable in terms of the same ideas that are used to explain attitudes and behaviour towards people in general. The next step is then to find ways of answering the new questions; that is what the government should do to reduce economic lynching?

Solution

- Educating the youth against racism which breed economic lynching. Because many African-Caribbean youths are disenchanted with their future: mass youth unemployment, poverty wages and educational cuts are forcing them to the edges of society. Education about the effect of economic lynching would help the society to wake up and examine the consequences of economic lynching is having on African-Caribbean people.
- Political participation among African-Caribbean people will enable them to have a say on matters concerning them. If they are not political active, their views will not be heard. People from other cultures cannot represent them because African-Caribbean problem will be seen from their own cultural point of view. Take for instance, if an Asian or white person represent the interest of

---

114   Keith, M., (1999) Rights and Wrongs: Youth, Community and Narratives of Racial Violence', in Cohen, P., (ed.), New Ethnicities, Old racisms. London: Zed Books.

115   Back, L., (1996) New Ethnicities and Urban Culture. London: UCL Press.

African-Caribbean people, let us say, community leader, most often, African-Caribbean people will see it as white or Asian organization which has nothing to do with them and would play a dormant role. Therefore political participation is important for them so that they would not been seen as service users but those who have got something to contribute to the society and would be in position to change the way other white and Asian sees them. It is political decision taken by others are responsible for their economic lynching. If they participate in taking that decision that affects them economic lynching will be ameliorated.

- African-Caribbean people should be encouraged to form organizations that will help them regenerate their community. The elite among them should be encouraged to train and educate those who are less well off on how to improve their situation. The less well off here comprises the single mothers who are going through rough time due to separation to unemployed young stars who want to support their partners and their children financially and emotionally. At the moment majority of the community projects for the African-Caribbean's are run by white or Asians; that is why instead of the problem going away it is recycled.

- The government should involve African-Caribbean people when drawing policies that affect them. If we look at the most social policies about ethnic minorities in Britain, most often, African-Caribbean's problems will not even be mention. What we could see addressed is the problem of Indians, Pakistani, and Bangladeshi because these ethnic minorities are involved in the policy making and that is why it reflect their own cultural background.

- The government should help to end the organic selection of teachers and encourage the African-Caribbean people who want to teach to become teachers. The government should also help to discourage the importation of foreign teacher from countries their colour are regarded as more acceptable than black colour. What we have discovered is that instead of giving an African-Caribbean person who has right to stay and work in UK, the educational authorities will go to India or Pakistan to employ someone; this type of practice aid economic lynching of African-Caribbean.

- There should be a policy on targeting employment. What that means is that some institutions should be encouraged to employ African-Caribbean people. For example, our banking institution hardly employ African-Caribbean's, if we walk into any bank in the high street you can hardly see any African-Caribbean staff all the faces you will see are white or Asian faces. That shows that African-Caribbean people are under-represented in the financial sector. The government should help in addressing the situation.

- There should be a promotion of good race relations shifting emphasis from 'diversity' to 'integration' because diversity is political enclosure which is a fertile ground for extremism but integration will increase racial harmony and reduces racial harassment and economic lynching. It will bring about the growth of positive attitudes and relationships between different ethnic groups. It will also reduce racial prejudice in the white population and increase the feelings of security and inclusion among African-Caribbean people.

Conclusion

The chapter has also shown that none of the elements in economic lynching is a sufficient explanation of majority behaviour at the same time none should equally, none can be overlooked. A significant amount of verbal hostility can be comprehended only in terms of the personality make-up of the individuals expressing it, but this does not explain it all. Everyone is at times inclined to vent his or her irritation upon a scapegoat. Almost everyone is to some degree ethnocentric. Such attitudes reinforce behaviour patterns, make economic lynching possible, and in turn are reinforced by social patterns. Questions about why some attitudes are learned rather than others prompt complementary lines of inquiry; they do not lead to a more inclusive or more powerful kind of explanation. Despite the defence given on why some people lynch others economically, does not warrant the economic lynching emitted against the African-Caribbean people. The majority attitude had been responsible for the economic lynching of African-Caribbean people and this kind of lynching lead to low educational achievement among black youths. The problem will not go away until the government come up a better policy that will address the issue rather than paying a lip service to the causes of the problem. There should be a legislation barring Politicians from playing a race card for their own selfish ends. African-Caribbean people should be encouraged to be political active because if they are not, their view and problems will be misrepresented. In drawing the policy, African-Caribbean themselves must be involved in it. It is morally wrong in using people who do not understand anything about the African-Caribbean way of life to be formulating policy that affect them while those making the policy are part of those practicing Economic lynching, which is an instrument for suppression. In the next chapter we shall show how repression was used as an instrument of economic exclusion and the devastated consequences it had on black community.

Chapter Two
Political Repression

Introduction

IN THIS CHAPTER we are going to demonstrate how repression contributed toward low educational achievement among African-Caribbean children. As a result of repression, there was high rate of unemployment among African-Caribbean families; they were unable to provide for their children the necessities of life. It is rational that we cannot have anything decent in life, without having money to pay for it and to have the money to pay for something we want, we must hold jobs i.e. be in employment. Employment becomes a necessary end to obtain, food, cloth and shelter. Without a job one cannot be able to buy food, cloth and pay for ones rent or mortgage. Commonsense told us that if a man cannot afford the basic things of life, the possibility of his children making it academically is very remote; before you know it petty argument will set in. On the basis of that bitterness will start to eat the fabric of the family relationship, within a twinkle of an eye the relationship is over. Because it is assume that these African-Caribbean men are failure that is why they cannot be able to provide their family the basic things of lives. What was forgotten was that these African-Caribbean men did not choose to be failures they were subjected to it by the state because of the colour of their skin.

That notwithstanding, it would be morally wrong to blame the African-Caribbean women for their behaviour or perception of their African-Caribbean men because the society made them victim and to have a man the society has castrated under their roof could be a means of making African-Caribbean women double victims. Because the colour of the African- Caribbean people offend the British people, and to limit their numbers, economic lynching became one of the instrument they can use to achieve this objective. We all know that economic lynching on the basis of colour is not new; it has been within the British institution for a very long time[116]. Whenever an incident happened in America, such as "white Americans oppressing the black", our commentators will tell us that such a thing cannot happen in Britain because the race relation here is very good. Such analysis of the race relation in Britain is bagging the question because we know it is not true. In America, if the white does not like the black person

---

116   Barton, M., (1987) Racial Theories. Cambridge: Cambridge University Press.

standing in front of him he will tell him straight away without mimicking words but here in Britain that is not the case, they will pretend as if they like you and go behind your back to destroy you. They can pretend to like you when they want to make use of you. When they finish exploiting you or feel that you have outgrown your usefulness they will dump you and start looking for a means to remove you from the labour market. That is exactly what is happening to the black people in Britain.

Political Repression & Technique of Lynching

Before we go further into the research we must define political repression so that lay people who have no knowledge of political economy can understand the issues we are discussing concerning political repression. So what is political repression? According to English Encyclopaedia, political repression is the oppression or persecution of an individual or group for political reasons, particularly for the purpose of restricting or preventing their ability to take part in political life of society. Political repression may be represented by economic lynching policies, surveillance abuse, police misconduct including police brutality, and violent action such as the murder or forced disappearance of political activists and dissidents. These techniques mentioned in the definition, most of them had been used against the African-Caribbean people; when put together, it amount to economic lynching. Having said that, economic lynching of the African-Caribbean man is not something new, it has been in existence for over 100 years now[117]. We are not debating about the present nor the past but the combination of both. If we cast our mind back to chapter one, during the definition of economic lynching, we stated that one of the definitions is killing someone with a blunt instrument by using a physical force. In this chapter two, we are going to talk about "physically killing" more and also examine how it was applied, as a means of denying African Caribbean people the resources for survival. When the British elite saw that physical lynching was causing them so much in terms of lives of white people that were killed by African-Caribbean people in self defence, they decided to change tactics: by using unemployment as a weapon to achieve their aim.

This is how it all started. When the first word war broke out, the African-Caribbean people were brought in to fight and die for their motherland, Britain[118]. They believed that conspiracy theory that fighting for Britain was the same as fighting for their mother land but they were wrong because immediately after the war, they were reminded that they were different because of the colour of their skin, it became a barrier that separate "them" from "us". "US" the civilized white people while "THEM" African-Caribbean people who are partly children and partly animals. And should be sent back to the jungle where they belong. On that note, lynching started, wherever and whenever, an African-Caribbean person was sighted: whistle would be blown; signalling the present of an African-Caribbean person and the white mob would run after him. If the police employed a delay tactics, to enable the white mob to finish the job they would kill the African-Caribbean man with their bay hands. Because they mob enjoyed the support of the security forces, sometimes, they went on "nigger hunting"[119]. Since they believed that by hunting down the "niggers", African-Caribbean people, and killing them, African-Caribbeans would be eliminated from the Whiteman's soil. And to achieve that objective mass unemployment was inevitable.

117   Gilroy, P., (1993a) the Black Atlantic: Modernity and Double Consciousness. London: Verso.
118   Boyer, C., (1983) Dreaming the Rational City. Cambridge, MA: MIT Press.
119   Calhoun, C., (ed.) (1992) Habermas and the Public Sphere. Cambridge, MA: MIT Press.

Mass Unemployment and Lynching of Black People

As soon as peace agreement was signed on 11 November 1918, the war-time boom for African-Caribbean labour fizzled out as quickly as it had begun[120]. During that period shipping companies at a time, was the largest employer in Britain and they chose to sign on white foreign seamen rather than African-Caribbean British seamen which left African-Caribbean people in unimaginable poverty. The National Sailors' and Firemen's Union and National Union of Ships' Stewards, Cooks, Butchers and Bakers, the two forerunners of the National Union of Seamen, were unequivocally opposed to the employment of African-Caribbean seamen when white crews were available. This economic repression prompted William P. Samuels from British Guiana, a seaman stranded in Cardiff, to write to the Colonial Office seven weeks after the war:

"We kindly beg to appeal to you for justice. We are seafaring men that have served this Country faithfully in her past difficulties either in the services of His Britannic Majesty or in Mercantile Marine. The Places of our birth are surely British Possessions or Protectorates and here in Great Britain which is the Capital of the British Empire we are badly treated by the British People. We do not want any favour all we want is fair play. Every morning we go down to shipping offices to find ourselves work so as to make honest bread and are bluntly refused on account of our colour: whereas, foreigners of all nationality get the preference. This is not only in Cardiff but throughout the United Kingdom. What is the British Motto? Are we not men and brothers whom Christ died for? Why take such filthy advantages of men who have done you no wrong? Is it because we have no one to fight our cause? Why treat us as mere brute? Is it because we are mere dogs which neither Bark nor bite? No sir, we are men, men that gives the British Empire little or no trouble we kindly ask to step in to ameliorate the situation[121]".

By the following spring after the colonial office had received Mr Samuel's letter the Ministry of Labour's Employment Department sent secret instructions to labour exchange managers that unemployed African-Caribbean seamen of British nationality should be left in ignorance of their rights: over 130 black British seamen were on the beach in Glasgow, and hundreds more elsewhere, it was these men who were cheated of their right and subjected them to economic slavery and unbearable hunger pain. The majority of these men were eligible for out-of-work donation or unemployment benefit but they had apparently not realised that, and it was not considered desirable to take any further steps to acquaint them of the position because they want them to starve to death just for the fact they were blacks.[122]

This unimaginable repression of African-Caribbean people by the state triggered the first so-called race riots in British ports which took place on Tyneside. According to some historical account Arab and Somali seamen are said to have settled in South Shields in the 1860s, and there were some African-Caribbean seamen in North Shields before the First World War. That will tell you how long the African-Caribbean people have been living in England. However, the war increased the black population fourfold. To give

---

120   Benhabib, S., (1992) 'Models of Public Space: Hannah Arendt, the Liberal Tradition, and Jurgen Habermas', in C., Calhoun (ed.), Habermas and the Public Sphere. Cambridge, MA: MIT Press.

121   Back, L., and Solomos, J., (2000) (eds) Theories of Race and Racism: A Reader. London and New York: Routledge.

122   Davis, M., (2000) Magical Urbanism: Latinos Reinvent the US Big City. London: Verso.

you the flavour at that time, in February 1919, e.g. some Arab seamen, all British subjects, having just paid £2 each to clear their union books, which had to be up to date before they could ship out, were then refused work. An official of the stewards' and cooks' union, J.B.Fye, incited a crowd of foreign white seamen against them; although he was later convicted of using language likely to cause a breach of the peace[123]. Fye hit one of the Arabs and called him a terrorist, who hit him back. The crowd chased the Arabs to Holborn, the district of South Shields where they lived. Here, they were joined by some compatriots armed with revolvers, who fired warning shots over the heads of their attackers. The Arabs then turned the tables by chasing the crowd of white people back to the shipping office, wrecking it pretty thoroughly, and beating up Fye and another union official. Army and navy patrols were called in and 12 Arabs were arrested. At Durham Assizes, where the judge expressed some sympathy for them, three were acquitted, 7 were sentenced to three months', and two to one month's, hard labour[124].

Demobilization

Demobilization of African-Caribbean soldiers had increased Liverpool's black population to a figure variously estimated at 2,000 and 5,000, of who large proportions were out of work. In one week alone, in the spring of 1919, about 120 black workers employed for years in the big Liverpool sugar refineries and oilcake mills were sacked because white workers now refused to work with them. These African-Caribbean people began to live on credit as a result of that these unemployed black workers, living on credit from day to day, were being turned out of their lodgings and lives became increasingly unbearable for these poor people.

Because of this harsh reality these innocent African-Caribbean people face, On 13 May, the secretary of the Liverpool Ethiopian Association, the merchant D.T.Aleifasakure Toummavah, went to see the lord mayor, crying to him like Moses did when he went to Pharaoh asking him to let his people go. He told him that between 500 and 600 African-Caribbean men, mostly discharged British soldiers and sailors were out of work and stranded in the area and anxious to go home before they start dying of starvation in the country they come to liberate. According to D.T.Toummavah some were 'practical starving, work having been refused to them on account of their colour'. He suggested that the Colonial Office repatriate them and give each man a bounty of £5, since most had pawned their clothes to buy food. Some, he added, have been wounded, and lost limbs an eyes fighting for the Britain. As this was going on, the mayor also received a deputation claiming to represent 5,000 jobless white ex-servicemen and complaining of the presence of African-Caribbean workers in the city competing for jobs. In a state of confusion, the lord mayor told the Colonial Office, that there were fights between the two races, and matters were not likely to improve in this direction as the position developed and probably grew worse. The initial reaction of one official at the Colonial Office to the £5 bounty suggestion was that the 'Lord Mayor' should be given a hint that if Liverpool wants to get rid of these men on these terms it was up to Liverpool city to find the £5. When their request was not granted many of the discharged African-Caribbean soldiers started losing their lives, not in the battle field but in the hand of men and women they have come to liberate.

---

123   Goffman, E., (1974) Frame Analysis: An Essay on the Organization of Experience. Boston: Northeastern University Press.

124   Solomon, M., (2001) the history of colonialism, Cambridge: Cambridge University Press.

What the African-Caribbean community did not realise was that their predicament was the State instrument to eliminate their numbers. Because politicians saw economic lynching as a means to advance their position, they started pandering to racism and as result tension began to rise between the locals and these aliens (African-Caribbean community). Liverpool police did little to lessen the tension; because in the same month, they fought a battle with African-Caribbean men alleged to be running an illegal gaming house[125].

Remember that in chapter one, we demonstrated how political opportunism can lead to discrimination as a means of advancing their political position. By the second half of May, The Union and the government in power at that time has poisoned the political atmosphere, making the street of Britain very dangerous. African-Caribbean men peacefully walking the Liverpool streets were being 'attacked again and again'. On 4 June two Scandinavians stabbed a West Indian, John Johnson, when he refused to give them a cigarette according to Peter Frayer's account. Johnson was severely wounded in the face, and the news spread quickly. Because of that African-Caribbean community can no longer bear to watch while their kinsmen were being lynched to death for no apparent reason. The new that they too would be lynched to death if they stand aside and look without putting up any resistance to these unprovoked attack on innocent African-Caribbean community. Next evening eight of John Johnson friends went to the pub where the Scandinavians use, threw beer over a group of them, and then attacked them with sticks, knives, razors, and pieces of iron taken from lamp-posts, knocking unconscious a policeman who tried to stop them. Five Scandinavians were taken to hospital, but only one was detained[126].

In an effort to arrest those involved, police raided boarding houses used by African-Caribbean seamen. The seamen defended themselves, one with a poker, others with revolvers, knives, and razors. One policeman was shot in the mouth, another in the neck, a third was slashed on face and neck, and a fourth had his wrist broken. At one of the raided houses, 18 Upper Pitt Street lived Charles Wotten, a 24-year-old ship's fireman, variously described as a Bermudan and a Trinidadian, who had been discharged from the navy in the previous March. Wotten ran from the house, he was closely pursued by two policemen and by a crowd of between 200 and 300 mob hurling missiles. The police caught him at the edge of Queen's Dock, and gave him to the lynch mob who tore him from their hands and threw him into the water. Shouting 'Let him drown!' they pelted him with stones as he swam around until he died; his corpse was dragged from the dock afterward and no arrests were made.

Since nothing was done, the signal was sent out that it was okay to lynch and kill any African-Caribbean man seen walking on English soil as a result of that anti-black reign of terror raged in Liverpool. On 8 June three African-Caribbeans were stabbed in the street. And on the 10 June mobs of youths and young men in 'well organised' gangs, their total strength varying from 2,000 to 10,000, roamed the streets 'savagely attacking, beating and stabbing every negro they could find[127]'. One senior police officer reported to the Colonial Office, which was naturally anxious about possible repercussions in African-Caribbean countries to do something to ameliorate the situation. When the "Daily Times" got hold of the news it reported that "Whenever a Negro was seen he was chased, and caught, severely beaten"[128]. When they were able to make a stand, in their own dwellings, black people did so, defending themselves as best

---

125   Wood, W., (1999) Keep the faith baby, London: The Bible Reading fellowship pp.10-16.
126   Bagley, C., (2000) Acting on Principle: An examination of Race and Ethnicity, London: BAAF
127   Goldberg, D., (2002) The Racial State, Oxford: Blackwell.
128   Carey, P., (2001) 30 Days in Sydney: A Wildly Distorted Account. London: Bloomsbury.

as they could. Hunted down in the streets as individuals all they could do was flee from their pursuers some of whom took their belts off and lashed their quarries' heads and shoulders with the buckle ends as they fled. 'Quite inoffensive' people were attacked in the streets, including an ex-serviceman who held three decorations for war service. A black man 'holding a good position on one of the Liverpool liners' was dragged from a car, beaten up, and robbed of £175". On the evening of 10 June Toxteth Park was reported to be in a wild state of excitement, thousands of people filling the thoroughfares.

Hysteria grew as house after house occupied by African-Caribbean people was wrecked, looted, and set on fire. In Jackson Street, a crowd of 2,000 wrecked a lodging house, breaking up chairs to use the legs as bludgeons. A boarding house on the corner of Chester and Dexter Streets had its windows and doors smashed with sticks and stones, the coping-stones and rails in front of the house torn down. The Elder Dumpster shipping line's hostel for black seamen, accommodating between 300 and 400, was wrecked. The David Lewis hostel for black ratings was attacked and its windows were smashed. A house in Stanhope Street was set on fire. In Mill Street, the furniture was carried from a house, piled up outside, and set on fire; then the house itself went up in flames. In Beaufort Street the mob tore down a house's shutters for battering rams, smashed doors and windows to splinters, dragged out furniture and bedding and made bonfire of them. Houses in Parliament Street and Chester Street were wrecked. Five white youths were seen on a roof, stripping off the slates and throwing them down on the occupants' heads[129].

There is a feeling of terror among the African-Caribbean people of the city, reported a local newspaper. All night long until sunrise, it added, 'black men could be seen in companies hastening along unfrequented throughout to the nearest police station'. Seventy people who left their homes to shelter in the Ethiopian Hall, the Ethiopian Association's social club, were transferred to the Cheapside bride-well in police vans for their protection. By 10 June, 700 men, women, and children had taken refuge in the bride wells and more were arriving hourly. Others sought sanctuary in fire stations[130].

At the height of the rioting, **the Liverpool "Courier"** poured oil on the flames with a feature article headed '*Where East Meets West*' and an editorial headed '*Black and White*'. *The former told how, on a visit to St James Place, You glimpse black figures beneath the gas lamps, and somehow you think of pimps, and bullies, and women, and birds of ill-omen generally, as now and again you notice a certain watchful callousness that seems to hint of nefarious trades and drunkenness in dark rooms*[131].

Behind the smashed glass of the upstairs rooms Negroes hide in the darkness, protected from violence by a cordon of police. An ambulance goes past, and the howl of the mob dies away on a delighted note when the word goes about that 'another blooming' nigger has been laid out[132].

129 Butler, J., (1990) Gender Trouble: Feminism and the Subversion of Identity. London: Routledge

130 Habermas, J., (1991) The Structural Transformation of the Public Sphere: An Inquiry into a Category of Bourgeois Society (Thomas Burger, trans.). Cambridge, MA: MIT Press.

131 Bhabha, H., (1997) Minority Culture and Creative Anxiet. From British Council (2003) Reinventing Britain web site.

132 Liverpool Currier (1918) quoted in Peter Fryers

The editorial, demanding 'the stern punishment of black scoundrels', was more inflammatory still:
"One of the chief reasons of popular anger behind the present disturbances lies in the fact that the average negro is nearer the animal than is the average white man, and that there are women in Liverpool who have no self-respect. The white man regards "the black man" as part child, part animal, and part savage. It is quite true that many of the blacks in Liverpool are of a low type, that they insult and threaten respectable women in the street, and that they are invariably unpleasant and provocative".

An 'experienced' police officer took a slightly different view. Attributing much of the trouble to outsiders, he told the Manchester Guardian: 'The people here understand the negroes. They know that most of them are only big children who when they get money like to make a show. The Negroes would not have been touched but for their relations with white women. This has caused the entire trouble[133]"

It was left to a local magistrate to say that it was the white mobs which were 'making the name of Liverpool an abomination and disgrace to the rest of the country[134]'.

That was not however the feeling in south Wales, which was experiencing at the same time 'one of the most vicious outbreaks of racial violence that has yet occurred in Britain'. During a week of anti- black rioting, three men were killed and dozens injured, and the damage caused to property cost Cardiff council over £3,000 to repair. The rioting 'left a scar on the race relations of the city which took more than a generation to heal[135].

Probably healing is not the right word to use because up to today in the 21st century African-Caribbean people are at the receiving end. Trouble began in Newport. On 6 June 1919, a crowd gathered together when an African-Caribbean man was alleged to have made an offensive remark to a white woman. One account said he put his arm round her and he was attacked by a soldier. There was a fight in which many people were hurt, crowds started smashing the windows of African-Caribbean people's homes, and the occupants defended themselves with pokers and staves and fired warning shots over their assailants' heads. Two houses in George Street were wrecked and ransacked by a mob of several thousands that smashed every window, tore out the window-frames, threw bedding and furniture, including a 'valuable piano', into a nearby railway siding, and set fire to them. In Dolphin Street, Chinese laundries and a Greek-owned lodging house were wrecked, at same time as African-Caribbean people' houses in Rupert Street and a restaurant in Commercial Road owned by a black man named Degrader[136]. Twenty black and two white men were arrested. Plain-clothes and mounted police were drafted into the town, but it took a baton charge to disperse crowds making fresh attacks on George Street boarding houses. 'We are all one in Newport and mean to clear these niggers out', one rioter told a reporter. The scene in Newport, said the South Wales Argus, looked like the aftermath of an air raid: 'Windows were smashed, furniture in the front rooms had been wrecked, and blood-stains were visible."

---

133   Manchester Guardian

134   Martin, B.,(2000) Between Camps: Nations, Culture and the Allure of Race. London: Allen Lane.

135   Hesse, B., (1993) Black to Front and Black Again: Racialization Through Contested Times and Spaces, in M., Keith and S., Pile (eds.), Place and the Politics of Identity. London: Routledge.

136   Keith, M., (1993) Race, Riots and Policing: Lore and Disorder in a Multi-Racist Society. London: UCL Press.

On 11 June, at Cadoxton near Barry, a 30-year-old demobilized white soldier named Frederick Henry Longman, a dock labourer by trade, accosted a 45-year-old seaman from the French West Indies named Charles Emanuel with the words 'Why don't you go into your own street?' then punched him on the forehead. Three other white men joined in, one of whom began hitting Emanuel on the back with a poker. Emanuel took out a clasp-knife and stabbed Longman, killing him instantly. Emanuel was chased by a large crowd and arrested with the knife still in his hand; he was later found guilty of manslaughter and sent to prison for five years[137]. But Tony Martin killed a burglary that break into his home he was set free on the ground of self defence. That does not apply to a black person because a black man has no right to defend himself when attacked. That is why Charles Emanuel was sent down for five years with hard labour. After his arrest crowds gathered outside the police station, smashed the windows of black people's homes, and 'paraded the streets of Camdenton looking for black men' until the early hours of the morning. Next day, extra police were drafted in, because of the attempts to wreck black people's homes by white mobs.

On 11 June a brake containing African-Caribbean men and their white wives, returning from an excursion, attracted a large and hostile crowd. Soon a crowd of whites and a crowd of blacks were lined up on opposite sides of Canal Parade Bridge. A reporter saw 'a howling mob of young fellows and girls facing the African-Caribbean's at about 100 yards distance'. With shouts of "Come on and set about them!" the whites made a rush from the north side throwing stones, whereupon revolver shots came from the African-Caribbean crowd and a white soldier was wounded in the thigh[138]. The whites pressed forward in an attempt to reach Bute Town, the narrow cluster of streets between the Glamorganshire Canal and the Taff Vale Railway where a large number of Cardiff's African-Caribbean citizens had their homes, but police managed to stop most of them.

The chief constable's report, which was issued a month later, blamed the white mobs for the original incident. 'If the crowd had overpowered the police and got through', he wrote, 'the result would have been disastrous, as the black population would probably have fought with desperation and inflicted great loss of life[139].

Some attackers did get into Bute Street, where they smashed the doors and windows of Arab owned lodging-houses with sticks one shop front was 'smashed to matchwood' and where a woman was arrested for flourishing a razor and 'vowing vengeance on "niggers"[140]. A house in Humphrey Street was set on fire and gutted, and in Caroline Street a white man died after his throat was cut by an Arab man, it was alleged, though no eyewitness ever came forward, no black man was found in the vicinity, and no one was ever charged with the crime. Because no one was charged a house owned by African-Caribbean people at the corner of Morgan Street and Adam Street were ransacked. Police broke into a house and dragged out a black man with blood streaming from his head: 'He was greeted by a howl from the crowd, and several kicks and punches were aimed at him.' A second soon appeared, 'in much the same condition as his compatriot'. Last to be brought out was 'a white girl, whose mouth was bleeding'. In the same house

137   Hines, V., (1972) The Black man and the future, London: Zulu Publication.
138   Vines, V.,(1995a) 'Ethnic Entrepreneurs and Street Rebels; Looking Inside the Inner City', in S., Pile and N., Thrift (eds.), Mapping the Subject. London: Routledge.
139   Henes, V., (1993b) Small Acts: Thoughts on the Politics of Black Cultures. London: Serpent's Tail.
140   Dominic, L., (1995b) 'Conclusion', in S. Pile and M. Keith (eds.), Geographies of Resistance. London: Routledge.

a black man called Norman Roberts was also brought out admitted to hospital with a severe knife wound in the abdomen. The disturbances went until around midnight[141].

This was only the prelude to a much more determined and organized attack on Cardiff's African-Caribbean community. Knowing what was about to take place, the whole of the city's police force was concentrated in the cordoned off area that The "Times" called 'nigger town'; a company of the Welsh Regiment was secretly drafted into Cardiff and held in readiness; and the stipendiary magistrate was preparing to read the Riot Act. Contemporary reports make it clear that 'Colonial soldiers' (i.e. Australians) armed with rifles placed themselves at the head of the lynch mobs. 'The methods adopted by the soldiers', said one report, 'were those of active service, because the men, after firing from the prone position upon the blacks, crawled back to safety.' Some of these riflemen were in khaki or blue uniforms, others in mufti with medal ribbons[142]. The Western Mail gave a vivid account of an attack on the former Princess Royal hotel in Millicent Street: Several Colonial soldiers present constituted themselves the ringleaders of the besieging party, which was largely made up of discharged soldiers.

The door of the house was attacked and it was quickly burst in. Men crowded into the narrow hall and began to ascend the stairs. A revolver shot rang out, and with it the exclamation, 'My God, I am hit!' Five other shots quickly followed.

The attackers dropped flat on their faces, crawling back and telling those behind to do the same. They held up a table as a shield, and the defenders backed to the wall of the room. 'Once at close quarters, each of the surviving attackers took his man, and soon desperate struggles were in progress around the room.' Meanwhile 'others of the raiding party were busily engaged in ransacking the premises. Kit bags containing clothing were hastily abstracted, and there were willing "receivers" outside.' After it had been looted the house was set on fire. It was in Millicent Street that 40-year-old John Donovan, wearing his Moms ribbon, was shot through the heart by a cornered Arab[143].

Ibrahim Ishmael, a Somali seaman and poet who was living in Cardiff at this time, refers to the Millicent Street fighting in his remarkable autobiography, completed in 1928 and recently discovered by Dr Richard Pankhurst. A Warsangeli, from the eastern part of what was then the British Somaliland protectorate; Ishmael was between 18 and 23 years old and worked as a ship's fireman. He and some companions had only just come to Cardiff at the time of the trouble:

"Shortly after our arrival the black people in Cardiff were attacked by crowds of white people. A Warsangeli named 'Abdi Langara had a boarding house in Millicent Street, right in the European part of the town. It is there that I used to have my dinner every day. 'Abdi acted as a sort of agent for the Warsangeli, who left their money with him when they went to sea, and also had their letters sent to his place. As soon as the fight started, all the Warsangeli who were in Cardiff went to Millicent Street to defend 'Abdi's house in case it was attacked. But to me and to my best friend who has since died in Mecca they said, "You are too young to come, and you have never faced difficulties of this kind[144]". We insisted, for we could not bear to stay away when our brothers were

141   Charles, M., (2004) After the Cosmopolitan. London: Routledge.

142   Kymlicka, W., (1995) Multicultural Citizenship: A Liberal Theory of Minority Rights. Oxford: Clarendon Press.

143   Malik, K., (1996) the Meaning of Race. London: Routledge.

144   Pollock, S., Breckenridge, C., and Chakrabarty, D., (2000) 'Cosmopolitanisms'. Public Culture, 12 (3): 577—91.

in danger of being killed, but our plea was of no avail So we went to the Somali boarding house of Headsail and there we waited, ready for an attack, as we expected that a crowd of white people might break in at any moment.

In Millicent Street, the fight started at about 7:30 p.m. and lasted a fairly long time. Seven or eight Warsangeli defended the house and most of them got badly wounded. Some of the white people also received wounds. In the end, the whites took possession of the first floor, soaked it with paraffin oil and set it alight. The Somalis managed to keep up the fight until the police arrived. One of them was left for dead in the front room and was later carried to the hospital where he recovered; some escaped through a neighbouring house and came to tell us the story of what had happened, the others gave themselves up to the police, and we did not see them for a long time[145].

Crowds led by soldiers were surging from street to street wherever the cry of 'blacks' went up. One victim had a crowd of about 1,000 after him. The newspaper accounts are eloquent: 'Always "the black man" was their quarry, and whenever one was rooted out by the police the mob rushed upon him, and he got away with difficulty' amid cries of "Kill him!" A black man spotted near the Wharf Bridge was first insulted and then attacked by three whites, one of whom blew a whistle. This seemed to be an expected signal, because hundreds of persons rushed up from the neighbouring streets, including many women and girls, who had sticks and flung them at the unfortunate African-Caribbean man as they chased him along the street.

Two men dragged out of their Bute Street house fought desperately with frying pans and pokers. A Somali priest, Hadji Mahomet, was prepared to face the mob, but his white wife pleaded with him to hide so he clambered up a drainpipe, hid on the roof, 'and with true Eastern stoicism watched his residence being reduced to a skeleton'. A Malayan boarding house in Bute Terrace was wrecked and the occupants, fleeing to the roof, were pelted with stones. In Humphrey Street an Arab named Au Abdul fired a revolver at his assailants; when he was arrested there were shouts of 'Now we've got him!' and 'Lynch him!' (Charged later with attempted murder, he 'had some difficulty in walking into court owing to an injured leg, and he also bore evidence on his forehead of having received injuries[146]'.)

One whom the lynch mob did succeed in killing, a young Arab named Mohammed Abdullah, died in hospital of a fractured skull after being savagely beaten in an attack on an Arab restaurant and boarding house, used chiefly by Somalis. The mob charged down the street, threw stones into the building from both sides, and smashed the windows. Shots were fired from upstairs. The mob surged in, and police arrived soon afterwards. The inquest on Abdullah could not decide whether he had been hit on the head with a chair leg or a police truncheon. Hundreds of African-Caribbean people attended his funeral. Murder charges against six white men were dropped for lack of evidence[147]. Whenever a white man kills a black man he never goes down for it, there is always lack of evidence for it. Just like when Stephen Lawrence was murdered by six white men none of them get convicted for that crime. What this demonstrates is systematic pertain used to lynch African-Caribbean people in the last ten decade or so.

---

145   Desmond, P., (1996) Democracy and Difference: Changing Boundaries of the Political. Princeton: Princeton University Press

146   Rattansi, A., (2003) 'Who's British? Prospect and the New Assimilationism', in Runnymede Trust (ed.), Cohesion, Community and Citizenship. London: Runnymede Trust.

147   Rex, J., and Mason, D., (1986) (eds.) Theories of Race and Ethnic Relations. Cambridge: Cambridge University Press.

Some former members of the British West Indies Regiment were daring enough to go about the streets with their uniforms on, which afforded them some protection. But not much. One black ex-serviceman, described in a local paper as 'a well-set-up young fellow', 'proved to be a brave man, and in perfect English appealed to the crowd not to molest him, but this did not prevent him receiving several blows' before police escorted him away.

For the most part however, in the words of the "Western Mail", 'the efforts of the police were confined to keeping the white men from damaging property'. Property being more important than people, the community under siege had two choices. They could leave the city; or they could turn their ghetto into a fortress[148]. A few did leave, on the afternoon of 13 June: a sad little procession of seamen with kit-bags on their backs and sticks in their hands, escorted by police and followed by jeering crowds[149]. The majority chose to stay and, if need be, fight.

As crowds gathered again that evening in St Mary Street, at the top end of Bute Road, the black citizens of Loudoun Square, Maria Street, Sophia Street, and Angelina Street 'established quietly determined means of self- protection'. They posted sentries, loaded their guns, and left no one in doubt of their mood, as a South Wales News reporter who got through the police cordon testified:
"The African-Caribbean men, while calm and collected, were well prepared for any attack, and had the mob from the city broken through the police cordon there would have been bloodshed on a big scale, and the attacking force would have suffered heavily. Hundreds of Negroes were collected, but these were very peaceful, and were amicably discussing the situation among them. Nevertheless, they were in a determined mood, and ready to defend 'their quarter of the city' at all costs. They had posted sentries at each entrance to give notice of the approach of any hostile crowd". "An old resident of Loudoun-square told me, the journalist continued, that he and his wife had watched the Negroes loading revolvers. They made no secret of it. As my informant put it, he added, 'There is enough arms and ammunition among them to stock an arsenal." Long-term black residents said: 'It will be hell let loose if the mob comes into our streets, if we are unprotected from hooligan rioters who can blame us for trying to protect ourselves[150].

As this trouble was going on African-Caribbean people have no one to speak for them. Dr Rufus Fennell volunteered himself to become their spoke man. He proved himself an outstanding leader of Cardiff's black community. He was West Indian, medically trained in the United States; he had survived 314 days of trench warfare and had been wounded three times while serving in Mesopotamia, where he had attended thousands of British troops. Lacking British medical qualifications, he had been practising as a dentist in Pontypridd and was refused to practice as a surgeon which he was trained. When the rioting started in Cardiff he went there. Neil Evans, interviewing old people in Cardiff in the 70s, found that Fennell was remembered for his courage and intelligence: 'During the riots he was said to have walked boldly into the centre of the town, despite warnings of the possible dire consequences of this action.' Aged

148   Rory, R., (1998) 'Justice as a Larger Loyalty', in P. Cheah and B. Robbins (eds.), Cosmopolitics: Thinking and Feeling Beyond the Nation. Minneapolis and London: University of Minnesota Press. .

149   Alexander, P., and Halpern, R., (2000) (eds.) Radicalizing Class, Classifying Race:

150   Anthias, F., and Yuvai D., (1992) Racialized Boundaries: Race, Nation, Gender, Colour and Class and the Anti-racist Struggle. London: Routledge.

31, about six feet tall, well dressed and highly articulate, Fennell acted as the community's spokesman in negotiations with the authorities; pressed the claims of those who wanted to be repatriated; told reporters 'that it is absolutely necessary to grip the evil, and not to play with it'; and told one of several protest meetings held at the docks by West Indians, Somalis, Arabs, Egyptians, and 'Portuguese subjects' that it was their duty to stay within the law, but 'if they did not protect their homes after remaining within the law they would be cowards, not men[151]'.

This lynching had given a reason to repatriate the wounded soldiers without compensation and by mid-September, 1919 600 African-Caribbean men had been repatriated. But not everyone involved wanted to be, and part of Cardiff's black population indignantly rejected the offer. What the chief constable, in a confidential report to Scotland Yard, called the 'militant section' insisted on their right as British subjects to get fair treatment and stay in the United Kingdom. And some of the militants, the chief constable added, 'expressed their willingness to be repatriated but openly stated that it would only be for the object of creating racial feeling against members of the white race domiciled in their countries[152].

Majority who wanted to be repatriated about Two hundred of them Egyptians, Somalis, and Arabs were sent to Plymouth by train, and Fennell went with them. Unhappy the way these men who fought for the empire were abused, he told the weekly paper John Bull how shamefully they were treated. That the men were penniless he said, but the tiny gratuity promised them was never paid. They were hungry, but were given nothing to eat on the journey. And when they went on board ship, the staffs were all off duty, the captain was asleep, and there was no food at all for them. 'These black Britons had all done first-class war work', reported John Bull, 'yet they were treated worse than repatriated enemy aliens[153].

Immediately after that episode Fennell was in London, complaining to MPs and the Home Office about the flaws in the repatriation process of the African-Caribbean war heroes. Some had been sent home before they were paid compensation for losses suffered in the riots; others, before receiving the back pay due to them. Fennell accused the Cardiff police of prejudice against African-Caribbean people and asked that police cease to supervise the departures[154]. But the officials were unsympathetic, almost immediately after leaving the Home Office Fennell found him under arrest on a trumped-up fraud charge. After being kept in custody in London for a while he came up in court in Cardiff on 22 July, accused of obtaining £2 by false pretences from Ahmed Ben Ahmed Demary, a boarding house master. Fennell's solicitor reminded the court that there was 'a great deal at the back of the case' and that 'certain men were anxious to keep the accused in prison because of the way he had watched the interests of the African-Caribbean men'. The magistrate set him down on the trumped-up evidence of the police as a way of removing another nigger from the street[155].

151   Rose, N., (1999) Powers of Freedom: Re framing Political Thought. Cambridge: Cambridge University Press.

152   Modood, T., (1997) Ethnic Minorities in Britain: Diversity and Disadvantage. London: Policy Studies Institute.

153   Rowthorn, B., (2003) 'A Question of Responsibility'. Open Democracy www. opendemocracy.net/ debateSIartic40964SS

154   Karl, C., (1987) 'Recent Marxist Theories of Nationalism and the Issue of Racism'. British Journal of Sociology, XXXVIII, 1: 24—43.

155   Cohen, P., (2002) 'Psychoanalysis and Racism: Reading the Other Scene', in D.T. Goldberg and J. Solomos (eds.), A Companion to Racial and Ethnic Studies. Oxford: Blackweil.

Since there was unholy alliance with every institution in UK, London was not spared sporadic outbreaks of anti-black rioting. On 16 April there was a 'serious trouble in Cable Street, Stepney. Shots were fired, a violent Street fighting took place, and several black seamen were injured. On 29 May a man named William Samuel, described by a Colonial Office servant as 'a burly negro, with an aggressive manner' wrote to the Sailors Home in St Anne Street, Lime house, to the secretary, complaining of attacks on black men. 'a sergeant of police said to William Samuel that night, "why; we want niggers out of our country this is a white man's country and not yours"[156]. That same evening large crowds gathered outside black people's Home in West India Dock Road, cat-calling and inning every black person who appeared and trying to force their way in and lynch them.

There were similar scenes outside lodging-houses used by African-Caribbean seamen. Outside the St Anne Street sailors' hostel 29-year old John Martin, a Jamaican on four weeks' leave from the Royal Navy was seized by the head from behind, knocked down by men with sticks, and kicked in the mouth. Alleged to have fire revolver towards the crowd, Martin was arrested with injuries head and face, and charged with wounding a ship's fireman, although he was found not guilty[157]. White mob were not happy with the result, on 16 June a coffee-shop in Cable Street use by African-Caribbean people was stormed by a crowd that seized one of the customers and beat him. Because of this barbaric act, the next day there were disturbances in Poppy where a gang attacked a house occupied by a Chinese cleared out the furniture, stacked it in the middle of the road set fire to it, causing a 'huge blaze' that gutted the house. However, the reason the Chinese houses were attacked had nothing to do with skin colour; the only explanation for it is that, British people believe that Chinese are communists and were trying to infect British capitalism with dangerous communism.

This explanation for riots was advanced by a former British colonial administrator, "Ralph Williams", who had served in Bechuanaland and Barbados and had been governor of the Windward Islands in 1906-9. His hobby was 'ceaseless travelling to far away countries, and when the riots reached their climax he wrote a letter to The "Times" summing up what he had learnt on his travels:
"To almost every white man and woman who has lived a life among African-Caribbean people, intimate association between black men and white women is a thing of horror. It is an instinctive certainty that sexual relations between white women and black men revolt our very nature what blame to those white men who, seeing these conditions and loathing them, resort to violence? We cannot forcibly repatriate British subjects of good character, but we can take such steps as will prevent the employment of an unusually large number of men of colour in our great shipping centres[158]*"*

Five days later The "*Times*" printed a stinging reply, drawing attention to the existence of hundreds of thousands of persons of mixed race in South Africa and the West Indies, where 'young girls of 13 and 14 years of age are used to gratify the base lust of white seducers'. These girls were left with children of mixed race on their hands 'to mourn the "honour" of the civilized white man'. The writer went on, "I do not believe that any excuse can be made for white men who take the law into their own hands because

156   Bonnett, A., (2000) White Identities: Historical and International Perspectives. Hemel Hempstead: Prentice Hall.

157   Eisenstein, Z., (1996) Hatreds: Racialized and Sexualized Conflicts in the Twenty First Century. New York: Routledge.

158   Carter, B., (2000) Realism and Racism: Concepts of Race in Sociological Research. London: Routledge.

they say they believe that the association between the men of black race and white women is degrading. Sir Ralph Williams and those who think like him should remember that writing in this way gives a stimulus to these racial riots and can only have one ultimate result, the downfall of the British Empire. If Sir Ralph Williams thinks that the problem can be solved by sending every black or coloured back to his own country, then we should be compelled to see that every white man is sent back to England from Africa and from the West India islands in order that the honour of our sisters and daughters there may be kept intact".[159]

The writer of this letter was Felix Eugene Michael Hercules, for a brief but key period one of the inspirers and leaders of the national liberation movement in the British West Indies.

To understand the anti-black riots in Britain and the black community's response we have to see them in the context of social unrest. The end of the First World War ushered in 'the most turbulent an age of profound social crisis ever known by Britain and that overwhelming majority of its people who toil to live. In 1919 a strikers demonstration in Glasgow was attacked by police and its leaders were mercilessly beaten; miners, railway and transport workers became highly in a militant mood; there was a lightning police strike; there were mutinies in army camps and depots, and thousands of Army Service Corps men commandeered lorries and poured into London to lay their grievances before the government[160].

Because of the divisive role of racism in Liverpool and Cardiff that year is obvious; white workers in bitter economic competition with African-Caribbean workers were mobilized into lynch mobs led by army officers. This was very far from the revolution that Britain's rulers feared. But the social unrest of 1919 was not limited to the heart of the British Empire and that was what gave Hercules' reply to Williams considerably more political bite than either, perhaps, could have realized when it was printed. A 'rising tide of colour' was bringing 'serious race riots in the United States, constitutional agitation in India, and economic and political unrest in several British African-Caribbean colonies, in South Africa, and the Belgian Congo. It was believed that this new race consciousness was a direct result of the Great War'. Events in Liverpool and Cardiff could not but stimulate the growth of black consciousness in Britain's colonies. In particular, they hastened the growth of anti-colonialism in the British African Caribbean's.

Because of economic downturn, the government began to talk about repatriation. In a communication on 'Repatriation of African-Caribbean Men', the colonial secretary, Lord Miner, pointed out that many of the black men attacked in the riots had served in the army, navy, and merchant service during the war and bitterly resented the ingratitude shown in the attacks. He feared the effect their return to the colonies would have on attitudes to white minorities there[161]. His fears were soon justified.

Some of the Trinidadians who had experienced the Cardiff riots, By mid-July were back home and within days of their return there was fighting in the streets against sailors from HMS Dartmouth. Four months later the Trinidad workers' fury erupted in a dock strike that brought British colonialism to its knees within days, when the governor persuaded the shipping agents to grant the strikers' demand for a 25 per

159   Dalal, F., (2002) Race, Colour and the Process of Racialization: New Perspectives from Analysis, Psychoanalysis, and Sociology. Hove: Brunner-Routledge.

160   Haralambos, M., and Holborn, M., (2000) Sociology, 5th edn. London: Collins.

161   Jacobson, M., (1998) Whiteness of a Different Color: European Immigrants and the Alchemy of Race. Cambridge, MA: Harvard University Press

cent wage increase[162]. Soldiers' demobilized from the British West Indies Regiment began an insurrection in Belize in July, and people were heard shouting: "This is our country and we want to get the white man out; the white man has no right here". In the same month five or six seamen from HMS Constance were wounded in hand-to-hand fighting in Kingston, Jamaica, and the captain landed an armed party to put down the outbreak which Jamaica's acting governor attributed to the treatment which had been received by African-Caribbean sailors at Cardiff and Liverpool [163].

By the October of that year the upsurge of black consciousness in the West Indies, the growing labour troubles there, and the start of the national liberation struggle had so alarmed the British government that it sent the State Department a confidential report on 'Unrest among the Negroes', a copy of which came to light in the United States National Archives in the 1960s. Britain's rulers feared that black radicalism in the USA might infect, and inflame, their black subjects in the Caribbean. They were pretty scared of Marcus Garvey's militant paper, the "Negro World". And the activities of Felix Hercules also caused them much concern. Herclus letter became the first general secretary of the Society of Peoples of African Origin and associate secretary of the African Progress Union.

Towards the end of June 1919 Hercules began a tour of the West Indies, with the dual aim of investigating conditions and recruiting for the Society of Peoples of African Origin. He spent two months in Jamaica and a few weeks in Trinidad, then went to British Guiana. Three months later he tried to get back into Trinidad, but the governor would not let him land. In the West Indies as in Britain, police kept close watch on him and reported every word he said. 'He is a very learned man', said one police report. But they could not pin anything on him. There is an air of frustration about Sir Basil Thomson's comment in December 1919: 'Though Hercules is careful what he says in public, in private he is inciting the negroes to take matters into their own hands.' Eleven days later Major-General Sir Newton James Moore, MP, former premier of Western Australia, was assuring the Commons that Hercules' activities had a great deal to do with the unrest in the African-Caribbean colonies[164].

He told them that after 1920 they lost sight of Hercules; but early in 1921, in an intelligence summary of economic and social conditions in the West Indies, Rear-Admiral Sir Allan Everett reported that 'agitators like Hercules and Marcus Garvey type, who thunder against white rule and preach the doctrine of self determination in countries where blacks greatly preponderate, are growing factors to be reckoned with as regards potential unrest' Hercules' published statements made it clear that he 'thundered' the Pan-Africanise tradition. He told readers of the "*African Telegraph*" that he had originally been an internationalist[165]. But 'England, with its barriers and its prejudices, its caste system, Western civilisation with its deification of Money and Force where one hoped to find Christ, these things it is that have driven him to the refuge of his own people'. Nonetheless he still believed, he added, "that the day will surely come when men of every nationality and of every race will look back at colour and see clearly the brotherhood in man". Toasting

162   Lewis, G., and Phoenix, A., (2004) '"Race", "Ethnicity" and Identity', in K. Woodward (ed.), Questioning Identity. London: Routledge.

163   Macey, D., (2000) Frantz Fanon: A Life. London: Gretna Books.

164   Walker, M., (1978) "The National front", New York: Fontana.

165   Rose, S., (1976) Scientific Racism and IQ, in Nicholas Rose (ed.) "The Political Economy of Science", London: Macmillan.

'The African Race' at the African Progress Union's inaugural dinner in 1918, he declared: "I believe in the destiny of the Race to which we have the honour to belong"[166].

When he spoke in Jamaica in 1919 on 'Unity of the Coloured Race', stressing the need for race pride and consciousness, and for cooperation among the black people of Africa, the West Indies, and the United States he comment was not reported in the island's press, but his telegrams were scrutinized and he himself was 'carefully watched[167].'

With graduate qualities Hercules showed his mettle and his political acumen above all in his reaction to the anti-black riots in Britain. He was not a member of the deputation, led by Archer as president of the African Progress Union that went to see Liverpool's deputy lord mayor on 16 June 1919. But Hercules was one of the speakers at a protest meeting in Hyde Park, convened by the Society of Peoples of African Origin. And, as the society's general secretary, he wrote to the colonial secretary asking whether the government intended 'to take adequate measures for the protection of British subjects in this country' and calling for an inquiry which never took place, into the death of Charles Wotten. His letter went on:

"Hundreds of Africans and West Indians have for years been living as law-abiding citizens in Liverpool, at Cardiff and in other large towns, some of them have married British Women and settled down, and the records of the Police will show, even better than we can profess to, what has been the incidence of law-breaking amongst them.
My Society has, however, learned with horror and regret that large numbers of Africans-Caribbeans who came here either as seamen or in a military capacity to help the Mother Country during a critical period have been 'signed off' and left stranded at various ports[168].

Lord Milner's bland reply promised that black British seamen, and black men from the colonies who had served in the Forces during the war, would be granted a resettlement allowance of £5 and a voyage allowance, provided that they applied within two months.

For Hercules, as for the entire black community in Britain, the final straw came a month after the riots, when it was decided not to allow any black troops to take part in London's victory celebrations: the much-trumpeted Peace March on 19 July 1919. In an "African Telegraph" editorial written on the eve of his departure for the West Indies, Hercules put into words what every black person in the country was feeling about British ingratitude, injury, and insult and went on to draw the necessary political conclusions. "*Every ounce of strength was put into the struggle by the African-Caribbean man. He fought with the white man to save the white man's home and the war was won. African-Caribbean men in the entire world are asking to-day, what have we got? What are we going to get out of it all? The answer, in effect, comes clear, convincing, and conclusive: 'Get back to your kennel, you damned dog of a nigger*[169]!'

His anger was that residences of African-Caribbean men were demolished; and were pounded in the streets, drowned, butchered in cold blood and terribly massacred and maimed, with the Imperial Cabinet looking on without a clear statement of policy on the subject. No black troops were allowed to take part

---

166   Edward, R., (1976) Socio-biology, "the New Synthesis, New York: Harvard University.
167   Donald, S., (1975) Cultural Bases of Racism and Group Aggression, Devon: Two Rider Press.
168   Goldberg, S., (1977) The Inevitability of Patriachy, London: Temple Smith.
169   Lawrence, M., (1980) Throwing a Naked Light on Political and Natural Gas, Daily Telegraph, 20 February.

in the Peace March. The quietness of the Imperial Government during the race riots drives home the fact that they approve of them.

Four years after the riots of 1919 they had been expunged from white memories. The author of an article on 'Britain's Negro Problem' in the Atlantic Review could assure his American readers that 'up to the present time, Great Britain has been spared the odium of race riots[170]'. Black memories, however, were not so conveniently short. For Britain's black community, 1919 illuminated reality like a flash of lightning. The lessons of the riots were etched into the consciousness of an entire generation[171]. Through the 1920s, 1930s, and 1 940s black people in Britain, struggling against the hidden and open attacks on them that went by the name of 'colour bar', knew very well what their fate would be if they failed to struggle. All they had to sustain them in this struggle against economic lynching was a pride and militancy that owed much to the work of 'agitators' like Felix Hercules who fought against propaganda like horror on the Rhine.

Horror on the Rhine

Horror on the Rhine is a Racist propaganda against the African-Caribbean people. It is important to note that attacks on black people were not the prerogative of right-wingers: One such attack came in 1920 from the pen of the prominent left-winger E.D.Morel, secretary and part-founder of the Union of Democratic Control and editor of its journal "Foreign Affairs". Morel, whose father was French and whose real name was Georges Edmond Pierre Achilles Morel-de-Ville, had founded the Congo Reform Association in 1904 and was 'more than any other individual: responsible for terminating King Leopold's infamous regime in the Congo'. The year was 1897; he was burly man in his mid-twenties with a handlebar moustache. He was confident and well spoken but his British speech was without the polish of Eton or Oxford. He was well dressed but the clothes were not from Bond Street. With an ailing mother and a wife and growing family to support, he was not the sort of person likely to get caught-up in an idealistic cause. His ideas were thoroughly conventional. His look was sober like that of a respectable businessman.

Edmund Dene Morel was a trusted employee of a Liverpool shipping line. A subsidiary of the company had the monopoly on all transport of cargo to and from the Congo Free State, as it was then called, the huge territory in central Africa that was the world's only colony claimed by one man. That man was king Leopold the 2nd of Belgium, a ruler much admired throughout Europe as a philanthropic monarch. He had welcomed Christian missionaries to his new colony: his troops, it was said, have fought and defeated local slave traders who pray on population; and for more than a decade European newspapers have praised him for investing his personal fortune in public works to benefit the Africans.

Because Morel speaks fluent French, his company sends him to Belgium every week to supervise the loading and unloading of ships on Congo run. Although the officials he worked with had been handling this shipping traffic for years without a second thought, morel began to notice things that unsettled him.

---

170   Foot, P., (1969) Immigration and Race in British Politics, London: Penguin.
171   Eysenck, J., (1971) Race, Intelligence and Education, Kent: Temple Smith

At the Docks of the big port of Antwerp he sees his Company's ships arriving filled to the hatch covers with valuable cargoes of rubber and Ivory. But when they cast off their hawsers to steam back to the Congo, while military bands play on the pier and eager young men in uniform line the ships rails, what they carry was mostly army officers, firearms, and ammunition. There was no trade going on here. Little or nothing was being exchanged for the rubber and Ivory. As Morel watched these riches streaming to Europe with almost no goods being sent to Africa to pay for them, he realised that there could be only one explanation for their source: "slave labour".

Brought face to face with evil, morel did not turn away. Instead, what he saw determined the course of an extraordinary movement, the first international human rights movement of the twentieth century. Seldom had one human being, impassioned, eloquent, blessed with brilliant organizing skills and nearly superhuman energy, managed almost single handily to put one subject on the world front pages for more than a decade. Only a few years after standing on the docks of Antwerp, Edmund Morel would be at the White House, insisting to President Theodore Roosevelt that United State of America had a special responsibility to do something about the Congo.

He would organise delegations to the British Foreign Office. He would mobilize everyone from Booker T. Washington to Anatolia France and to Archbishop of Canterbury to join his cause. More than two hundred mass meetings to protect slave labour in the Congo would be held across the United States. A large number of gatherings in England, nearly three hundred a year at the crusade's peak, would draw as many as five thousand people at a time. In London, one letter of protest to the "Times", on Congo would be signed by eleven peers, nineteen Bishops, seventy-six members of Parliament, the Presidents of several chambers of Commerce, Thirteen editors of major newspapers, and every Lord Mayor in the Country. Speeches about the horrors of King Leopold's Congo would be given as far away as Australia. In Italy, two men would fight a duel over the issue. The British Foreign Secretary, Sir Edward Grey, a man not given to overstatement, would declare that "no external question for at least thirty years has moved the country so strongly and so vehemently[172]. He called it a story of savage crime, with a long period of exploitation on the way the world had forgotten one of the great mass killings of recent history[173]. A member of the Independent Labour Party and later a Labour MP, Morel was 'the most powerful driving force in the U.D.C.' and suffered 'agonies of sympathy with his beloved black man'. These agonies, exquisite though they may have been, did not stop his attacking the object of his affections as an oversexed, syphilitic rapist. The attack was made in the "Daily Herald", then Britain's leading left-wing daily and, with a circulation of 329,000, 'probably at the height of its power[174].

Morel was protesting against France's use of black troops in occupied Germany. His article was printed under front-page banner headlines that proclaimed: "BLACK SCOURGE IN EUROPE: Sexual Horror Let Loose by France on the Rhine[175]".

172   Megan, C., (1996) Economic dependency of the empire, Oxford University press.
173   Hochschild, A., (1999) King Leopold's Chost, A Story of Greed, Terror and Heroism in Colonial Africa; London: Macmillan.
174   Forman, E., (1977) The Anatomy of Human Destructiveness, London: Penguin.
175   Michel, C., (1919) The trouble of our Times: Daily Times pp4

According to Morel, France was thrusting her black savages into the heart of Germany. Primitive African barbarians, spreaders of syphilis, had become a terror and a horror unimaginable to the German countryside and an "abominable outrage upon womanhood". The barely restrainable bestiality of the black troops' had led to many rapes; particularly serious problems since Africans were 'the most developed sexually of any race and for well-known physiological reasons, the raping of white women by a Negro is nearly always accompanied by serious injury and not infrequently has fatal results. The corpses of young women had been found under manure heaps. German local authorities were forced to provide brothels for these oversexed blacks otherwise "German women, girls, and boys" would pay the penalty. And the Herald warned that whereas today, with British connivance, the French were using black troops against the Germans, tomorrow they might use African mercenaries against white workers elsewhere[176].

Because of this style of attack this French man won the heart and of many union members who dislike blacks. On that note, Morel repeated and elaborated his attack in a pamphlet called The Horror on the Rhine, in which he claimed that black troops "must be satisfied upon the bodies of white women". The first two editions each sold out in less than a month and by April 1921 eight editions had appeared. A free copy was presented to every delegate attending the 1920 Trades Union Congress and, according to one of Morel's colleagues; it left delegates with a feeling of physical and spiritual revulsion. Sober journals joined in the chorus. The Commonwealth referred to as "a horde of Senegalese savages" and "the lust of a black soldiery", The Nation to "savages" and "terrorists[177]"

Conclusion

On a closer examination, there are three reasons for this prejudices and economic lynching. One, some of the white men cannot stand a black man going out with a white woman and to stop that happening they have to lynch the black people out of existence. Inside them, they have the notion that those white women that are going out with black men have no shame and have brought a cause to the British soil. Secondly, they associate black with anything evil so whenever they see a black man they think they have seen the real devil. Thirdly, they believe that the presence of a black will bring them bad luck, therefore to stop bad omen happening, Black people have to be lynched out of existence. They never thought that Black people, when attacked could defend themselves, so when they try and Black people stand up for them they decided to change tactics. Some intellectuals saw that the best way to send them back to jungle is not by fighting them but through economic lynching. They turned economic lynching as a means of social control, knowing full well, that without jobs these Black men can hardly provide for their families the necessities of life. Those who can will be framed and put away for life in prison where they will garnish their teeth. In attempt to have and keep a family, many will get involve into crime and prison will become their permanent home. Of course, children born in this type of homes will be perpetually damage because the environment they were born will not allow them to rise above their "stations". In most cases where they have opportunity to go to school, they are bound to fail. Therefore political repression is a powerful instrument of economic lynching and a powerful means or barrier to higher educational achievement. For African-Caribbean people to start achieving academically, political repression must be ameliorated.

---

176   James, N., (1919) African Soldiery: Daily Herald pp1
177   Morel, D., (1920) the horror on the Rhine, London: MB Press.

Chapter Three

Unemployment

Households

AFRICAN CARIBBEAN HOUSEHOLDS tended to be smaller than those of other ethnic groups we have in average 3.3people: compare to Bangladeshi households which have on average 4.7 people, Pakistani households 4.2 people. African-Caribbean children are more likely to be brought up by one single family due to socio-economic factors.

Income

- African Caribbean People were more likely than White and Asian people to live in low income households.
- 60% of African-Caribbean groups were living in low income housing.
- Minority ethnic groups have lower levels of household income than the White population.
- Majority of the African-Caribbean people were heavily reliant on social security benefits and least likely to obtain income from earnings, reflecting their higher unemployment rate; they were also more reliant on earnings from self-employment than any other group[178].

---

178   Marsh, K., (1994) Ethnic Minorities and the Labour Market, London, Tailstock.

Unemployment and the labour market

Figure 6

Unemployment figure compare to other ethnic   groups among men
(*Source: Population Trends, 2002*).

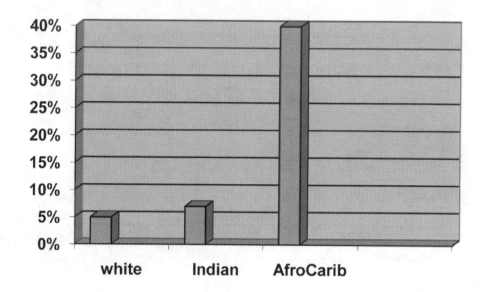

Unemployment rates were:

- 5% for White men;
- 7% for Indians, Pakistanis and Bangladesh men;
- 40% for African-Caribbean men;
- between two to three times higher than White men for all other ethnic groups.

Other unemployment Variables:

- Indians, Pakistanis and Bangladesh are dominant in Transport and communication Industries; while African-Caribbean's have no dominant work place.
- 71% of Chinese people worked in distribution, hotel and restaurant sectors compared to an average of 18% working in these areas.
- A report from the Prime Minister's Strategy Unit[179] argued that "Britain's ethnic minority population is increasingly important in the labour market". Yet African-Caribbean are lacking behind other ethnic groups in accessing the labour market.
- Indian and Chinese people are doing well and often out-performing White people in schools and

---

179   Prime Minister's Strategy Unit Ethnic Minorities and the Labour Market, March 2003

in the labour market[180].

- Africans-Caribbean experience significantly higher unemployment and lower earnings than White people.

- Black Elites are least among other ethnic minority groups to get jobs, even those doing relatively well, are not doing as well as they should be, given their education and other characteristics.

If we impose the question "why black people are more likely to be unemployed than other racial groups?" we shall come to the conclusion that economic lynching is to blame because it is embedded within the British Economic System and disseminate to every institution within its economic sphere. Take for example, on Tuesday, 25 October 2005; the media reported how a law firm have got a blanket ban on recruiting black Solicitors. An undercover Journalist made the claim when he discover how Osita Mba, a Jew, from Eastern Nigeria (Ibo) failed to get job interview within Oxford Company because he is a Jew and secondly he is black[181]. He exposed how Marshall & Galpin had a policy not to hire a black solicitor and have not done so in the last 10years. When Mba, a 32year old, graduated as a British Solicitor in January 2005 and was told by his agent that Marshall & Galpin was looking for a newly qualified solicitor. Few days after applying for the job he got an email from the company that they were looking for legal executive and not a Jewish private client lawyer. A month later an Asian muslam joined the firm as a private client lawyer on £28,000.00 a year. When the case went to industrial tribunal, the company claim that Mba's CV was simply not good enough for him to get an interview; while the reason behind his deselection could have been the colour of his skin.

Furthermore, a survey was carried out on the department of Art, what was discovered was that there is no African-Caribbean man working for the organisation. The only people holding jobs within the Art department are white and Asians and nothing was being done to change that economic lynching against African-Caribbean people in "Art World". According to Guardian, the only position available for the black people is security guard or receptionist[182]. The spokeswoman for Museums and Galleries agreed that Museums and Galleries are institutionally racist in her recruitment and argued that it is common with every other institution in Britain but they would do their best to address the issue. Instead of addressing the issue black people are losing their jobs in the name of efficiency. Efficiency becomes the buzz word to justify economic lynching of African-Caribbean people. This economic oppression is not something new; it has been in existence even before the Second World War in 1945, during the Hitler reign of terror as we have demonstrated in chapter 2 above.

The British people went to the African-Caribbean people they have disposed off and asked them to come to Britain and work because "their mother land" as they put it needs them. On those bases, African-Caribbean people came to Britain to reconstruct her war torn economy. British firms actively take on workers from the Commonwealth and Colonies, during the 1950s, 60s and 70s, including British

---

180   (National Statistics 2003)
181   Mark, M., (2005) Metro, Tuesday 25 October 2005, p2
182   Mandy, T., (2005) Guardian news paper pp4.

Transport and the National Health Service. Government ministers at the time described these men and women of African descend as 'model citizens'[183].

Sir Winston Churchill declared to the people of Caribbean after World War 11, "The Mother Country needs you. Come and help rebuild her. "Think British. Be British. You are British." It was believed that Churchill made that speech in light of the fact that large numbers of African-Caribbean men were contracted by the USA Government as farm labourers in the Southern States. The African-Caribbean people believed Churchill.

On that note, 22nd June, 1948, the Empire Windrush brought to Tilbury Docks 492 Jamaicans to help Britain achieve a higher standard of living for themselves and their families. The Empire Windrush was a historic symbolism, which pioneered the way for other Shipping Liners to start transporting steady stream of African-Caribbean immigrants to England. By June 1949, Britain received her first thousand African-Caribbean immigrants. Ten years later, according to Peter Fryers[184], 125,000 African-Caribbean's arrived in England, since the end of World War II. This compared with 55,000 Indians and Pakistanis for the same period. As we progress into the essay, you will find out that due to repression as a means of social control against the African-Caribbean people, the population of India as a country has outstrip the population of the entire African-Caribbean Continent According to the home office figure published in 2005 www.statistics.gov.uk[185].

183   Conquest, R., (1977) "Socialism's", Defeat is not Enough: Daily Telegraph, 25 June.
184   Frayer, P., (1999) "Staying in power", London: Hodder and Stroughton.
185   www.statistics.gov.uk

Figure 7

Population Size

7.9% from a minority ethnic group

	Total Population		Minority ethnic population
	Count	%	%
White	54153898	92.1	n/a
Mixed	677117	1.2	14.6
Asian or Asian British			
Indian	1053411	1.8	22.7
Pakistani	747286	1.3	16.1
Bangladeshi	283063	0.5	6.1
Other Asian	247664	0.4	5.3
Black or Black British			
Black Caribbean	565876	1.0	12.2
Black African	485277	0.8	10.5
Black others	97585	0.2	2.1
Chinese	247403	0.4	5.3
Others	230615	0.4	5.3
All minority Ethnic population	4635296	7.9	100
All Population	58789194	100	n/a

The size of the minority ethnic population was 4.6million in 2001 or 7.9 per cent of the total population of the United Kingdom.

Indians were the largest minority group, followed by Pakistanis, those of mixed ethnic backgrounds, Black Caribbeans, Black Africans and Bangladeshis. The remaining minority ethnic groups each account for less 0.5 per cent but together account for a further 1.4 per cent of the UK population.

Ethnic group data were not collect on the Northern Ireland Census in 1991. However, in Great Britain the minority ethnic population grew by 53 per cent between 1991

Prime Minister Churchill, in making his pitch for the African-Caribbean to come to 'Mother Britain was addressing people mostly of African origins, who were made to live and work as slaves during the 16 and 19th century, by the ancestors of many of the very same type of people whom Winston Churchill and Morel were representing. The African-Caribbean people were brought in chains to the Caribbean islands to work on British (White) sugar plantations. Other people from India and China made their homes on the Islands subsequently[186].

Those from India were contracted by the plantation owners as indentured labourers. The Indian and Chinese were not slaves; but cheap labour. According to Alma Smith, freelance researcher, she stated "most of the people are farmers or fishermen, and in spite of poor wages, high unemployment and the resulting low standard of living on many of the Islands, the people generally adopted a fairly light-hearted attitude towards life. Most have a strong religious background, and this tradition has continued with the migrants who travelled to the United Kingdom[187]

Due to intimidation, harassment, suppression, torture and lynching of black people by the union members and to put a stop to this barbaric act, Churchill introduced the 1948 British Nationality Act providing British citizenship to the people from the British Commonwealth and Colonies, giving a right to enter, reside and work in Britain indefinitely. Evidently, the African-Caribbean's fielded the majority of immigrants to Britain during the 1950s and 60s. After they had arrived in Britain and gave their all, members of the African-Caribbean Communities were often projected by sections of the media as 'problems', associated with drugs, lawlessness, under achievements and a 'drain' on the social fabric of society. A situation created by the left wing institutions of the state itself to prevent upward mobility of the African-Caribbean people as we have seen Morel done through incitement against innocent black people who have done him no wrong.

It immediately escapes their memory that Black people from the British Commonwealth fought side by side British and allied troops in Europe, during 1939 and 1945 War, the aim of which was to rid Europe of racism and fascism. Liberation came in 1945, but by 1955, it was as though there was no liberation. Racism and fascism of sorts became bona fide to Black ex-servicemen and women, their relatives and country men and women who were joining them in Britain[188].

African-Caribbean people were received by the White 'liberated' with 'no coloured', 'no dogs', 'no Irish', when many of them sought the essential things of life such as housing, jobs, food and clothing, to sustain independent living in England. Members of White Britain were to enjoy the fruits of 'liberation', but not members of the African-Caribbean immigrant community, invitees of the British Government. They were quickly reminded that they were product of slavery[189]. The opportunity to develop good community and race relations was missed, and what followed was racial denunciation of black people which shape the future of race relations in Britain today.

---

186   Dawkins, R., (1976) the Selfish Gene, Oxford: Oxford University Press.
187   Billings, M., (1978) "Fascists", London: Academic press
188   Booker, C., (1980) These Striking Time, Daily Telegraph, 27 January
189   Barker, M., (1979) Racism the New Inheritors, Radical Philosophy, vol.21, 1979

Denunciation

The denunciation of Black people began the process of White Britain's social construction of a black monster. 100 years later, the end results of that construction are revealed as they haunt a multi-cultural Britain. In sincerity that types of social construction suits those who had a long term hidden agenda to frustrate the real aspirations and inevitable upward mobile movement of African-Caribbean people, in Europe and elsewhere, people like Morel and his trade union movement because African-Caribbean colour is considered to be offensive[190].

What the enemies of multi-culturalism did not realise was that The British National Health Service and transport system could not have functioned efficiently without the support of African-Caribbean nurses, midwives, doctors bus drivers and conductors.

When the trade union thought that African-Caribbean people have exhausted their usefulness, and Winston Churchill majority in house of common was dwindling the far left seized the opportunity to advance their own political career by urging, The Prime Minister, to seek ways of keeping African-Caribbean people out of the Home Civil Service. Mr R.A. Butler was asked by Sir Winston Churchill's Cabinet in 1954 to produce a report on ways of stopping the demand of opportunistic left wing MPs who were taking a filthy advantage of African-Caribbean people who for over a century have served this country well during her most difficult times. Since Sir Churchill majority had been wiped out he had no other choice but to succumb to the demand of this scrupulous MPs. Whenever a party is in opposition they pander to racism in order to get elected into power. They create racism as a political culture to suit their purpose and racism will be orchestrated in unimaginable scale to yield expected result, economic lynching (***See Political Culture in Chapter five***). This institutional racism was haunting the African Caribbean people unto this day.

That is why people from African-Caribbean countries are hardly employed as teachers because British people thought that they are not good to teach White children. Secondly, Black colour is not palatable in the classroom. If there is any shortage of teachers, it would be better to go to India, Pakistan, Bangladesh or any other Muslim country in Asia to recruit teachers rather than employing African-Caribbean people who have got right to work and leave here. The request to Butler, who, as Chancellor of the Exchequer, was responsible for Civil Service matters, reflected the deep anxiety of Churchill's Government's policy on immigration from the African-Caribbean's[191].

In the late autumn of 1954 the Home Office produced figures showing that immigration from the African-Caribbean had increased to 10,000 a year[192]. On that report, nothing was said about India, Pakistan or Bangladesh because these people are considered to be friendly and their colour is acceptable. According to the official minutes at the time, the Cabinet agonised over several sessions, discussing new rules for deporting African-Caribbean people convicted of offences or those who were a charge on public funds.

---

190   Conly, C., (1976) on the possibility of Action beyond Ideology, Social Praxis, vol.1, no.4.

191   Brown, A., (2001) Mixed Feelings: The Complex Lives of Mixed-race Britons, London: The Woman's Press.

192   Gurburg, L.(2000) Ethnic minority in Britain, London: Macmillan.

The Cabinet minutes recorded Prime Minister Churchill to have said: "The rapid improvement of communications need to be found urgently, without it the future is fearful and that will create panic among the poor African-Caribbean people: which will make them want to come to Britain. Panic will inevitably or likely to lead to a continuing increase in the numbers of African-Caribbean people coming to this country, and their presence here would sooner or later come to be resented by large sections of the British people[193]". Sir Churchill had got the right ideas but what he had not got was the majority in the house to enable him carryout the right policies that would give everyone a chance to partake into this newly found liberty and nurtured their talent to blossom reality. The moment Churchill's administration fall and Labour party took over government, Manchester, Liverpool, Paddington and London became trouble spots; the issue was seen by the Cabinet as non-partisan.

However, majority of Labour MPs were worried about this development and because of Labour small majority in the house of common, Clement Attlee said that he would consult Sir Churchill on necessary measures. Lord Swindon, Secretary for Commonwealth Relations, wanted a policy of welcoming the comparatively few "good young" Canadians or New Zealanders (both white skin people) who wished to work in Britain, and legislation to restrict African-Caribbean people was called for urgently. Cabinet papers for 1954 declassified on 19 October, 1985 and available for public view at the Public Record Office at Kew showed how even before Britain acquired significant numbers of non-white inhabitants, public officials were worried about the social effects[194].

The Home Secretary, Gwllym Lloyd-George, predicted ominously that foreign ship-owners would soon cash in by speeding up the flow of Indians and African-Caribbean's to Britain. It was not until eight years after both Labour and Conservative governments raised the spectre of immigration controls, Mr Harold Macmillan's Conservative Government introduced in 1962 Britain's first immigration Act because of that prediction. By then mass immigration had increased the number of African-Caribbean people living in Britain considerably. Based on the above background to government and official thinking during the 1950s and 60s, the stage was set for a period of considerable social repression of African-Caribbean people by the State. Nearly all social, economic and political considerations which followed had their roots in the foundation, which was laid by the Morel and his trade union movement. What was being said to the African-Caribbean immigrants, by the government and large numbers of the population was: 'cheap labour yes - social mobility no'. That message was clearly understood by the White indigenous majority population, from which members of the British police forces were recruited. From here on social repression against African-Caribbean people in Britain seemed to have been the order of the decades. Britain, has forgotten very quickly that the choice to come to Britain was not that of black community but that of the British government.

Choice to Come To Britain

BLACK PEOPLE sacrificed many lives for 'mother' Britain during the 1939-45 War, when the cream, the youth of the Commonwealth, came and fought side by side with British troops to defeat fascism in Europe. African-Caribbean men and women, served in the British Navy, Army and Air Force, as enlisted men and officers. Those ordinary African-Caribbean men, women and children in Africa and Caribbean

---

193   Antony, M., (1999) The theory of segregation, New York: Harper Collin.
194   Antonovsky, A., (1990) Towards a refinement of the "marginal man" concept, Social Forces, 35(1): 57-62.

and other parts of the British Commonwealth, who did not travel to Britain, contributed to the war efforts by growing and shipping foods to the British people to keep them fed, during the difficult times of the war[195].

Let us not forget that Britain did not pay market rate for the foods she received, because she could not pay and there was no question of 'market forces' then. The foods were not shipped to Germany, Italy or Japan only to Britain 'Mother Britain'. Then, African-Caribbean people in the British colonies were heroes to the British media and the entire population. The line was clearly drawn, Black sailors, soldiers and airmen, fighters at the time, were told by the British government, and they believed it, that they were fighting for Britain, and once fascism and anti-Semitism were defeated, African-Caribbean service men and women felt assured that their children and grand children would have earned the rights to the benefits of a 'liberated' Britain. 'Rule Britannia - let the bells of freedom ring loud and clears but they were wrong[196].

The war ended and the hugs and kisses faded with it, immediately replaced by economic lynching, insults and institutionalised racism. British public seemed to have forgotten the citations of their Black war heroes and the contributions Black people in the colonies made to feed and liberate British people[197]. Africans-Caribbean ex-servicemen and women recalled how same members of the White Community in Britain, saying to them 'the war is over' when are you going home? The African-Caribbean ex-servicemen and women said that they often replied that they too fought and were entitled to their bit of freedom in Britain as well as other loyal citizens which is correct. They fought hard to win this liberation and many black people lost their lives for Britain.

In this 21st century, very few post war and contemporary children know of the contributions African-Caribbean people made to the war efforts. On grand occasions, such as the Remembrance Day Celebration at the Cenotaph, in Whitehall Central London, and elsewhere in Britain, it is a rarity to see Black ex-servicemen and women marching with their White colleagues. This event is televised throughout the nation. This is community education; this tells the people that African-Caribbean people are noting but the product of slavery that should be excluded from the main stream of British economy through mass unemployment.

The ordinary citizens - Black and White - should be forgiven to conclude that African-Caribbean people made no contribution to Britain's war efforts, and that they had nothing to commemorate. This is a deliberate distortion, by implication, of history, by the leaders of our British Establishment who do not want to see social mobility of black people in a country they helped to shape, defended in her time of trouble, laid their lives to preserve our freedom and defeated the terrorists and the Nazi criminals[198].

Most often many black people asked "Where is the Royal British Legion embrace, overt or covert, which commemorates the memory of fallen Black servicemen and women? Europe's wars - I and II, were not the Blackman's wars. At the time, African-Caribbean people were under the yoke of colonialism in the

195   Back, L., (1999) New Ethnicities and Urban Culture: Racism and Multiculture in Young Lives,London: UCL Press.
196   Clark, K., (1989) Prejudice and Your Child, Boston, MA: Beacon Press.
197   Haugaard, J., (2000) Research and policy on transracial Discrimination: Adoption Quarterly, 3(4): 35-41.
198   Little, K., (1997) African-Caribbeans in Britian, London: Routledge and Kegan Paul.

Caribbean, Africa and indeed parts of Asia, by the major players of the wars, albeit less so by Germany. Black people were involved by their colonial administrators to take sides. The 1960s, 70s, 80s and 90s were to see the overt return of the enemies which were believed to have been defeated twenty years earlier, racism, fascism, anti- Semitism xenophobia and religious intolerance become the order of the day[199].

Today, African-Caribbean ex-servicemen and women of the 1940s are grandparents, and many are still residing in Britain. They lived to witness Britain's core politics telling their grand children that they had no 'real' moral claim on Britain, and the ex-service men and women asked, 'what was the fighting about?'

This lack of true historical focus, as it affected members of the African-Caribbean Community, began during the 1950s. At the time, Britain was still having an influx of immigrants from the British Commonwealth and colonies. Black people again responded to Britain's call for help and they came in their thousands in 1950s to help Britain, and to gain the livelihood denied them in their own countries, because of the stronghold which Britain and other Western powers exercised over their economies, and have exercised for hundreds of years as a result of colonialism. The vast majority of the new immigrants were strong, healthy, young men and women, who came from humble villages, they were ordinary and even simple people. They were above all sincere, religious, honest, ambitious and hard working. What was certain, they knew nothing about economic lynching, racial discrimination or colour bar, as they existed in Britain[200].

Britain's so-called right wing politicians and hard left wing politicians like George Galloway Respect Party: made sure that the new comers learned quickly about racial discrimination. On the streets, White 'Teddy Boys', part of Britain's working class youth culture, which moved on later to 'Skinheads', were aggressive and anti-black mobs. Teddy Boys and Skinheads attacked African-Caribbean people on the streets, simply because their skins were black. In 2005 general election George Galloway MP and his allies, the Muslim fanatics collided together to lynch black people out of Westminster politics.[201]. Not all White youth cultures were hostile to the immigrants and not every Conservative is a natural enemy of the immigrants as Churchill had proved.

Black Economic migrant to Britain

Black workers came to Britain for two main reasons (a) there was a labour shortage in Britain, and industry and government went out of their way to attract Commonwealth citizens and other foreigners to come and work in Britain. The Aliens Order of 1920 was relaxed to admit foreigners under Ministry of Labour permit to work in certain industries. In 1948, the British Nationality Act gave free entry to citizens in the Black Commonwealth, Barbados in the West Indies, for example, was a central area, where London Transport recruitment was at the highest; and (b) the centuries of British Imperialism in the British Commonwealth impoverished these countries: Unemployment and poverty forced Black people to leave their homes and look for jobs in Britain[202].

---

199   Banks, N., (1995) Mixed up Kid, Social Work Today 24(3): 12-13
200   Barton, M., (1992) The Idea of Race, London: Tavistock.
201   Collins, P., (2000) Black Feminist Thought, Cambridge, MA:Unwin Hyman
202   Hall, S., (1996) The Question of Cultural Identity, London: Sage, pp1-17

Because of the devastation of World War II, it left behind a great gap in labour. Some British industries, like the car industry, were expanding and productivity could be increased either by modernising, in order that a large part of the work was automated, or by getting more labour. Getting more labour was the answer because automation created more jobs that were labour intensive. At that time the population rate of growth was declining; Britain had to look outside for labour supply[203].

At the same period, British White workers were leaving certain industries. These were the more boring, tedious, arduous, unpleasant and low paid jobs. White workers were deserting them as other opportunities arose in that period of growth. The new arrivals lived mainly in the urban industrial areas of England: London, the South East, the West Midlands and the North. The largest number of Black people worked in textiles: clothing: small manufacturers; plastics; foundries; metal work; transport (as railway guards, porters, bus conductors) and service industries (kitchen hands, waiters, hospital orderlies) as well as engineering and electrical goods.

The immigrants also worked in the construction industry and few in agriculture. The British Health Service was well known for the number of Black doctors and nurses it attracted. African-Caribbean people were overwhelmingly in the labourer category, the most menial and lowest paid grades. As the Asians were brought in the 70s black doctors and nurses were quickly replaced with the new comers whose colours were acceptable.

The work African-Caribbean people do involved pushing, pulling and dragging; but with the development of a continuous process of production, it became impossible to determine where traditional labouring work finished and other classification begins.

In the past, for example, manufacturing industries hired African-Caribbean workers; it was possible for labourers to be upgraded to semi-skilled jobs. Night work was another labourer category that many White workers avoided. The African-Caribbean workers were hired in large numbers to the northern textile factories which were manned at night almost entirely by African-Caribbean workers. African-Caribbean worker got the hard and dirty jobs in the foundry and small manufacturing industries, like the North London cluster. African-Caribbean workers were concentrated in small firms, which could only operate profitably with cheap labour, where conditions were often Victorian, with 12 hours shifts, no tea breaks, no canteen and no proper ventilation[204].

In 1962, a survey showed that black workers earned 30% less than the average for manual work in Britain. In 1966 the average earning for all male workers was £20 per week. The average pay of an African-Caribbean worker in Manchester was £16-£18 (£14-£16 take home pay) that is 15-18 % less than the national average. Taking income per head as the measure, in 1966 the average for African-Caribbean worker was 22% below the white population. When people from Pakistan began to arrive in West Midlands the factory work, mainly the night job that was predominantly African-Caribbean, were

---

203   Robins, D., (1992) Tarnished Vision: Crime and Conflict in the Inner City. Glossary page 131. Published by Oxford University Press.
204   Haskey, J., (1998) The Ethnic Minority Populations Resident in Private Households, estimates by county and Metropolitan Districts of England and Wales: Population Trends, 63 (Spring): 22-25.

given to them, as a result a lot of African-Caribbean people were made jobless. Due to their joblessness police use it as a platform for social control and repression[205].

Black People and the Police

The 1824 Vagrancy Act, Section 4, Contributed to Civil Unrests among members of the Black Community and the Police during the 1970s and 80s, particularly among Black youth, who were invariably charged with "being a suspected person loitering with intent to commit an arrestable offence contrary to section 4 of the Vagrancy Act, 1924".

This was commonly known as the 'sus law' by members of the Black Community, partly because the charge referred to a person acting 'suspiciously' with intent to commit a crime. Charges for carrying fire arms and possession of, or using, Class A drugs were very rare, at this era of Black Community development. The Police often used the 'sus law' to harass and criminalise African-Caribbean youth. This created bad feelings among the youth, which subsequently led to serious and dramatic civil unrests in Brittan's inner cities[206].

African-Caribbean people (and their White sympathisers), the youth in particular, complained bitterly about police harassment, and set up organisations to put a stop to that harassment; instead of police to stop it they escalated their repression against innocent youth who have done them no wrong. The mental scars they received left a hole in their lives and made it practically impossible for them to do well at school. In a meeting organised to improve the situation between the instrument of the state and the African-Caribbean youth: Andrea Shervington, a 47 year old Guyanese, living in Notting Hill Gate during 1970, he came to Britain in 1950. He explained: "I can remember in 1950 when the exodus of African-Caribbean people started arriving in Britain to fill the 'Mother Country's' labour gap, left by the 'war of liberation'. We had our minor tiffs with the police, but never anything in the line of race - usually matters rose out of our attitudes, being a gay people". "The noises we made on the buses and trains, the parties we held, and so on. Soon things changed, when we began to own properties, like cars and homes. It was then that we noticed the police repression[207]. "The police often saw four of us in a car and automatically assumed that the car was stolen. Should the car contain a White girl, the police tended to be more offensive? We were invariably taken to a police station and questioned about our car," said Andrea. Because of that the situation between the Police and members of the Black community deteriorated.

What made the situation worse was when the First Secretary of the Nigerian High Commission in London was "brutally beaten by the police in Brixton, South East London." The Diplomat was driving a white Mercedes Benz at the time. At the Brixton police station, the identity of the diplomat was discovered, but it was too late. The arresting officers "assumed the Nigerian stole the car'. Prejudice, because every white

---

205   Jones, B., (1994) The end of Africanity: The bi-racial assault on blackness: The Western Journal of Black Studies, 18(4): 201-210

206   Mackey, H., (1972) The complexion of the accused: The Black Revolutionary: Negro Educational Review,23: 132-147.

207   Benson, S., (1990) Ambiguous Ethnicity, Cambridge: Cambridge University Press.

man assumes that every African-Caribbean person is a criminal even when they have not done anything[208] (**see Chapter one**).

In the same meeting Rudy Narayan, an Indian Barrister at Law in London, born in Guyana, and deeply involved in helping to keep African-Caribbean people out of British jails, explained: "The Black man in Britain has got to be a 'criminal or violent'. To divert from that set pattern, he will be harassed and even crushed by the police. If Black people showed that they have pride, and stand up against repression, the police will find ways of charging them with obstruction, assault and/or insulting behaviour[209]. "What we are seeing here is a general assumption by the police of guilt of imaginary crimes, whenever they see African-Caribbean people gathering in threes or fours in the streets. There is also an assumption of helplessness. Helpless In deed, because no one defenceless as they are can endure the brutality of the state or cope with this state repression on the law abiding citizens of Britain. The police believe that they can pull up Black people any time and anyhow, without having to account for their actions. Rudy continued, "I handled a case recently, of one Mr. St. Louis, living in Islington, London. He suffered four broken ribs, intense bleeding and vomiting while in police custody. The case was sent to the police Commissioner and he replied that there was not enough evidence to warrant a prosecution against the police officers who attacked my client. "If this society was a just one, the police would not have the powers they now have. But this society is one of inequalities and struggles, which uses the police as instrument of repression," Rudy concluded.

Another Seminar was held, when the state repression show no sign of abating, at the West Indian Student Centre in Collingham Gardens, South West London, on 27 September, 1970, to discuss 'the deteriorating relationships, the growing mistrust and lack of confidence, between African-Caribbean people and the Police[210]'.

West Indian Students in the United Kingdom thought that 'A solution was absolutely necessary if peaceful community relations are to exist'. The Seminar was chaired by Mr 0. S. Chung, and speakers were Gary Burton, born in Antigua, President of the West Indian Student Union, Jeff Crawford, born in Barbados, General Secretary of the West Indian Standing Conference, Rudy Narayan, Jonathan Guinness, Caucasian, of the Monday Club, John Lambert, Senior Research Associate for Urban and Regional Studies, Birmingham University and Inspector Reg. Gale, Chairman of the Police Federation. Inspector Gale said: it is difficult to argue that we are not agents of the Establishment. But we do not make the laws that we have to enforce. They are made by people that you never see. "I see the whole problem as a social one, and I don't know what the answer is. I am quite content to have an independent element in the present complaint procedure [of the police] to make the public satisfied[211]". Inspector Gale continued: "I do not believe that all policemen are perfect. We try to cure their imperfections if there are any. But you cannot blame the police for lack of government leadership. You cannot blame the police for carrying out their jobs." Of course, you cannot blame the police because the music they are dancing, the drum is biting by the politicians, far left politicians, MPs, and trade unionist who do not want to work alongside black people; who think that the only way to eliminate them is through economic lynching as

---

208   Durojaiye, A., (1979) Patterns of Friendship Choice in an Ethnically Mixed Junior School: Race, 13(2): 189-200.

209   Holmes, R., (2001) How Young Children Percieve Race, Thousand Oaks, CA: Sage.

210   Miles, R., (2000) Britain, the Black Man, and the Future, London: Routledge.

211   Economist (2001) Primary Colours, 17 March.

a result the gulf between the Police and members of the Black Community widened, which led to mass demonstrations in major English cities by African-Caribbean people against police repression[212].

This resulted in one of many clashes between members of the Police and the Black Community, the children of those who came to liberate them from Garman terrorism on August 1970 during a demonstration in Notting Hill Gate against "police brutality of African-Caribbean people". The clashed happened at Portland Road. Thirty Black people were charged with incitement to riot, assault on police. One man, Roddy Kentish, born in Jamaica, was charged with attempted murder of a police officer, "who fainted during the heat of the arrest[213]".

However, as the situation get worse and Complaints of police malpractice became evidence and extensive during the 1970s and 1980s. The BBC Television programme "Cause for Concern", broadcast in August, 1968, documented cases where appeals against convictions of members of the Black Community were upheld, and examples of police malpractice shown up: planted evidence, perjured statements in court, and trumped-up charges[214]. The facts were there, that was in 1968. A spokesman for the Metropolitan Police at Scotland Yard explained: "The police have made genuine attempts to remedy these complaints by setting up a Community Relations Division and Liaison Officers in local immigrant areas." He continued: "The police treat Black and White people alike. When approached by the police, African-Caribbean youth tend to be arrogant and argumentative, asserting their rights[215]. I agree that it is at that point the man on the beat is called upon to judge his client. Unless he is well-trained in Race Relations, his judgement is in danger of being clouded by his prejudices." Now it is becoming clear that those in authority are beginning to admit their prejudices against African-Caribbean people. Implying that what they are doing as police officers are wrong but cannot stop because that is what the society expect from them; They are not suppressing the African-Caribbean people because they enjoy doing it, repression against the black community is one of their assignment[216].

Conclusion

African Caribbean households tended to be smaller than those of other ethnic groups they have in average 3.3people: compare to Bangladeshi households which have on average 4.7 people, Pakistani households 4.2 people. African Caribbean People were more likely than White and Asian people to live in low income households. 60% of African-Caribbean groups were living in low income housing; 5% for White men; 40% for African-Caribbean men, Africans-Caribbean experience significantly higher unemployment and lower earnings than White people. The reason behind the mass unemployment among African-Caribbean people is efficiency. It becomes the buzz word to justify economic lynching of African-Caribbean people. The denunciation of African-Caribbean people began the process of White Britain's social construction of a black monster. This institutional racism was haunting the African-Caribbean people unto this day. That

212   Katz, I., (1996) The construction of Racial Identity in Children of Mixed Parentage: London Jessica Kingsley.

213   Heron, L., (2000) (ed) Truth, Dare or Promise, Black youth growing up in the Fifties, London:Virago.

214   Ogilvy, B., (1990) Staff attitudes and perceptions in multi-cultural nursery school: British Juornals of Developmental Psychology, 10:85-97

215   Ramdin, R., (1997) The Making of Black working Class in Britain, Aldershot: Wildwood House.

216   Mullahs, P., (2000) Second generation African Youth: Identity and Ethnicity: New Community, 12:310-320

is why people from African-Caribbean countries are hardly employed as teachers because British people thought that they are not good to teach White children. From here on social repression against African-Caribbean people in Britain seemed to have been the order of the decades. During the ww11, African-Caribbean people in the British colonies were heroes to the British media and the entire population. British public seemed to have forgotten the citations of their Black war heroes and the contributions African-Caribbean people in the colonies made to feed and liberate British people. African-Caribbean people were involved by their colonial administrators to take sides. That loyalty did not stop Teddy Boys and Skinheads attacking African-Caribbean people on the streets, simply because their skins were black. Even though African-Caribbean people were overwhelmingly in the labourer category, the most menial and lowest paid grades. They were still harassed and criminalized by the police just for being what they are. This harsh economic condition facing the African-Caribbean people made it difficult for their youth to do well academically.

Chapter Four
Educational System

Introduction

SOME SOCIOLOGISTS SEE education as a crucial determinant of life chances in modern societies as the link between education and destination strengthens and the link between origins and education weakens. The stable link between class origin and education is consistent with a reproductive framework while the decreasing link between sex origin and education is consistent with the meritocratic thesis. What about the link between ethnic origins and education? When we disaggregate the Asian group we find that the underachievement of African-Caribbean pupils is masked by the success of African Asian pupils. Performance of African-Caribbean boys is more consistent with a reproductive framework: because the system does not want them to rise above their stations. Due to that reason African-Caribbean children seems to be doing badly at schools.

Road to Educational Equality.

Due to insurmountable complaints about inequality among different races, educational authorities began to develop policies to address that concerns. Since then, educational development in Britain has been preoccupied for much of the post-war period with one central issue. The issue is of course that of social inequality, with 'the major focus of traditional concern, being, with social class[217].

The idea that industrial societies are moving towards meritocracy has provided the setting for much of this investigation. According to this view, the logic of industrialisation entails a transition from a situation where status is ascribed at birth to a situation where status is achieved through one's own efforts. Class origins become increasingly less influential in accounting for class destinations as educational qualifications become the key determinant of occupational placement. The argument predicts that, with the expansion

---

217   Halsey, A., (1995) "Change in British Society" 4th (ed), Oxford University Press, Oxford.

of educational opportunities, the path from origin to education (a) will decline. In addition it anticipates that employers' recruiting strategies will ensure that the path from origin to destination (b) also declines while the path from education to destination (c) increases[218]

Even though research in Britain has indeed confirmed that there is a trend for link (b) to weaken and link (c) to strengthen[219] its primary concern has been with link (a). At this point, a range of studies, using odds ratios to calculate the relative chances of children from different class origins attending selective secondary schools obtaining one or more passes at GCE (General Certificate of Education) Ordinary level (equivalent to GCSE (General Certificate of Secondary Education) grades A-C) and entering higher education[220] have demonstrated, contrary to the predictions of the meritocratic idea, that no change was evident among different birth cohorts during the twentieth century. The upshot of this research programme is clear. Despite a significant expansion in educational opportunities, which has benefited all social classes, class relativities have remained remarkably constant.

218   Heath, A., and Clifford, P., (1996) "Class inequalities and Educational reform in Twentieth Century Britain", London: Longman

219   Halsey, A., and Ridge, J., (1980) Family, Class and Education in Modern Britain, Oxford: Oxford University Press.

220   James, W., (1993) Migration, Racism and Identity Formation: the Caribbean Experience in Britain, London: Verso.

Figure 8

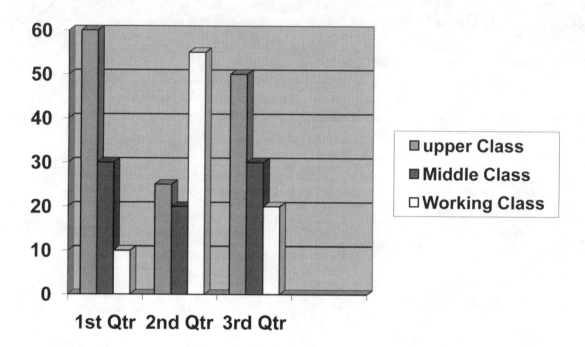

At the first Qtr this is what the class system look like at the begining.
At the second Qtr, improvement in inquality.
Third Qtr, Research shows no improvement.

In the face of continuing significance of class for educational attainment, increasingly within the sociology of education attention has turned to gender and ethnicity. These comprise 'giant steps in the path of aspirations towards equality'. For sex discrimination still 'excludes women from the top jobs and highest earnings and economic lynching results, as we have already seen, in African-Caribbean groups failing to gain 'the same returns on their investments, in education as do, native-born Whites'[221]. Contrary to the expectations of the meritocratic thesis, ascribed status is still clearly significant when the link between education and destination is examined.

What about the link between origin and education? Here change rather than continuity is evident in relation to gender. And the change is in the direction predicted by the meritocratic thesis of a declining link between origin and education. For the central empirical trend is of general and relative improvement in the levels of female educational attainment. While the evidence points then to a pattern of unchanging relative social class disadvantage it indicates 'decreasing disadvantage for women. The issue we now need to address is the link between ethnic origin and education.

---

221   Karn, V., (1998) Race and Ethnicity in Housing: A Diversity of Experience, London: Routledge.

African-Caribbean underachievement:

There is no doubt whatsoever that educational opportunity has expanded considerably. Nevertheless, as we saw in the previous section, many sociologists still wish to argue that groups still do not have equal chances of acquiring valued qualifications. The working class, for example, still do not have the same chances as the middle class. In this view, the most appropriate indicator of the degree of opportunity is a measure of the relative educational achievements of different groups. 'It is in this sense that we can speak of a group underachieving in relation to other groups within the population'[222]. Hence it is that some academicians talk of working-class underachievement and, more recently, of the underachievement of boys. When it comes to ethnicity, what has struck most academicians is the comparatively lower educational attainment of African-Caribbean children. The Committee of Inquiry into the Education of Children from Ethnic Minority Groups, which was itself set up, at least in part, in response to widespread concern about the educational performance of 'African-Caribbean' pupils, took this line. The interim (Brampton) report outlined the results of the Department of Education and Science (DES) annual school leavers' survey in 6 local education authorities (LEAs) for 1978/9 and the final (Swann) report reported the findings of the same survey in 5 LEAs for 1981/2. After comparing the achievements of White, Asian and African-Caribbean pupils, the interim report concluded that African-Caribbean children as a group are underachieving in our education system[223] while the final report concluded that 'there is no doubt that African-Caribbean children, as a group, and on average, are underachieving, both by comparison with their school fellows in the White majority; as well as in terms of their potential, notwithstanding that some are doing well. The prominence given to this official inquiry meant the notion of African-Caribbean underachievement received wide coverage and was widely disseminated.

The view of underachievement has proved to be highly contentious, in spite of this, One critic has argued that it assumes that groups are equal in all 'relevant respects'[224] and that this condition is not fulfilled in the case of Afro-Caribbeans because of evidence that they are inherently less able. Flew, is correct in indicating that the concept does presuppose that ability is randomly distributed between groups, but as we shall see in the next section this is not an unreasonable assumption. Another critic has argued that the concept of underachievement, privileges one aim of education, namely the pursuit of educational qualifications, over others and that other aims are more desirable. While we may sympathise with this position, educational qualifications are none the less critical to people's life chances with the tightening link between education and destination and, given racial discrimination, are of the utmost importance to minority ethnic groups. A third critic has argued that the concept of underachievement implicitly blames the group deemed to be underachieving and that the notion of African-Caribbean for example, underachievement is particularly dangerous because it is likely to reinforce the common stereotype of Black people as inherently less able[225].

It seems he is right to warn of possible connotations of the term but it is used here in a purely descriptive way to refer to demonstrable differences in relative achievement between groups and does not privilege

222   Gillborn, D., (1995) Racism and Antiracism in Real Schools, Milton Keynes: Open University Press.
223   Geddes, A., (1996) "The Politics of Immigration and Race", Manchester: Baseline.
224   Dummett, A., (2000) "Tackling Racism: From Legislation to Integration", Basingstoke: Macmillan.
225   Fitzgerald, M., (1998) "Race and Criminal Justice System", London: Routledge.

any particular social explanation for such differences, although it does of course expressly rule out a genetic explanation.

Having said that, more than a decade has passed since the official inquiry drew our attention to African-Caribbean underachievement. Since then more reliable findings have emerged which move beyond the rather crude ethnic breakdown employed by Rampton/Swann and enable us to address simultaneously issues of class, gender and ethnic background[226]. The two most significant overviews of research on ethnic differences in levels of achievement have been published by the Office for Standards in Education (OFSTED). These reviews draw on two main sources of data. The first derives from LEAs, while the second derives from the Youth Cohort Survey (YCS), which comprises a longitudinal nationally representative survey of young people and represents a massive improvement on previous data.

While it cannot be said that ethnic monitoring is undertaken in a consistent way by LEAs or is even a universal feature of LEA data gathering, it is none the less interesting to note that for each of the main ethnic groups studied there is at least one LEA where that group is the highest attaining[227]. While we cannot read too much into such local

Figure 9

GCSE attainment by ethnicity, in state schools, England and Wales, 1988, 1995 and 1997

Ethnic Group	Five or more higher grade passes (%)			Improvement (%)	
	1988	1995	1997	1995-97	1988-97
White	26	42	44	+2	+18
Black	17	21	28	+7	+11
India	23	44	49	+5	+26
Pakistani	20	22	28	+6	+8
Bangladish	13	23	32	+9	+19

Source: YCS, adopted from Gillborn and Mirza (2000)

variability (which is anyway quite limited), this finding does remind us that there is no 'necessary or pre-determined ethnic ordering' and that 'no ethnic group is inherently less capable of academic success'. We need to bear this in mind when looking at the more reliable national data on ethnic difference in

226   Green, D., (2000) Institutional Racism and the Police, "Institute of Study of Civil Society", London: Cambridge University Press.
227   Home Office (2000) Code of Practice on Reporting and Recording Racist Incidents, London: Home Office.

educational achievement from the YCS according to Gillborn and Mirza. The diagram above presents a comparison of changes in the attainment of five ethnic groups at GCSE level (grades A-C) between 1988 and 1997.

Averages mask 'considerable variation in performance within ethnic groups and significant overlap between groups'[228], but the average differences evident in the diagram above are none the less significant. The most recent results from 1997 confirm the finding of the Brampton and Swann reports that African-Caribbean pupils are underachieving relative to White pupils but at the same time point to significant variability among Asian pupils, with Indians attaining better results than Whites but Pakistanis and Bangladeshis performing slightly better than Black pupils because Asians were given better opportunities than Black people. Though, the proportion of pupils attaining five or more higher-grade passes has increased in all ethnic groups since the introduction of the GCSE, and between 1995 and 1997 relative inequalities of attainment for minority groups declined, over a longer period from 1988 to 1997 the differences in attainment between Indians and White pupils, on the one hand, and African-Caribbean, Pakistani and Bangladeshi young people, on the other hand, widened.

Indian pupils have made the greatest gains in the last decade: enough to overtake their white peers as a group... Bangladeshi pupils have improved significantly but the gap between themselves and white youngsters is much the same. African-Caribbean pupils have drawn least benefit from the rising levels of attainment: the gap between them and their white peers is now bigger than a decade ago due economic lynching suffered by their parents.

In many ways, it is the performance of African-Caribbean pupils which continues to constitute the greatest cause for concern. For a while 'the performance of Pakistani and Bangladeshi pupils in the early years of schooling remains depressed' but manifests improvement 'once they become proficient in English. African-Caribbean pupils make a sound start in primary schools but their performance shows a marked decline at secondary level'[229]. This is evident from baseline data supplied by some LEAs which 'suggests that the inequalities of attainment for African-Caribbean pupils become progressively greater as they move through the school system' with 'differences becoming more pronounced between the end of primary school and the end of secondary education. The YCS enables us to analyse a nationally representative sample of young people not only by ethnicity but also by gender and social class. We saw earlier that among young people as a whole there is an association between classes and (to a lesser extent) gender, on the one hand, and success in education, on the other hand. What is evident when Tables below are examined is that this familiar association holds within each of the ethnic groups identified. Girls attain better results than boys and, even more markedly in most groups, middle-class pupils attain better results than working-class pupils.

The Diagram below compares the proportion of pupils from seven ethnic groups, after controlling for gender, attaining five or more higher-grade passes at GCSE. Ethnic inequalities persist when a comparison is made of pupils of the same number from different ethnic backgrounds with a considerable gap evident

228   Gillborn, D., and Mirza, H., (2000) Educational Inquality: Mapping Race, Class and Gender, London: OFSTED.
229   Leslie, D., (1998) An Investigation of Racial Disadvantage, Manchester: Manchester University Press.

between Chinese, Indian and White girls, on the one hand, and Pakistani, Bangladeshi and Black girls, on the other hand.

Figure 10

GCSE attainment by ethnicity, controlling for gender, in state schools, 1995

Ethnic group	5 + Higher grade GCSE passes (%)		
	Male	Female	All
White	37	47	42
Black	15**	26	21
Indian	39	49	44
Pakistani	16	28	22
Bangladeshi	23**	24**	23
Chinese	63*	63*	63**
Other	37	45	41
All	36	46	41

* subsample 30 or less. ** subsample greater than 30 but less than 100. Source: YCS, adapted from Demack et al. (2000)

11

GCSE attainment by ethnicity, controlling for gender, in state schools, 1995

Ethnic group	5 + Higher grade GCSE passes (%)		
	Non-manual	Manual (Skilled & semi-skilled)	Unskilled/unclassified
White	55	27	19
Black	30**	25**	19**
Indian	64	40	12**
Pakistani/Bangladeshi	41**	25	17
Other	63	41**	25
All	55	28	19

* subsample 30 or less. ** subsample greater than 30 but less than 100. Source: YCS, adapted from Demack et al. (2000)

The table above compares the proportion of pupils from five ethnic groups attaining five or more higher-grade passes at GCSE. While this table points to class differences within each ethnic group, social class differences do not override the influence of ethnic inequality: when comparing pupils with similar class backgrounds there are still marked inequalities of attainment between different ethnic groups. Indeed in some respects the analysis reveals new inequalities; showing that Black pupils from relatively advantaged backgrounds are little better placed, as a group, than white peers from manual backgrounds and, worse placed than Indian peers from manual backgrounds. When we compare pupils from different ethnic groups, after putting into consideration both gender and social class, the results demonstrate that in 1995,

'Indian pupils did best, followed by white, Pakistani/Bangladeshi and Black pupils respectively'[230]. Placing gender, class and ethnicity in a relative perspective, we discover that the ethnic differences were larger than the gender differences and the social class differences were the largest of all. We have to remember [however] that those ethnic groups with the lowest educational attainment (Pakistanis, Bangladeshis, African-Caribbean's) are those with disproportionately large numbers in the lowest social class groups, Their problems are therefore ones of both 'race' and social disadvantage[231].

The data from the YCS that we have examined so far refers to pupils at a single point in time, notably at the end of compulsory schooling, whether that was in 1988, 1995 or 1997, Young people from African-Caribbean groups are, however, much more likely than White pupils to stay on in post-compulsory education. Indeed Drew found that, once attainment was taken into account, ethnic origin was the single most important factor in determining the chances of staying on. This finding is echoed by the analysis of the participation rates of 16-19-year-olds in full-time education in the 1991 Census, which revealed 'the almost uniformly higher participation rate of African-Caribbean ethnic groups during the post 16 period in comparison with the White group', a phenomenon 'little altered when differences associated with gender and social class are taken into account'[232]. Likewise, investigation of the participation in full-time education of 16-24 year olds in the 1994 PSI survey indicated that 'no ethnic minority group had a lower participation rate in post 16 educations than white people and that people from ethnic minorities in general are also staying on for longer periods. Among those who had already gained GCE O-level or higher qualification, about twice as many ethnic minority as white persons were likely to be continuing in education, with the higher participation rate in post-compulsory education of Asian men being particularly striking. This clearly represents a significant 'ethnic minority drive for qualifications'. For staying on longer allows pupils more opportunity 'to upgrade existing qualifications and obtain further qualifications of value in the labour market[233].

Evidence that the greater likelihood of members from minority ethnic groups staying on pays off, emerges from an analysis over time of the experience of 16-19-year-old youngsters who reached the minimum school leaving age in the mid-1980s according to Drew's findings. Although this study uses a rather crude ethnic breakdown (Afro-Caribbean; Asian; White) and is now somewhat outdated, it does show how young people from minority ethnic groups are more likely than those from the majority ethnic group to improve their qualifications over time. By the age of 18, 'Afro- Caribbean' students had caught up a little on White students in terms of proportions obtaining four or more 0-levels (or their equivalent). Their relatively lower achievements at 16, however, had ramifications leading them to be more likely to study vocational rather than academic courses from which at 18 they emerged as the best vocationally qualified group, a finding consistent with the PSI study, which confirms that African-Caribbean's have a higher proportion of vocational qualifications than other ethnic groups but they do not have is the opportunity to nourish it to blossom reality. Meanwhile Asian students, who at 16 had been slightly behind White students in terms of proportions obtaining four or more 0-levels, by 18 had not only caught them up but overtaken them, emerging at this age as the best academically qualified group.

230   MacMaster, N., (2001) Racism in Europe, London Palgrave Macmillan.
231   Litlewood, P., (1999) " Social Exclusion", Social Science teacher, Vol.29, no. 1
232   MacDonald, R., (1997) "The Underclass and Social Exclusion", London: Routledge.
233   Law, I., (1996) Racism, Ethnicity and Social Policy, London: Prentice Hall.

What is striking overall, as modood put it, is that 'ethnic minorities manifest a radical diversity, indeed extreme contrasts, in their educational attainment levels[234]. By no means can the minorities be seen to be in the same position. This becomes clearly evident when ethnic groups are compared in terms of their highest qualification. While this classification of qualifications is rather crude so that it shows, for example, the proportion whose highest qualification is any 0-level or equivalent where the equivalents may be vocational rather than, as in the YCS, the proportion with five higher-grade passes at GCSE (five 0-levels)[235] Looking at modood, work, Jones acknowledged that, the results are none the less revealing. Among people of working age, the PSI survey indicates that 'the Chinese, Africans, and Asians are much the best qualified groups, among men, then come Whites, with Caribbean's and Pakistanis being less qualified: but Africans are the least to be employed among all these ethnic groups.

Among women, by contrast, Caribbean's are more likely to be qualified than Whites, with Pakistanis and especially Africans generally much less qualified. This picture reflects the different starting-points of different groups as well as their different experiences of education in Britain. To ascertain what progress, if any, has been made, we need to look at different generations.

A good number of those who came to Britain as adults, the migrants, did not have qualifications. There were, however, significant group differences, with Caribbean's, Pakistanis and Bangladeshis being poorly qualified while more than a third of Indians, African Asians and Chinese had a higher qualification (A-level or equivalent or higher). 'In most groups, the second generation (25-44-year-olds who were born in Britain or came as children) had made significant progress[236] . This was particularly evident in the case of Caribbean's but generally much less so in the case of Pakistanis and not evident at all in the case of Bangladeshis. Comparison of the qualifications held by this second generation leads Modood to amend 'the two-way division between ethnic groups of migrants with a new middling or mixed category. While, on the one hand, Africans, Asians and the Chinese generally had better qualifications than Whites and, on the other hand, Pakistanis and especially Bangladeshis generally had markedly worse qualifications than Whites, Indians and Caribbeans were in an intermediate situation, generally somewhat less well qualified than Whites. This second generation distinguished is, however, something of a ragbag, which includes people not fully educated in Britain. More revealing is the comparison of 16-24 year old men and women, the new generation.

The new generation distinguished here includes many still in education and therefore many who have not yet 'achieved their ultimate highest qualification. This means 'that in comparing them with their elders one is not comparing like with like'. What is more, 'ethnic minority, especially South Asian, participation in post-compulsory full-time education is much higher than that of Whites; moreover, ethnic minority persons on average acquire some of their qualifications at a later age than Whites'. Although there is evidence that this latter factor is declining over time, 'the effect of these two factors is that... ethnic minority qualification levels, especially those of South Asians, are disproportionately understated[237] Modood found out that despite this caveat, the illustration below indicates that the position of Indians, Africans, Asians and Chinese is similar to that of Whites except at degree level where their position is generally distinctly

234   Kymlika, W., (2000) Nation Building and Minority Rights: Comparing West and East, Journal of Ethnic and Migration Studies, vol.26, no.2.

235   Miles, R., (1993) Racism After Race relation, London: Routledge.

236   McGrew, A., (1992) A Global Society, in Hall, S., (ed.) Modernity and its Futures, Cambridge: Polity.

237   Brown, D., (1991) "Recial Justice at Work", London: Policy Studies Institute.

better. By contrast, and despite some progress, the attainment of Pakistanis and especially Bangladeshis continues to be markedly worse on the whole than other ethnic groups. But white employers are likely to employ them rather than Africans because of the colour of their skin which is considered acceptable. Even though Africans are better qualified than the Asian they are the most likely to be unemployed

Figure 12

Highest qualification held by 16-24 year old men and women, by ethnic group, 1994

Ethnic group	White	Caribbean	Indian	African Asian	Pakistani	Bangladhi	Chinese
Non or below O-level							
Men	22	31	27	22	44	42	17
Women	26	18	21	17	40	52	10
O-level or equivalent							
Men	33	31	27	27	22	38	[40]
Women	31	30	24	31	31	29	[49]
A-Level or equivent or higher degree in parctheses							
Men	46	38	46	50	34	19	[44]
women	43	53	54	51	31	19	[41]

O-level is equivalent to A-C GCSEs: GCSEs were introduced in 1988. Figures in squere bracket denote small sample size. Source: PSI survey 1994, adapted from Modood et al (1997)

Caribbean's seem to be in an intermediate situation, with young men having faltered in their progress and now not in a dissimilar position to Pakistanis, while young women have made significant strides. The reason being, that they have seen the economic situation at home; which made it impossible for them to pursue education further because their parents would not afford it.

Having said that, the overall situation of the different ethnic minorities manifests continuities with their different starting points. Mortimer, thinks that it is borne out by the 'correlation between the levels of qualifications of those born outside the UK and the levels of qualifications of those born in the UK[238] .He also pointed out that there are at least two other striking development', however. 'One is the strong educational drive found in the ethnic minorities' which has allowed many to make significant progress. The other 'is the special progress of women' a phenomenon not confined to ethnic minorities but one particularly evident there.

---

238   Crompton, R., (1997) "Economic Restructuring and Social Exclusion", London: University College London Press.

Mortimer then conclude that it could have been a mistake because much emphasis of the research on ethnic differentials in educational achievement since the late 1970s has been on the underachievement of West Indians or Caribbean's. Even though, the 1985 committee of inquiry emphasised 'that West Indian children, as a group, and on average are underachieving[239] . The terminology has changed over time, with the 1996 OFSTED report preferring the term 'African-Caribbean's' and avoiding the term 'underachieving', but the same emphasis is apparent. 'Recent research tends to show African Caribbean pupils as relatively less successful than their "Asian" and white peers[240]. Such a conclusion, however, deserves amendment in the light of our analysis of more recent research, which involves nationally representative samples and involves disaggregating ethnic groups by gender and national origin. While there are some differences in the results of research that focuses on the performance of pupils in schools and the results of studies that look at young people's highest qualifications together they suggest that it is Caribbean young men rather than young women who are underachieving and that the position of two Asian groups is at best not markedly better and may even be worse.

In view of the fact that most of the existing research has focused on African-Caribbean underachievement. We shall therefore focus on different explanations for the lower educational attainment of this group, African-Caribbean people. It should be noted, however, that the explanations, which we shall be exploring, have been used to account for social class differentials in educational attainment and, with modifications, are used also to explain Pakistani and Bangladeshi underachievement. It will be evident that the debate between competing explanations is deeply political.

Parekh illustrates this well: For example, an explanation in terms of genetic inferiority the structure of the family or lack of cultural depth (**see Chapter 1**) fastens the blame on the African-Caribbean community; an explanation in terms of the African-Caribbean child's low self- esteem, ethnocentric curriculum, racist textbooks and the ethos of the school lays the blame at the door of the school and the educational system; and one that stresses racism and economic inequalities puts the responsibility upon the white society and police heavy handedness against innocent black youths who have done nothing wrong (**see chapter 2 & 3**). Not surprisingly, the group which suspects that it might be blamed and asked to change its ways tends to marshal whatever arguments it can against the threatening explanation, or to demand impossible standards of proof and conceptual rigour from it while not bothering to provide these for its own alternative explanation; or to point the finger at the intellectual judgement and honesty of its advocates[241] .

The fact 'that African-Caribbean children tend to score lower than white children on tests of intelligence[242] has suggested to some people that the differences in educational attainment are primarily attributable to differences in intelligence, and that these differences are in turn genetically determined (**see chapter 1**). One of the critics of the educational system, Bernard Coard, disagreed with this intellectual propaganda of Jensen and Eysenck, this how he put it:

239   Modood, T., (1997) "The Politics of Multi-Culturalism in the New Europe", London: Zed Book Ltd.
240   Pacione, M., (1997) "Britain's Cities: Geographies of Division in Urban Britain", London: Zulu
241   Milner, D., (1993) "Children and Race Ten Years On", London: Ward Lock Education.
242   Moore, R., (1997) "Migration and the class Structure of Western Europe", London: Allen & Unwin.

emotional-disturbance, apply just as much to the actual questions asked on the IQ test administered to the children The 1Q test has three biases against the African-Caribbean child, cultural, middle class, and, the very nature of 'the test situation'. The vocabulary and style of all these IQ tests is white middle class. Many of the questions are capable of being answered by a white middle class boy, who, because of being middle class, has the right background of experiences with which to answer the questions regardless of his real intelligence. The Black working class child, who has different life experiences, finds great difficulty in answering many of the questions, even if he is very intelligent.

The very fact of being 'tested' is a foreign experience to many Black children. The white middle class child is used to tests. The questions that are asked on these tests have to do with the sort of life he lives. He is therefore confident when doing these tests. Thus the white middle class child can be expected to do these tests better than the white working class or Black child and he does. If white middle class people make up these IQ tests, and if they also do the testing, is it really any surprise that their own children score the highest? Does this have anything to do with the real abilities of the children? None.

Similarly, it should be pointed out that an emotionally disturbed child is highly likely to do badly in tests, since the act of sitting in one place for an hour or more, and answering a series of questions and doing a series of different tasks in a special order is likely to be too frustrating and confining an experience for him.

IQ tests can only be claimed to measure intellectual functioning at a particular moment in time; without being able to give the reasons why the functioning is at that particular level or say which factors are more important than which for each child tested This point is vital to grasp if one is to understand why the IQ test is meaningless in so many cases.

The child may be functioning below normal because of being emotionally disturbed, or because of being in a bad mood on the day of the test. It could be because of racial resentment at being tested by a white person or the fear of being placed in an ESN school as a result of the test. It could be the result of low motivation to do or succeed on the test; or it could be the fact that the act of being tested is a foreign or unusual experience, and hence the child is nervous and possibly upset. Any or all of these factors is enough to upset his true score by as much as 20 or more points. And all of this is assuming that the questions on the test itself are not culturally biased which they are!

Now some of the less honest educational psychologists will say that they take account of these factors by stating in their report on the test that the child seemed upset, or disturbed, etc. But this does not 'take account' of these vital factors. There is no assessment or scoring procedure on the IQ test that can add on points to a child's score to take into account any of the disturbance factors. What is most disturbing about the use of the IQ test is that it is the children with difficulties who are on the whole tested. Therefore the test is being used in an area where the factors discussed above would most distort the test results; in fact, make it a mockery of an exercise. Since 20 to 25 points can in many cases decide a child's future, and the test result is very often wrong by a wider margin when dealing with 'problem children', the test is not only a shambles but a tragedy for many".

As we have seen the notion that racial differences in ability are inherited was thoroughly discredited, not only presently but since after the Second World War, by the scientific community. This bias has been given renewed respectability by Jensen in an article entitled, '**How much can we boost IQ and scholastic achievement?**' and has been popularised in this country by Eysenck, with a renewed lease of life.

Justifying educational inequality.

It is intellectual absurd to devote space to an examination of the alleged genetic inferiority of Caribbean children is to confer 'intellectual legitimacy and social respectability upon an illogical view[243]. Despite how ridiculous it might seems, this view is still, however, propagated by some academics and popularised through the media and cannot be left unchallenged. Parekh argues that the Swann report has analysed paradigm and expose the genetic explanation given and published in "The **Bell Curve**".

The central thesis of The Bell Curve is that the United States is becoming a meritocracy, with intelligence becoming the key determinant of status. The result is a system of 'cognitive classes', with those at the top tending to be the most intelligent members of society and those at the bottom tending to be the least intelligent members of society. Examining the links between origin, education and destination in Britain, we challenged the meritocratic thesis in the first section. For Herrnstein and Murray, however, and those who sympathise with their position in Britain[244], the thesis cannot be so easily dismissed. IQ (intelligence quotient) measures intelligence and it is individual differences in IQ (itself seen as primarily inherited) which explain differences in the class positions which individuals achieve.

Even though the question of group differences in intelligence is irrelevant to their central argument, Herrnstein and Murray do bring up the question. They point to the significant 15-point gap in the average IQ scores between Whites and Blacks and, relying heavily on the work of Jensen, arguing that there are good reasons for believing that the IQ differences are primarily genetic in origin. Although they are careful enough in the end to conclude that they are 'resolutely pessimistic' on the precise mix of environment and genes. That notwithstanding, the overall tenor of their argument is clear. The over-representation of Black people in the lower cognitive classes is explicable in terms of their lower IQ scores and there is nothing which can be or indeed should be done to try to change this situation. They went further to argue that instead of African-Caribbean people bemoaning the fact that Blacks are intellectually inferior to Whites, "They should celebrate the fact that they possess different qualities: 'It is possible to look ahead to a world in which the glorious Hodge-bodge of inequalities of ethnic groups, genetic and environmental, permanent and temporary can be not only accepted but celebrated"[245].If we purse for a moment and ask what is this "Hodge-Bodge" we shall come to discover why they think blacks are inferior. "Hodge simply means a name used to represent a typical agricultural labourer (archaic) and Bodge means a clumsy piece of work or badly done repair". What they are implying is that African-Caribbean people are archaic, clumsy and badly looking colour. The question now is what should Africn-Caribbean people celebrate about being clumsy and with the wrong colour?

Judging from that, there is no doubt that the publication of The Bell Curve caused a huge furore, with the contention that there are inherent racial differences in intelligence. That is why Jones insist that the arguments which cumulatively indicate that 'the evidence for the mental superiority of one or the other race is as flimsy, confused and full of intellectual dishonesty as to be scarcely worth considering[246].

---

243   Morris, L., (2001) "Rights and Controls in the Management of Migration: the Case of Germany", Socialogical Review, vol.48,no.2.

244   Owen, D., (2001) "Minority Ethnic Participation and Achievements in Education, Traing and the Labour Market", Department for Education and Employment,London: HMSO.

245   Nuttall, D., (1998) Differential School Effectiveness, "International Journal of Educational Research", vol.13.

246   Blair, M., (1992) Racism and Education, Milton Keynes: Open University Press.

First of all, it is questionable whether race is a biologically meaningful concept. Although we can of course distinguish people on the basis of skin colour, those classified as White or Black do not, as we illustrated, constitute distinct populations. Intermarriage is common in Britain, for example, and geneticists have shown that there is vastly more genetic variation within so-called races as between them.

Secondly, it is questionable whether IQ measures intelligence. Gardner for example challenges the notion that there is such a thing as general intelligence and claims instead that there is distinct kinds of intelligence. IQ tests only measure some of these intelligences and are as a result culturally biased[247].
Thirdly, Although studies in the United States indicate a gap of 15 points in the average IQ scores of Whites and Blacks 'there are signs that the gap between black and white is narrowing' , a phenomenon acknowledged even by Herrnstein and Murray. What is more, studies in Britain indicate that 'the overall difference is considerably smaller[248].

Fourthly in Britain differences between the social and economic circumstances of White and Black families are primarily responsible for the IQ gap. This is fundamental, because it is the only reason why the gap exists.

 Nevertheless, when Swann report was published, Mackintosh and Marcie-Taylor, were commissioned to look into the IQ question, they concluded that 'the often quoted gap between African-Caribbean and White IQ scores is sharply reduced when account is taken of socio-economic factors as we have mentioned above'. A crucial difference in the environments between Blacks and Whites depends on whether individuals are classified as Black or White. This factor "racism" 'cannot be pinned down to controlling conventional environmental variables'. In a study which critically examines Herrnstein and Murray's thesis, the authors argue that attention need to be given not only to socio-economic deprivation but in the segregation and stigmatised identity of African-Caribbean people in this country. Once these three effects of racism are taken into account, the IQ gap becomes understandable[249].

To strengthen their position Herrnstein and Murray argue that environmental factors cannot explain IQ differences because studies of identical twins reared apart in different environments from an early stage show that the heritability of IQ is too high. There are two problems here. Firstly, estimates of heritability (the proportion of the variation of a trait that can be attributed to genetic variation) differ, with Jensen putting it as high as 80 per cent but Jencks putting it much lower at 45 per cent. Secondly, estimates of heritability are based on tests administered to particular groups and cannot properly be generalised to other groups. Thus 'the heritability of height might be extremely high in both a poor Third World village and a wealthy First World suburb; taller parents would produce taller children in both places. The richer population might be taller than the poor, but this does not preclude the possibility that a better nourished generation in America for example, might in the future grow as tall as its distant peers in the presently developing world. The correlation between the heights of parents and children might remain just as strong, but the heights themselves might change[250].

247   Parekh, B., (1996) united Colour of Equality, New Statesman, 13 December.
248   Osgerby, B., (1998) Youth in Britain Since 1945, Oxford: Blackwell.
249   Parker, D., (1994) "Encounters Across the Counter: Black People in Britain", New Community, vol.20, no4.
250   Butler, T., and Savage, M., (1996) "Social Change and the Middle Classes", London: University College London Press.

It seems, from Swann point of view, that the only evidence which could convincingly show that Black White differences in IQ were genetic in origin 'would be the demonstration of a difference in IQ scores between randomly selected groups of black and white children brought up in strictly comparable conditions'. Only three studies 'have even attempted to approximate these ideal conditions (albeit not very successfully)' and in these studies what is striking is that 'such differences have been extremely small[251]. There is considerable evidence that IQ scores, which hereditarianism assume are relatively stable, are in fact rising considerably[252]. Flynn, who has found this phenomenon in over twenty countries, concludes that 'IQ tests "cannot bridge the cultural distance that separates one generation from another". And if the tests cannot bridge the gap between generations, they may be incapable of bridging other cultural gaps, such as those between ethnic groups'.

In view of these arguments, the Swann report's somewhat cautiously concluded 'that IQ is not a significant factor in underachievement' which seems to be more plausible.

Economic deprivation, culture and the home.

Economic and cultural factors at one stage were considered by sociologists to be critical to an explanation of group differences in achievement. They are still considered important by many. Although the 1944 Education Act removed some financial barriers which had previously reduced access to secondary education for the working class, 'material factors' continued to be responsible for class differences in staying on after compulsory schooling. As for the more recent 1988 Education Reform Act, it has been argued that 'choice and the market provide a way for the middle classes to reassert their reproductive advantages in education[253]. This is partly because of their more favourable economic situation which allows private transport, childcare, and so on, to be affordable but also because of their 'cultural capital' which enables more informed choices of schools to be made. If we turn to ethnic differences in achievement, again economic and cultural factors are significant. Thus the underachievement of African-Caribbean people is explicable in terms of both extreme economic deprivations, which exceeds that of other ethnic groups. The same factors, economic deprivation and lack of fluency in English go some way also towards explaining the underachievement of Africans. The Swann report points out that ethnic minority are 'particularly disadvantaged in social and economic terms'. This is evidenced for example in the higher rate of unemployment of all minority ethnic groups which stems at least in part from economic lynching. 'This extra deprivation over and above that of disadvantaged Whites leads in many instances to an extra element of underachievement[254]. The report recognises that underachievement cannot be wholly accounted for in these terms because groups similarly subject to discrimination and disadvantage differ in their levels of achievement. Since the report was published, evidence has mounted, as we have already noted in the previous chapters, to indicate that, although minority ethnic groups may all be subject to racial discrimination, Indians and Pakistanis can no longer be considered to be as a group economically disadvantaged in the same way as African-Caribbean people are. This goes some way to accounting for the educational achievement of Indian pupils, Nevertheless, the differences in achievement between African-

251   Cohen, A., (1993) Multi-Cultural Education, Cambridge: Harper & Row.

252   Phizacklea, A., (1990) Labour and Racism, Oxford: Oxford University Press

253   Paul, K., (1997) Whitewashing Britain, London: Cornell University Press.

254   Sagger, S., (1992) the Dog that didn't Bark, Manchester: Manchester University Press.

Caribbean's and Asians overall, many of whom are equally disadvantaged, needs to be explained. And here many, including both the Rampton and Swann reports, have turned somewhat cautiously to a cultural explanation for it.

According to Rampton report:

"A disproportionate number of African-Caribbean women are forced to go out to work because of their economic circumstances, The percentage of African-Caribbean men employed on night shift is almost double that of white males and the incidence of one parent families is higher for African-Caribbean people than for Whites. African-Caribbean parents may therefore face particular pressures affecting their children in the vital pre-school formative years. While it is now generally accepted that young children need to form a stable and consistent relationship with only a limited number of adults we are faced with a situation where African-Caribbean parents are stretched in ways which make steady, relaxed care of their children hard to achieve. Many African-Caribbean parents may not be aware of the pre-school facilities that are available and may not fully appreciate the contribution that they can make to the progress of their child before he enters school"[255].

Here is the Swann report:

"Seeking to grapple with the differences in achievement between frican-Caribbean's and Asians: It has been put to us, that Asians Are use to 'keeping their heads down' and adopting a 'low profile', thereby making it easier to succeed in a hostile environment. African-Caribbean's, by contrast, are given to 'protest' and 'a high profile', with the reverse effect. Given the very different histories of the two groups, it is not an improbable explanation. It has also been put to us that the explanation lies in the particularly tightly knit structure of the Asian community and the Asian family, more tightly knit than is either the case with whites or African-Caribbean's[256].

Nonetheless, the two report failed to mention that Asian where given an economic advantage over the African-Caribbean people because white prefer Asian colour and regard it as more acceptable than Black. Even though, Swann report, seems to imply that indirectly; because when you critically examine his report you might have the impression that he was saying that Asians are cool headed and have a strong family structure and because of that they were given a little bit of economic opportunity and that the same opportunity was denied to African-Caribbean's because of their attitude which was not supported with enough evidence.

That notwithstanding, By contrast, the 1996 and 2000 OFSTED reports make no reference to cultural factors at all. There are three reasons for this. Firstly, OFSTED's remit is narrower than that of the other two reports, being focused 'on issues that directly influence pupils' achievements, especially where they relate to education policy, schools and matters that teachers might wish to address as part of their work[257]. Secondly, certain cultural factors, which previously had been thought to be important in accounting for African-Caribbean underachievement, have been found empirically to be insignificant.

Milner, for example, who earlier had been very influential in pointing to a negative self-image among African-Caribbean children because of the inability of their culture to insulate them from racism, recognises 'that black children are now quite clear about their racial identity and view it positively'.

255   Robinson, V., (1998) Transients, Settlers and Refugees, Oxford: Clarendon.
256   Ratliffe, P., (1996) Geographical Spread, Spatial Concentration and Internal Migration, London: HMSO.
257   Scarman, L., (1981) The scarman Report: The Brixton Disorders, London: HMSO.

What is true of negative self-image is also true of language. The Caribbean dialect known as Creole or patois, once thought to play a role in underachievement, is now generally recognised to be of minimal significance in this regard[258].

Thirdly, there has been widespread rejection of cultural explanations because they are taken to imply that Caribbean culture is deficient, effectively blame parents for the underachievement of their children and in the process absolve the education system of responsibility.

There clearly is a series of problems in pointing to cultural differences. The boundaries between ethnic groups are fuzzy; there is a great deal of variation within ethnic groups; and there is the danger of overstating differences. Rampton's picture of the West Indian family is also applicable to many White families, for example. The risk of ethnocentrism is high, with other cultures being inappropriately judged by the standards of one's own. Thus Creole or patois was once seen as bad English when it is in fact a dialect of English and linguistically no better or worse than any other ethnic minority. As a result of that pupils are disproportionately sent to less effective schools. Although Smith and Tomlinson's findings suggested, that the schools examined were not nationally representative[259]. It is noticeable that 'the expectations of what all the pupils in these urban schools could achieve was low', so that it is questionable how effective even the effective schools are in the areas where ethnic minorities tend to receive their education.

The other study of note is that of Nuttall which was much more extensive covering 30,000 pupils in 140 Inner London Education Authority (ILEA) secondary schools. They found that the progress of ethnic minority pupils was generally as good as, if not better than, White pupils. The one exception comprised African-Caribbean pupils, who made slightly less progress. They also discovered that some schools were on average more effective than others, but in addition noted differential effectiveness in relation to African-Caribbean and Pakistani pupils. Although this study is also suggestive in pointing to differences between schools, there are problems. Unlike Smith and Tomlinson's study, class is not controlled for and doubts have been expressed about the validity of the prior attainment scores which were partially based on teacher assessments.

School effectiveness research is still at an early stage. There is evidence that schools differ in their effectiveness. On the other hand it is questionable how useful the concept of overall effectiveness is. For there is also evidence 'that the variation between departmental effectiveness is often greater than the differences between schools' overall levels of effectiveness[260]. In addition there is the question of differential effectiveness, with Nuttall et al.'s study indicating that not all pupils benefit equally from attending apparently 'effective' schools. The research shows that schools do make a difference but as yet we cannot tell how much and for whom.

258   Taylor, P., (1992) The Politics of Race and Immigration in Britain, Developments in Politics, vol.4.
259   Tomlinson, S., (2000) Ethnic Minorities and Education: New disadvantages, London: Falmer.
260   Swann, M., (1995) Education for All: A Review of Research into the Education of Pupils of West Indian Origin, Windsor: NFER Nelson.

Racism and multi-ethnic classrooms

A second strand of research on schools is not concerned so much with differences between schools as the features that schools share. In the view of some writers, schools are immersed with ethnocentric values. The curriculum reflects the outlook of one culture and as such is biased against children from African-Caribbean ethnic groups, who find that their own cultures are either ignored or belittled.

In the view of some professionals, the bias against African-Caribbean's is particularly severe and takes a racist form. An early piece of research which involved 510 teachers from 25 schools around the country revealed 'a high degree of consensus of opinion concerning the academic and social behaviour' of African-Caribbean pupils, with more than two-thirds of teachers agreeing in effect that such pupils are less able and give rise to more disciplinary problems. Since the teachers exhibited a much greater willingness to accept unfavourable generalisations about pupils of African-Caribbean origin than those of Asian or European origin, it does indeed seem 'that there is large scale stereotyping of African-Caribbean pupils[261]. Although we do not have recent evidence from questionnaires on teachers' attitudes towards ethnic minority pupils, a series of qualitative studies in schools indicate that 'African Caribbean's and Asian pupils can be subject to different expectations'. One study of a boys' comprehensive in the early 1980s noted, 'There was a tendency for Asian male students to be seen by the teachers as technically of "high ability" and socially as conformist. Afro-Caribbean male students tended to be seen as having "low ability" and potential discipline problems[262].

Having said that, the argument that some teachers hold, stereotypical views, does not necessarily mean that they treat pupils differently in practice. If we wish to explore this question we need to study multi-ethnic classrooms. The first study to gain widespread recognition and referred to in the Swann report studied 70 White teachers in primary and middle school classrooms. Using a modified version of the Flanders schedule to measure pupil teacher talk, Green discovered that Caribbean boys were much more likely to be criticised than other pupils and that, in the case of ethnocentric teachers, Caribbean girls were also much more likely to be criticised. He concluded that 'boys and girls of different ethnic origins taught in the same multi-ethnic classroom by the same teacher are likely to receive widely different educational experiences'. Green's work does not, however, explore the processes which underlie teacher pupil relationships. To do this we need to turn to ethnographic studies.

Our staring point will be the ethnographic study Wright conducted of two multi-ethnic comprehensive schools between 1982 and 1984, focusing, especially on the fourth and fifth years. She found the teachers to be critical of rather than encouraging towards African-Caribbean pupils. The result was that 'the classroom encounters observed for both schools showed the interaction between the teacher and the individual Afro-Caribbean student to be frequently characterised by confrontation and conflict[263]. 'Behavioural criteria rather than cognitive ones' influenced the teachers' assessment of African-Caribbean pupils with the result that they 'were likely to be placed in ability bands and examination sets well below their actual academic ability' as measured in one school by their performance in the third year examination. The response of African-Caribbean pupils to the labelling process was to resist, in the process confirming

261   Van, T., (1991) Racism and the Press, London: Routledge.

262   Solomos, J., (2001) Racism and Migration in Western Europe", Oxford, Berg.

263   Troyna, B., (1990) Beyond Reasonable Doubt? Researching "Race" in Educational settings, Oxford Review of Education, vol.21,no4.

their teachers' expectations and entering into a self-fulfilling prophecy which in some cases resulted in suspension or expulsion.

Gillborn studied a coeducational 11-16 comprehensive in the mid- 1980s. Despite the fact that the teachers seemed much more committed to the goal of equality of opportunity than those studied by Wright, they believed 'that Afro-Caribbean pupils represented a greater challenge to their authority than any other group in the school'. Believing 'the myth of an Afro-Caribbean challenge' they sought to nip it in the bud. The result was that 'Afro-Caribbean pupils experienced a disproportionate amount of punishment, and that they were sometimes exclusively criticised even when peers of other ethnic groups shared in the offence[264]. A high level of tension and indeed conflict was evident between White teachers and African-Caribbean pupils, who responded to their differential treatment in some cases by resistance, in other cases by accommodation.

Mark and Ghaffi studied a boys' in a comprehensive and a sixth form college in the early 1980s. Again conflict was evident between White teachers and Black pupils. The boys' comprehensive was rigidly streamed, with behavioural criteria rather than cognitive. He discovered that there are African-Caribbean boys of relatively higher ability in the lower sets, especially among the West Indians. He quoted a teacher saying "I've told you before Johnson and Brian were marvellous at Maths, especially problem-solving. But it's their, the West Indians' attitude and that must decide it in the end. You can't promote a boy who is known to be a troublemaker who's a dodger. It will look like a reward for bad behaviour"[265].

The response of Caribbean's often took the form of resistance, with the formation of a distinct subculture, the Rasta Heads. Some Asians also resisted, but their subculture the Warriors adopted a lower profile. The response of the African-Caribbean and Asian students at the sixth form college was different again. The Black Sisters adopted a policy of 'resistance within accommodation', being, like other young Black women studied in two comprehensive schools in London), anti-school but pro-education according to Mirza .

While Wright studied four inner-cities primary schools in 1988-89: his 'classroom observation indicated that teachers tended to treat Afro-Caribbean children (especially boys) in a more restrictive way than other pupil groups. For instance issuing orders rather than encouraging them to express their ideas. Asian children, on the other hand, received more individual attention; in other words they tend not to be overlooked or underestimated by teachers[266] . What is of particular concern 'in addition to the frequency of critical and controlling statements which Afro-Caribbean pupils received was the observation that they were likely to be singled out for criticism even though several pupils of different groups were engaged in the same act of behaviour'. The following extract from a nursery group of four-year-olds illustrates this: Teacher: Let's do one song before home time. (White boy): Humpty Dumpty.

Teacher: No, I'm choosing today. Let's do something we have not done for a while. Chukwuemeka: (a black boy) I know, we'll do the autumn song.
Teacher: What about the autumn song we sing. Don't shout out; put your hand up nicely: ones again disadvantaging African-Caribbean pupils. On another study carried out on the same subject between

264   Mayor, B., (1992) Racism and Education, London: Sage.
265   Young, H., (2001) The Right to be British, The Guardian, 12 November
266   Walvin, J., (1998) "Black Caricature: the roots of Racialism", London Hutchinson

1985 and 1987 in a multi-ethnic comprehensive. Unlike the other studies, the author 'found no evidence of differential treatment of students on ethnic or racial lines either in classrooms or in wider school processes'[267]?

In support of their claim, they argued that minority students, especially African-Caribbean girls, in fact achieved better results than White pupils, even in a school where the standards expected of them were very low. The school differed from the others studied in being located in a community with a long history of cooperation between different ethnic groups. It was generously staffed and the staff had a high level of awareness of race, being engaged in the implementation of an anti-racist programme.

Although Foster recognised that the distinct features of the school he studied may have resulted in him reaching different conclusions than the other ethnographic studies, he has, together with Gomm and Hamersley, since attacked the credibility of these studies. A series of articles have culminated in a book attacking ethnographic and other studies which purport to show that school processes contribute to educational inequality. Their conclusions are worth quoting. On studies claiming to show that schools are discriminatory in their allocation of students to different levels of course, they conclude: 'Taken overall this body of research fails to establish that discrimination against working class and black students occurs on any scale in the allocation of students to courses or through the effects of this allocation[268]'. On studies claiming to show discriminatory treatment in the classroom they conclude: There are also some serious problems with the evidential base on which descriptive claims about differential treatment rely. Sometimes no evidence at all is presented to maintain their assertion. And when evidence is provided it is often of a kind which cannot effectively support the sort of claim made: for instance one or two examples are offered to establish the different frequency of particular sorts of teacher action in relation to different categories of students. Moreover many of the interpretations made of data are questionable.

Given such scepticism towards evidence which points to inequalities at school level and in the classroom, their overall conclusion comes as no surprise: 'There is no convincing evidence currently available for any substantial role on the part of schools in generating inequalities in educational outcomes between social classes, genders or ethnic groups'. How satisfactory is this critique when applied to ethnicity, where the central concern has been with the attainment of African-Caribbean pupils? We shall begin by examining the evidence on discrimination in allocation to different levels of course.

Here there is considerable evidence that African-Caribbean pupils are under-represented in top sets and over-represented in bottom sets. Even the 1992/3 report of HM Chief Inspector of Schools acknowledged that they, along with other minority ethnic pupils, were in general under represented in the top ability sets[269].

There is also evidence that placement is often not based on ability alone and that this disadvantages African-Caribbean pupils. We have already pointed to the evidence from Wright, Mac and Gail, which indicates that behavioural criteria and not purely cognitive ones were used in the allocation of pupils to examination sets and streams and that this practice disadvantaged African-Caribbean pupils in particular.

---

267   Stewart, A., (2000) "Social Inclusion: An Introduction", London: Macmillan.
268   Troyna, B., (1984) "Fact or Artefact? The Eductional Underachievement of Black Pupils", British Journal of Sociology of Education, vol.5, no.2.
269   Werbner, P., (1992) "The Dialectics of Cultural Hybridity", London: Zed.

And there is other evidence pointing in the same direction. For example, a study of one local education authority shows that when there was a mismatch between the VR (verbal reasoning) band in which a pupil had been placed by teachers and that based on test performance. African-Caribbean pupils were more likely to be placed in the lower VR band while ESWI (English. Scottish. Welsh and Irish) pupils were more likely to be placed in a higher VR band than their test scores would suggest.

Foster indeed noted that behaviour rather than ability influenced allocation in his own ethnographic study. As he puts it:

"The behaviour of older Afro/Caribbean boys tended to be regarded less favourably. In a sense their youth cultural norms conformed less closely to the teachers' conceptions of the 'ideal' and as a result they seemed somewhat more likely to be allocated to lower status groups in the school's system of differentiation[270]".

Foster arrived at the same conclusion Bernard Coard arrived in the 70s when he wrote his book titled, "How the West Indian Child is made educationally subnormal in the British School System: the Scandal of the Black Child in Schools in Britain".

And in a revealing footnote to their damning critique of evidence of discrimination, Foster also recognise that 'it may be wise to depart from what would be expected on the basis of measured ability that have been found within and across studies, which tend to be always in the same direction. This indicates that more thorough investigation is justified' Foster went further to argue that indirect discrimination is probably occurring since allocation on behavioural criteria has been shown to result, however unintentionally, among disadvantaging African-Caribbean pupils.

As for the consequences of streaming, Wright, Gillborn, **Mac and Gail** do point to a tendency for the attitudes of different streams to polarise, with those in the bottom streams tending to engage in resistance, and at some points in their book, Foster, also acknowledge 'the operation of a differentiation polarisation effect[271].

Let us move on to look at the evidence on inequalities in the classroom. Foster et al critique is valuable in alerting us to some potential pitfalls of ethnographic studies. Although they can provide a rich understanding of classroom processes, there is the danger of selective perception, with one's observations being interpreted through the prism of a pre-existing theory. Other interpretations are always possible. Take the extract above about Chukwuemaka. We are led to assume that Chukwuemaka is particularly subject to censure because he is African-Caribbean. Could there not be other reasons? Are other African-Caribbean pupils also particularly subject to censure? In this particular study, Wright does in fact provide evidence to suggest that White teachers in general discriminated against African-Caribbean boys in general[272]. And this is crucial. For it is only by using different sources of evidence which corroborate each other that ethnographic studies are convincing. The ethnographic studies we have looked at are of variable quality in this respect, but all use a variety of methods to triangulate their findings. He also point to a relatively high level of conflict between White teachers and Caribbean pupils. Where Foster differs from Wright is in seeing teachers responding appropriately to the behaviour of Caribbean pupils and playing no real part in generating conflict.

---

270   Pilkington, A., (1993) Race and Ethnicity, Milton Keynes: Open University

271   Peach, C., (1999) the force of West Indian Island Identities in Britain, London: Allen and Unwin.

272   Mynott, E., (2000) The Asylum Debate, Runnymade Bulletin, no.322.

Foster argues that teacher deifications are based on observations of students' behaviour and academic ability in the classroom. He may be substantially correct. However, observations are not innocent and may be influenced by prior deifications, here is a student on teaching practice in a boys' comprehensive learning the ropes from school management:

"I was told that I had to look out for the African-Caribbean's and what to do. When they went mad, one just had to leave them alone to cool down. There was nothing we could do and things like that: if they swore at us in their own language we must report it. We had trouble from them in the past".
The student was subsequently appointed to the school. Here he is, a year later:

"The African-Caribbean's are tough". "I tried not to let anyone influence me in how I treat them but they look at you with wild eyes if you tell them to sit down. They are looking, expecting trouble. They are more prejudiced than white people. The Asians are better, you tell them to do something an' then meek mild they go an' do it"[273].

In addition to evidence that old hands may influence teacher, deification, there is also evidence from the studies by Gillborn and Wright and, more recently from OFSTED that the same behaviour may be treated differently by teachers. This is particularly disturbing if it results in Caribbean's being particularly subject to censure early in their school career, as in the case of Chukwuemaka. For Smith and Tomlinson indicate that students who are subject to constant criticism tend to underachieve.

To point to evidence which suggests that African Caribbean pupils are subject sometimes to differential treatment in the classroom does not mean, however, that Foster's ethnographic study were ensuing critique of research in this area, such a notion should be summarily dismissed. Having said that there is substantial agreement that, at least in the latter stages of schooling, the behaviour of some African-Caribbean pupils is not only defined by teachers as deviant but in fact is deviant. Where Foster and his critics fundamentally disagree is over their explanation of 'bad behaviour'. For Foster, primacy is given to extra-school factors. 'There may be a general tendency for Afro-Caribbean students on average to be less well behaved in schools[274] because of their adoption of a distinctive subculture consequent on a recognition on their part of poor post-school prospects and rejection of racism in the wider society. For the others, primacy is given to school processes, with some African-Caribbean pupils pictured as turning towards a distinctive subculture in order to resist their differential treatment in schools. The debate between Foster and his critics is important to the debate over the criminalisation of African-Caribbean people. For some writers, the greater involvement of African-Caribbean young men in street crime is primarily responsible for their greater criminalisation; for others, racism in the criminal justice system is primarily responsible for their greater criminalisation. More recently, however, there have been attempts by some criminologists 'to move beyond the either/or of racist criminal justice v black criminality[275] to recognise that both reinforce and feed off one another in a vicious circle of amplification. By analogy, we might suggest that in schools both differential treatment and 'bad behaviour' may result in the development of a vicious cycle.

This suggestion has been taken up by some recent ethnographic studies which seek to show how societal definitions of both ethnicity and gender impact upon the schooling experiences of African-Caribbean

---

273   Nazroo, J., (1997) The Mental Health of Ethnic Minorities, London: Policy Studies Institute.
274   Morrison, M., (2000) Inspecting Schools for Racial Equality, Stoke on Trent: Trentham.
275   Murry, C., (1984) "Losing Ground", New York: Basic

pupils and create a vicious cycle. Connolly provides one example from his study of a multi-ethnic primary school. Here the over disciplining of Black boys tends to construct an image of them among their peers, as being 'bad' and typically masculine. This, in turn, provides the context where African-Caribbean boys are more likely to be drawn into fights and to develop 'hardened' identities, which then means they are more likely to be noticed by teachers and disciplined for being aggressive; the cycle is thus complete[276].

While Connolly attributes primary responsibility for the generation of this cycle to teachers, Sewell, in a study of a boys' secondary school, challenges the notion 'that teacher racism alone' leads African-Caribbean boys 'to adopt a culture of resistance to schooling'. While he acknowledges that teachers tend to accept what Gillborn labels 'the myth of an African Caribbean challenge' and see boys in particular as threatening their authority, he also emphasises the role of the black pupils' subculture which 'helps to feed the stereotype that African-Caribbean boys are more openly aggressive and rude than their "weak" white counterparts'.

Both the teachers and pupils are envisaged as influenced by cultural representations of Black males acquired outside the classroom. The teachers tended to share the ethnocentric assumptions of the wider society and assume 'that African-Caribbean boys were instinctively against authority while Asian boys were the complete opposite[277]. The result was that African-Caribbean boys received a disproportionate amount of control and criticism compared to other ethnic groups. At the same time the Black subculture in the school drew on a wider street culture and placed emphasis 'on a Black collectivist anti- school ideology, on pro-consumerism and phallocentrism'. While this subculture enabled the boys to resist the racism of the wider society and maintain a positive Black identity, its adoption of a macho form of masculinity was not conducive to academic success. The equation, for some boys, of academic achievement with being gay or effeminate was evident here and constituted a significant barrier to those pupils seeking educational qualifications. The focus of conflict between teachers and Black pupils often revolved around displays of ethnicity from the boys. Black hairstyles were a particular bone of contention. The school sought to ban Black boys from having patterns in their hair while no such prohibition was made in relation to White boys who wore ponytails. The result was that Black hairstyles became 'a key factor in the display of an African-Caribbean masculine subculture that became an alternative to schooling[278].

In this way a vicious cycle can develop, in which what is perceived as a lack of respect from teachers is met by an aggressive response from pupils who in turn are punished for their behaviour. Such a cycle can, as in this school, have devastating consequences resulting in 'black young people being proportionately more likely to be excluded than members of other ethnic groups[279]. Permanent exclusions are the most extreme sanction schools have. The sanction is now not only being more widely used for disobedience of various kinds but is being used disproportionately with Black pupils, especially Caribbean's.

The evidence gathered during OFSTED inspections in 199 3/4.

To acknowledge that the evidence for indirect discrimination at the level of the school and to acknowledge that the evidence for differential treatment at the level of the classroom are stronger than Foster earlier

276   Gillborn, D., (1995) Racism and Antiracism in Real Schools, Milton Keynes: Open University Press.

277   Peters, G., (1990) There Ain't No Black in the Union Jack, London: Hutchinson.

278   Glasgow Media Group, (1997) "Race", Migration and Media, Glasgow: GMG

279   Peterson, P., (1992) the Urban Underclass and the Poverty Paradox, Washington, DC: Brookings Institution.

suggest does not mean that it is schools that are most central 'in generating inequalities in education outcomes between ethnic groups'.

Foster is correct in reminding us that we cannot generalise from particular schools and particular classrooms to all schools and all classrooms. Indeed it is questionable whether the rationale for ethnographic research is to generate generalisations at all[280]. And even if there are common school processes as suggested by the similar picture conveyed by most ethnographic studies, we cannot reach an informed judgement about the 'causal effectiveness' of school processes in the absence of a comparison with the contribution of extra-school factors. The research on school effectiveness, which does seek to control for factors such as prior attainment and social class, suggests that variations between schools do make a difference but that extra-school factors are generally much more significant in

Figure 13

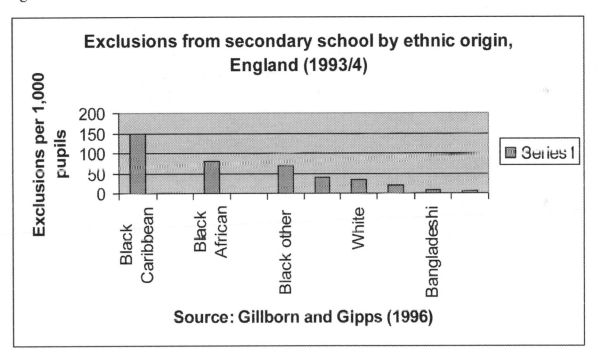

Determining student progress[281]. Although this research, according to Drew and Demack is concerned with differences between schools rather than purportedly common discriminatory practices within schools and thus cannot be used to refute the suggestion that racism in schools is of critical importance in accounting for ethnic differences in achievement, what it does suggest is that we should be extremely circumspect before reaching a definitive judgement.

The need for caution is reinforced when we remember the complexity in patterns of ethnic educational achievement, which indicates that, while some minority ethnic groups are doing better than Whites,

280   OFSTED, (1999) Raising the Attainment of Minority Ethnic Pupils, London: OFSTED
281   Drew, D. and Demack, S. (1998) "A League Apart: Statistics in the Study of "Race" and Education", Milton Keynes: Open University Press.

African-Caribbean boys are underachieving and that both Pakistani and Bangladeshi pupils are performing no better even though their parents have better economic integration than the African-Caribbean parents[282] Modood argued. The role of racism in accounting for this complex pattern is unclear. "Are all minority ethnic groups subject to discriminatory treatment? If so, how do some groups and indeed some individuals successfully resist such treatment? Evidence of racism in schools may be stronger than Foster work suggest, but this does not mean that such racism is the major factor in accounting for ethnic differentials in educational achievement. **(See chapter 2 & 3)**

The debate, which we have been examining, about the contribution which school processes play in accounting for Caribbean underachievement is part of a wider debate about the purposes of educational research. Foster adopts a 'methodological purist' stance, stressing that 'the purpose of research in this area should be to produce knowledge relevant to public debates, not to eradicate inequality'.

By contrast, Troyna and others adopt a partisan, or what Gillborn prefers to call a 'critical' position, seeing the purpose of research as that of documenting what is going on in order to challenge injustices[283]. The methodological purists contend that researchers who adopt an avowedly anti-racist position too readily accept evidence pointing to indirect discrimination and differential treatment. The latter retort that at least they are explicit about their value commitments, whereas the methodological purists, by imposing extremely stringent criteria to evaluate studies pointing to indirect discrimination and differential treatment, are implicitly concerned to defend teachers. Despite disagreement between those who adopt a methodological purist and a partisan stance, both in fact are opposed to 'falsifying data and suppressing "unhelpful" findings' and both recognise the need for 'assessment of factual claims in terms of logical consistency and empirical adequacy[284].

Where methodological purists and partisan researchers disagree is over whether the research on school processes meets these criteria. The former adopt extremely stringent criteria, argue that existing studies do not convince them 'beyond reasonable doubt' and on that basis conclude that 'it seems unfair and unwise to criticise current practices'. By contrast, the latter show that it is always possible to challenge researchers' interpretations, argue that their ethnographic studies present convincing interpretations and on that basis conclude that it is incumbent on schools to re-examine their current practices.

The political implications of the positions adopted by the two sides are clear. The first leans to a conservative privileging of current practices; the latter leads to a radical challenging of current practices. Somewhat ironically, given the explicit adherence of methodological purists to a scientific methodology, it is the partisan researchers who remain closer to a Popperian philosophy of social science. For at least they do put forward a theory to account for African-Caribbean underachievement. By contrast, the methodological purists content themselves with critiques 'mostly constructed in negative terms[285] and do not at least in their joint book put forward any theory at all: towards a multifactorial explanation of educational inequality.

---

282   Modood, T., (1997) Ethnic Minorities in Britain, London: Policy Studies Institute.
283   Foster, P., (1991) Case Still not Proven: a Reply to Wright, C., "British Educational Research Journal", Vol.17, no.2.
284   Health, A., Mills, C., and Roberts, J (1992) "Towards Meritocracy? Recent evidence on an Old Problem", in Crouch, C., (ed.) Social Research and Social Reform, Oxford: Oxford University Press.
285   Foster, P., (1992) Teacher Attitudes and Afro-Caribbean Educational Attainment, Oxford Review of Education, Vol.18, no.3.

When we explore divergent explanations for ethnic differentials in educational attainment (the primary focus of which here has been that of the underachievement of African-Caribbean children) we enter a politically highly charged terrain. Although sociologists are now less inclined to fall into the trap of the 'fallacy of the single factor[286] and frequently acknowledge that a range of factors operating in a complex way are needed to explain African-Caribbean underachievement, there is still a tendency to prioritise some factors to the exclusion of others. In particular we have noted the inclination of some to dismiss cultural factors and of others to reject the role of school processes. Steering a path through these tortuous rapids, we can conclude that IQ is not a major factor but that there is evidence to suggest that a range of social factors are significant: economic deprivation, which itself stems at least in part from economic lynching (See chapter 2&3); cultural factors, which need to be carefully contextualised to avoid 'blaming the victim'; ineffective schools, which themselves are often located in disadvantaged areas; and (the often unintentional) racial discrimination in schools. Sometimes the state deliberately put ineffective head teacher in schools that are predominantly black just to do one thing and one thing only, destroy it together with the future of those vulnerable black children.

Ethnicity and educational policy.

Central government policy on ethnicity and education has never been underpinned by a clearly formulated coherent philosophy. Neither has it generally involved specific policies aimed at ethnic minorities. For some, this is to be welcomed; with one writer considering that the 'racially inexplicit' policy characteristic of the UK in contrast to the 'racially explicit' policy characteristic of the United States was 'doing well in secrecy[287]. For others, the lack of explicit reference to 'race' and ethnicity in policy formulation constitutes what should be regarded as bogus 'decriminalisation', signalling a failure to tackle the central issue of racism.

Troyna and Williams work of 1986 shows that despite differing evaluations of government policy, there is still widespread agreement that the state has not attempted to take a lead in the area of ethnicity and education but has responded in an ad hoc manner. It is true that 'an enduring commitment to assimilation' has been evident throughout the post-war period, but this does not mean that we cannot distinguish different policy phases. Indeed it is not uncommon to identify three such phases "assimilation, integration and cultural pluralism". What we must remember, however, is that these phases overlap each other; that they cannot easily be periodised; and that their influence on educational practice has been variable.

The initial response of the education system was foretold on the need for the 'successful assimilation of immigrant children[288]. The major obstacle to achieving this was seen as the children's lack of proficiency in the English language. 'The emphasis was therefore on the teaching of English as a second language to immigrant children, often in specialist language or reception centres which also provided some basic pastoral support to counter 'culture shock'. Once this obstacle had been overcome, it was assumed that immigrant pupils would be absorbed within the overall school population. By 1965, however, the

---

286   Hammersley, M., (1997) "Constructing Educational Inequality", Lewes: Falmer.

287   Troyna, B., and Williams, J., (1986) Racism, Education and the State, London: Croom Helm

288   Taylor, S., (1992) The Politics of Race and Immigration in Britain, Developments in Politics, vol.4.

central government was concerned that 'as the proportion of immigrant children increases, the problems will become more difficult to solve, and the chances of assimilation more remote'. The response was to recommend to LEAs that they disperse immigrant pupils 'between different schools in an attempt to "spread the problem" and avoid any school becoming predominantly immigrant in character[289] . Such a recommendation was clearly designed to placate White parents and in the process identified immigrant pupils as the problem. A sentence italicised in the 1965 DES circular is revealing in this context:

"It will be helpful if the parents of non-immigrant children can see that practical measures have been taken to deal with the problems in the schools, and that the progress of their own children is not being restricted by the undue preoccupation of the teaching staff with the linguistic and other difficulties of immigrant children".

In order to implement the dispersal policy and discover the extent of language need, statistics were collected on 'immigrant children'. The latter were defined as both those who were themselves immigrant and those born in Britain to immigrant parents who had been in this country less than ten years. To enable local authorities to make special provision for immigrant children, the government provided under Section 11 of the 1966 Local Government Act some financial support. The definition of 'immigrant children' adopted by the government implied that the problems caused by increasing numbers of minority ethnic children in schools were temporary and would disappear after they had spent ten years in Britain.

The assimilation phase lasted until the late 1960s. It clearly rested on a number of highly problematic assumptions: that minimal changes were needed to the education system; that the presence of immigrant pupils caused problems; that the problems faced by immigrant pupils stemmed primarily from lack of proficiency in English; and that assimilation, which placed the onus on ethnic minorities to change, was both achievable and desirable. Some of these assumptions began to be increasingly challenged during the l960s. To many educationalists, the assumption that the 'problem' of ethnicity and education would evaporate once children had lived in Britain for ten years seemed overly optimistic. In particular, it was argued, attention should be paid to the cultural backgrounds of minority pupils and some recognition given to cultural diversity in schools.

The integrationist phase was born. Although this phase shared with the previous phase 'the common aim of absorbing ethnic minority communities within society with as little disruption to the life of the majority community as possible[290], it did at least recognise that the needs of minority ethnic pupils could not simply be met by limited remedial provision. Two responses were particularly evident. The first involved some acknowledgement that ethnic minorities have special needs while the second stressed that other groups have similar needs. Multicultural education (MCE) exemplified the first, and the conceptualisation of the educational needs of minority ethnic pupils as part of a broader problem of inner city disadvantage, which has remained the central thrust of urban policy, the second. In the absence of any central lead, multicultural initiatives varied widely between LEAS and schools.
 In practice, MCE was rarely evident in all-White areas and even in multi-ethnic communities did not entail a reappraisal of the curriculum. Rather it was tacked on and 'preoccupied with exotic aspects of cultural differences[291], the concern often being to portray 'positive images' in order to compensate for

289   Banton, M., (1972) Promoting Racial Harmony, Cambridge: Cambridge University Press.
290   Brake, M., (1986) Comparative Youth Culture, London: Routledge.
291   Skellington, K., (1992) Racism and Anti Racism, London: Sage.

an assumed cultural deficit. In a similar way, subsuming the needs of ethnic minorities within a wider category of the disadvantaged effectively identified them as a problem.

During the 1970s, recognition that integrationism constituted an inadequate response to the issue of ethnicity and education gradually filtered through, with the Select Committee on Race Relations and Immigration eventually recommending setting up an official 'inquiry into the causes of the underachievement of children of African-Caribbean origin[292]. The creation in 1989 of an inquiry with the broader remit to report on the education of children from minority ethnic groups signalled the temporary, collapse of integrationism.

As a result, cultural pluralism emerged and with it a somewhat different vision. For a pluralist society is one 'which enables, expects and encourages members of all ethnic groups, both minority and majority, to participate fully in shaping the society as a whole within a framework of commonly accepted values, practices and procedures, whilst also allowing and, where necessary, assisting the ethnic minority communities in maintaining their distinct ethnic identities within this common framework', which is responsible for today cultural extremism. Pluralist society may sound good and plausible but under critical examination you will find out that it is a claver way of hiding the truth; which is to maintain the social control of African-Caribbean people where every family is a single parent.**(see chapter 6)** Although there is still an assimilationist thrust evident and therefore some continuity with the two previous phases, more significant is the change of emphasis[293]. Rampton interim report, comprises the first official recognition of the significance of racism inside schools, while the final report Swann, advocates a form of multicultural education which incorporated an anti-racist element and was aimed at all pupils. At the same time some left-wing local authorities, woken from their slumbers by inner city disturbances, began to take the issue of racism seriously. Sceptical of the likelihood of the central government tackling racism, they pursued a number of anti- racist initiatives as part of a wider equal opportunities strategy[294] . 'This culminated in the 1980s with the adoption of anti-racist or multicultural policies and practices in over three-quarters of British LEAs'. Such initiatives were highly controversial, but along with the official reports helped to 'radicalise' the issue of ethnicity and education in the sense that racism became an explicit object of public debate and policy formulation. Nevertheless, the central government was not wholly inactive. Although reluctant to address the issue of racism because it benefit the political elite in their fight to exclude and repress the vulnerable African-Caribbean people who have done them no wrong. However, it did support a number of initiatives which signalled its belief in the importance of education for an ethnically diverse society. The upshot of all this was that the 1980s witnessed 'a growing awareness of the political, social and economic reasons for developing an education system relevant to an ethnically diverse society because 1980 became a period of racial upheaval, a period of social and economic lynching of African-Caribbean people. A period when it was political unacceptable to have black in our means, even the word black is no longer use to associate with the African-Caribbean's, it become a slogan used to identify the Asian. Any political appointment that should be for African-Caribbean people went to Asians. After the 7/7/05 terrorist bombing that killed innocent people that have done nothing wrong, the rule of the game changed: African-Caribbean's who were being driven to extinction had a lease of life and reclaim their identity. [295].

---

292   Solomos, J., (1999) Ethnic and Racial Studies Today, London: Routledge.

293   Rampton, A., (1981) West Indian Children in Our Schools, London: HMSO Cmnd. 8273.

294   Ratcliffe, P., (1999) Housing Inequality and "Race": some Critical Reflections on the Concept of "Social Exclusion, Ethnic and Racial Studies, vol.22, no.1.

295   Bryant, C., (1997) Citizenship, National Identity and the Accommodation of Difference: Reflections on the

Unfortunately, internal warfare ensued between advocates of multicultural and anti-racist education. For the former, 'the key issue facing schools is how to create tolerance for African-Caribbean minorities and their cultures in a white nation now characterised by cultural diversity. The basic educational prescription is the sympathetic teaching of "other cultures" in order to dispel the ignorance which is seen to be at the root of prejudice and intolerance'. For the latter, the key issue is racism, which is not characterised merely as prejudice but instead is seen as embedded in structures and institutions.

Combating racism 'requires a dismantling of institutionalised practices of racism as well as a direct confrontation with racist ideologies, for example, in the school curriculum[296]. It is of course questionable how significant the 'bitter arguments between anti-racism and multiculturalism' were for teachers, but before the ink run dry on the Swann report's attempt 'to move beyond the multicultural/anti-racist deadlock' the whole enterprise was savaged by more powerful voices. The New Right attacked what it saw as the politicisation of education, effectively identifying the central problem as anti-racism rather than racism. Much of the media joined in the attack, lampooning loony lefties for diluting and thereby undermining national culture that was designed to exclude the African-Caribbean people from the main British economy; often this involved significant misrepresentation. This was most marked in coverage of the Burnage inquiry[297]. The latter, which had been set up to investigate the background to the murder of an Asian student by a White peer, criticised the particular form of anti-racist education practised at Burnage. Although, he was adamant about the reality of racism and the need for a more sensitive and subtle form of anti-racism; 'The national press tended to represent the report as "proof" that antiracism is a damaging extremist political creed'. In this context, it is not altogether surprising that a mere three and a half years after the Swann report, it was branded by Minister of State at the DES as stemming from a different era: in essence the Government has taken on board Swann's recommendation, but it feels that the way in which one deals with the whole of this problem is perhaps changing with time and one perhaps cannot go back to something which was thought through and presented in a time and in an era which is very different from today. The whole idea of the debate is to enable the government introduce a reform, inform of Grant-maintained schools and City technology Colleges that would enable them to alienate the African-Caribbean people.

1988 Education Reform Act

A new era had arrived; the 1988 Education Reform Act (ERA) involved three major changes. The first of these was the introduction of a national curriculum for all state schools alongside a national system of assessment for pupils from 5-16 years. The second major change concerned the introduction of a system of school management known as the Local Management of Schools. The third major change involved the creation of a new tier of schooling comprising City Technology Colleges and Grant-Maintained Schools[298].

German, French, Dutch and British cases, New Community, vol.23, no2.

296   Swann, M., (1985) Education for All, London: HMSO Comnd. 9453.
297   Townend, P., (1992) Inequality in Health, Harmondsworth: Penguin.
298   Young, H., (2001) Labour's Law of Ethnic Punishment Shames us all, The Guardian, 8 may.

These changes deliberately eroded the power of local education authorities and embodied instead a concern for schooling to be both subject to market forces and under central control. League tables were introduced to expedite choice and a new inspection regime set up to maintain standards. The Act reflected two somewhat contrary principles. Moves to open up competition between schools indicated adherence to a neo-liberal market philosophy, while the introduction of a National Curriculum pointed to the espousal of conservative and trade union values centred on the preservation of a distinct national culture.

In many ways the 1988 Act and its successor, the 1993 Act represented something of a paradigm shift in the discourse surrounding educational policy. The concern with equality of opportunity, which had characterised much educational debate in the post-war period, was replaced by a concern with, to quote one former Secretary of State for Education, John Patten 'choice, diversity and, above all, standards'. Such a context has not been conducive to 'education towards racial equality[299]. Pessimism has been engendered by much of this legislation and the way it has been implemented. Take, for example, the introduction of the National Curriculum and the rationale given for it by the chief executive of the School Curriculum and Assessment Authority.

A fundamental purpose of the school curriculum is to transmit an appreciation of and commitment to the best of the culture we have inherited. That is why our statutory curriculum emphasises the centrality of British history. Britain's changing relations with the rest of the world. The English literary heritage and the study of Christianity, while (some argue) it ought to follow the example of our European neighbours in emphasising more than it currently does the roots of our civilisation in Greece and Rome[300].

While Tate acknowledged the need for pupils to learn about 'other cultures', he emphasised that this was 'subsidiary', integrationism rather than cultural pluralism which was back on the agenda. 'There was, of course, the "multicultural dimension" in the National Curriculum. NCC (National Curriculum Council) non-statutory guidance 1991 asserted that "multicultural education is the professional responsibility of all teachers in all schools". It sings Swann's song. But inequality and injustice did not get mentioned in it. And no attempt has been made to link even the most stimulating of multicultural initiatives to assessed performance indicators of either pupils or schools. Although in short MCE still had some official support, in practice, it was seen as of peripheral significance.

Other changes were also greeted with dismay. Wider parental choice, it was argued, leads 'to an increased likelihood of racial and religious segregation in schools where Moslems would not like to send their children to schools were there are infidel children at the same time white people would like to send their children to schools that are predominantly white[301], while the erosion of the power of LEAs means that 'the struggle for the promotion and infusion of anti-racist education must now take place at the meetings of every school governing body'. Concern was also expressed with the new funding arrangements for schools, with the 'reduced amount of monies now available' scarcely being conducive to 'progress in racial equality'.

299   Walvin, C., (2000) Black Caricature: the Root of Racialism, London: Hutchinson.
300   Woodward, K., (1997) Identity and Difference, Oxford: Oxford University Press.
301   Peterson, W., (2001) Race and Inquality in Education, Milton Keynes: Open University Press.

The advent of a Labour Government in 1997, committed to increase spending on 'education, education, education' has meant that, in contrast to the previous administration, equality of opportunity has been explicitly resurrected as a key objective. In his foreword to the White Paper, Excellence in Schools, which sets out the government's thinking behind subsequent reforms, the then Secretary for Education and Employment, David Blunkett, described the government's key objectives as 'equality of opportunity and high standards for all[302]. Has this objectives been achieved? The answer is no, it is only talk but no delivery, in reality the standard of education for African-Caribbean youth has got worse. They are the least likely to go to school, the least likely to pass GCSE examination and the least likely to hold down a job.

The emphasis on the overriding importance of standards, however, and the consequent commitment to parental choice, the maintenance of diverse types of school, a revamped National Curriculum, league tables and inspections represent significant continuities with the previous administration. For some researchers, the concern to raise standards has in practice taken precedence and the reliance on employing market mechanisms to this end has meant increased inequalities. The response of schools to a competitive environment generated by league tables, which rank schools in terms of the proportion of students gaining five or more higher grades at GCSE, has been to be more selective and to give extra support to those pupils identified as likely to meet this threshold. The result, it is argued, is 'a new IQism[303], which labels African-Caribbean students as likely failures and justifies rationing provision to support those, often middle-class White students, marked for success. In this way national education policy entails increased inequalities. What is more, successful schools are eligible for more funding. The urban location and socio-economic position, however, of many parents from minority ethnic groups inhibit their ability to choose such schools for their children, thereby, it is argued, 'segregating most minority students in under-funded and under-staffed schools in urban areas'.

While it is important to examine the unintended consequences of a market in education, the government's support of equality of opportunity cannot be dismissed as an empty form of words. The government has addressed equality issues primarily though it's social exclusion agenda. This has meant for example, in the case of education, creating Education Action Zones. Such initiatives are attempts to combat social disadvantage and are not specifically targeted at minority ethnic groups, the assumption being that measures benefiting all disadvantaged groups will disproportionately benefit minority ethnic groups. Since the publication of the McPherson report, however, the government has become rather less colour blind in addressing the issue of racial equality. An Ethnic Minority Achievement Grant (EMAG) was created in 1999 to replace the special funding previously available under Section 11 of the 1966 Local Government Act. Since LEAs have to bid for this funding, its advent, along with other initiatives, has encouraged LEAs and schools, whose arrangements for monitoring have been generally poor[304] (OFSTED in 1999, adopted a more systematic approach to ethnic monitoring. At the same time, OFSTED, criticised for its failure in its inspections to report on racism in schools[305], has been given new guidance and training to enable it to tackle racial equality in schools more seriously. The government has even made some hesitant moves to give multiculturalism a greater emphasis in the curriculum. From 2002, all secondary school pupils will be obliged to study citizenship and both this and personal and social education has

302   Klein, G., (1993) Education towards Race Equality, London: Cassell.
303   Pierson, J., and Hallam, S., (2001) Ability Grouping in Education, London: Chapman.
304   Rattansi, A., (2000) "Changing the Subject?" in Donald, A. and Rattansi, A. (eds) "Race, Culture and Difference, London: Sage.
305   Modood, T., and Werbner, P., (1997) the Politics of Multi Culturalism in New Europe, London: Zed Book.

a multicultural component. Curriculum 2000 has moved a little away from the previous colour-blind National Curriculum by making explicit, albeit piecemeal, references to race and cultural issues. It still remains the case; however, that multiculturalism is not included in the overarching statement of the curriculum's aims and values. To this extent multicultural education still remains somewhat peripheral and integrationism remains the order of the day.

The unwillingness of the government not to move further on multicultural education and develop more targeted initiatives to promote racial equality is not surprising, given the crisis of confidence which has occurred in the movement concerned with promoting racial equality. With notable exceptions, there is widespread agreement that the dispute between the proponents of multicultural education (MCE) and anti-racist education (ARE) is now outmoded. Rather than seeing MCE and ARE as embodying contrary principles and therefore irreconcilable, we are instead enjoined to respect their relative merits and seek amalgamation of the two 'anti-racist multicultural education[306]. This view is consistent with the discovery by some social theorists of a purportedly new phenomenon, cultural racism. The re-emergence of 'Africaphobia' has prompted Modood to emphasise the importance of 'cultural racism' as well as 'colour racism' while analysis of cultural representations has led Gilroy to conclude that 'a form of cultural racism which has taken a necessary distance from crude ideas of biological inferiority now seeks to present an imaginary definition of the nation as a unified cultural community[307].

While the emphasis on cultural racism confirms the need for a rapprochement between MCE and ARE, social theorists have more recently raised serious misgivings with the practice of both approaches. For not only do representations of the notion frequently assume that there are essential differences between cultures but so do MCE and ARE. The former tends to assume that the boundaries between ethnic groups are clear and that each ethnic group has a distinct culture which warrants respect. Such an approach, however, underestimates the degree to which globalisation dissolves boundaries. It implies 'some form of ethnic essentialism[308] Rattansi added, and thereby accepts the same assumption as cultural racism that groups are inherently different. It ignores intra-cultural differences and conflicts, and, in its refusal to judge other cultures, privileges the maintenance of existing cultural differences despite the self-contradiction involved in such a relativist position, ARE fares no better. For the tendency to assume that racism is the defining feature of the experience of minority ethnic groups entails a representation of ethnic minorities as essentially the same part of the Black community. As such, it amounts to a form of 'cultural essentialism', which ignores both inter- and intra-cultural differences. In the version of ARE criticised by the Burnage inquiry, a similar unwillingness to recognise difference characters the representation of the majority ethnic group 'White people' who are pictured as inherently racist. The concern of both MCE and ARE to counter ethnic stereotypes by presenting positive images has also been criticised. As Rattansi points out, 'There is an unacknowledged disingenuity involved in replacing one lot of selective images with another set of partial representations'. Such criticisms from people concerned to promote racial equality exemplify a crisis of confidence in the MCE/ARE movement.

Our brief review of post-war policy responses to the education of minority ethnic pupils clearly does not point to steady progress to equality. Instead it points to a return to at best integrationist assumptions and

---

306   Gilroy, P., (1993) "Small Acts", London: Serpent's Tail.

307   Gillborn, D., (1998) Racism and the Politics of Qualitative Research: Learning from Controversy and Critique in Connolly, P., and Troyna, N., (eds) Researching Racism in Education, Buckingham: Open University Press.

308   Stephen, S., (1996) Children and the Politics of Culture, Princeton: Princeton University Press.

a return to what has been called a 'spuriously deracialized' discourse. Initiatives designed to promote racial equality, such as MCE and ARE, are in retreat with the rise of what Tomlinson[309] has called 'educational nationalism', a discourse which seeks to preserve British culture in the face of threats from 'alien' cultures and claims that ethnic minorities face no obstacles to assimilation. We should not overstate, however, the dominance of educational nationalism. For this discourse is by no means uncontested. MCE is still official policy. There are successful MCE and ARE initiatives. A theoretical defence for a critical multiculturalism, which avoids essentialism, has been mounted in May 1999 and non-essentialist forms of education for racial equality have been devised[310]. What is more, the McPherson report has encouraged the government to acknowledge the seriousness of racism and develop action plans to combat it. This has encouraged it to become less colour blind and develop more targeted measures to promote racial equality. Whether these initiatives are able to counter the egalitarian consequences which seem to flow from the maintenance of a market in education is yet to be seen.

Conclusion

During the post-war period, the gap between poor and rich are very wide, especially among the ethnic minorities. This inequality was as a result of economic lynching of certain minority group, mainly African-Caribbean people. As a result, the sociology of education was preoccupied for much of the post-war period with the question of social inequality. And within this field two theoretical frameworks had loomed large. Liberal theorists had put forward the meritocratic thesis, while radical theorists had advocated a reproductive framework. The former see education as a crucial determinant of life chances in modern societies as the link between education and destination strengthens and the link between origins and education weakens. The latter, by contrast, presented a critical picture of education as a mechanism which maintains a strong link between origins and destinations. The stable link between class origin and education is consistent with a reproductive framework while the decreasing link between ethnic origin and education is consistent with the meritocratic thesis. In the context of ethnic origins and education our research has discovered that, even though there are significant average differences in achievement between pupils of Asian and African-Caribbean origin, there are also differences to be found within these two groups. When we disaggregate the Asian group we find that the underachievement of African-Caribbean pupils is masked by the success of African Asian pupils. When we do a similar exercise with the African-Caribbean group, we discover that it is boys especially who are underachieving. The performance of Indian, African Asian and Chinese pupils is more consistent with the meritocratic thesis while the Performance of African-Caribbean boys are more consistent with a reproductive framework.

When we turn to explanations for such underachievement, we enter a politically highly charged terrain, with advocates of competing explanatory frameworks often at loggerheads with each other. While sceptical of IQ being a major factor, it is argued that a range of social factors are significant: economic deprivation, which itself stems at least in part from Economic lynching, racial discrimination; cultural factors, which need to be carefully contextualised to avoid 'blaming the victim'; ineffective schools, which themselves are often located in disadvantaged areas; and (the often unintentional) racial discrimination in schools.

---

309   Hakim, C., (1998) Issues of Racism at Work, London: Athlone.
310   Tomlinson, S., (2000) Ethnic Minority and Education: New Disadvantages, in Cox, T., (ed.) Combating Educational Disadvantage, London: Falmer.

Turning finally to education policy, our research was unable to locate a clearly formulated coherent philosophy underpinning the state's pronouncements and practices in relation to ethnicity. Even though assimilationist assumptions have tended to be dominant in the post-war period, there have been different policy phases: assimilationism, integrationism and cultural pluralism. For a brief period in the 1980s, cultural pluralism encouraged those concerned with 'education towards racial equality' to believe that progress was being made, but since then pessimism has become more prevalent as assimilations and integrationist assumptions have renewed their manipulation against one another. What seems to be the general consensus was that African-Caribbean people were of low IQ, which is why they are at the bottom of social ladder and there is nothing anyone can do to help them because any effort made would be a wasted one. The philosophy behind this ideology cause the African-Caribbean people to underperforms academically. To keep on recycling educational underachievement among the African-Caribbean people, the debate of low IQ become an excuse to justify economic oppression. Because they know very well that if they lift up economic repression African-Caribbean people will outperform their competitors.

Chapter Five

Family structures of African-Caribbean people in Britain

Introduction

THE WAY AFRICAN-CARIBBEAN families are structured is what some sociologists called Modern Individualism[311]. Therefore, "Modern Individualism" is a contemporary way of living especially among African-Caribbean origin. The reason for the increase in the so called "modern Individualism" could be attributed to "Nigger hunting", hopelessness, unemployment, suppression and discrimination. African-Caribbean people did not choose to live like this, a life of singleness. Left for them to choose, they would choose a life where two partners live together and bring up their children in a loving family relation which give the children confidence to grow into adulthood; and become in a position to transmit that culture to their own children. When repression is endemic among a certain community, it creates a culture of hopelessness and inject low moral to the young ones. The result is that they can hardly do well at school; they would become least or at the bottom of educational attainment. The structure of this modern living is not by choice but by force. They were subjected to it by the state and institutionalise so that they cannot be able to provide their children that necessity of life. Glorifying the misery of these innocent people who have done the British people no wrong is worse than glorifying terrorism.

Modern individualism

Before, we go any further, we must define "individualism", and what exactly does it mean? According to "Powell and Smith" "Individualism is a term used to describe a moral, political, or social outlook that stresses human independence and the importance of individual self-reliance and liberty[312]. Individualists

---

311   Micheal, C., (2000) The sharing of Global Cake, Auckland, NZ: Heinemann.
312   Powell, W., and Smith-Doerr, L., (1994) Networks and Economic Life, in N., Smelser and R.., Swedberg (eds.), The Handbook of Economic Sociology, Princeton University Press and New York: Russell Sage Foundation, pp. 368—402.

promote the unrestricted exercise of individual goals and desires. They oppose any internal interference with an individual's choices whether by society, state, or any other group or institution. Individualism is therefore opposed to collectivism, which stresses community and societal goals over individual goals. Individualism has a controversial relationship with egoism (selfishness) [313]. While many individuals are egoists, they usually do not argue that selfishness is inherently good. Rather, they argue that individuals should not be constrained by any socially imposed morality; they believe that individuals should be free to choose to be selfish (or to choose any other lifestyle) if they so desire".

Etymology

The concept of "individualism" was first used by the French saint-Simonian socialists, to describe what they believed was the cause of the disintegration of French society after the 1789 Revolution. The term however, was already used (pejoratively) by reactionary thinkers of the French Theocratic School, such as Joseph de Maistre, in their opposition to political liberalism. However, The Saint-Simonians did not see political liberalism as the problem though, but saw in "individualism" a form of "egoism" or "anarchy", the ruthless exploitation of man by man in modern industry". While the conservative anti-individualists attacked the political egalitarianism brought about by the Revolution, the Saint-Simonians criticized Laissez-faire (economic liberalism), for its perceived failure to cope with the increasing inequality between the rich and the poor. In English language, the word "individualism" was first introduced, as a fault-finding, by the Owenites in the 1830s, although it is unclear if they were influenced by Saint-Simonianism or came up with it independently.

Alexis de Tocqueville, whose book Democracy in America was translated in English in 1840 (published in French in 1835) used the term as well. He was very critical of the concept, describing it as a sort of "moderate Selfishness" that disposed human beings to be concerned only with themselves and their families, leading to a decline of society. He thought that by calling individualism "moderate selfishness" would not convey the meaning he really wanted, he went further to describe the word "selfishness" as a passionate and exaggerated love of self, which leads a man to connect everything with himself and to prefer himself to everything in the world. He went on and said that individualism is a mature and calm feeling, which disposes each member of the community to sever himself from the mass of his fellows and to draw apart with his families and friends, so that after he has thus formed a little circle of his own, he willingly leaves society at large to itself. He also added that selfishness originates in blind instinct; while individualism proceeds from erroneous judgment more than from depraved feelings; which originates as much in deficiencies of mind as in perversity of heart. He then comes to the conclusion that selfishness blights the germ of all virtue; individualism at first, only saps the virtues of public life; but in the long run it attacks and destroys all others. It is from this Alexis de Tocqueville theory that Modood came up with the idea of African-Caribbean's "Modern individualism". What exactly was he implying, that African-Caribbean community are destroyed because of their selfishness, passionate and exaggerated love of self which leads African-Caribbean's to think of themselves and disposes members of their community. In other words, African-Caribbean's have blind instinct, deprived feelings, deficiencies of mind and as well as perversity of heart. That is why they are likely to be single instead of married, likely to be service users

---

313   Cliff, K., (2002) patriotic politics and economic dispensation, Cambridge mass: Harvard University.

instead of service providers, likely to commit crime instead of being a law abiding citizens, likely to go to prison rather than to have their freedom. That seems to be an incorrect assessment of African-Caribbean people without putting into consideration other factors such as economic lynching, racial discrimination and economic exclusion. However, it does not mean that Modood has not got a point here because he actually has. In this 21st century, African-Caribbean's are more likely to be single rather than married. African-Caribbean children are more likely to come from broken homes than any other group; they are more likely to be unemployed than any other group. That does not mean that underlying cause of the problem is psychological. The main cause of this new lifestyle "individualism" is a social problem due to economic lynching and exclusion.

Having said that we need to find out in detail why African-Caribbean people choose to live a life of single parenthood in Britain. To have more insight about it we have to ask the question, "Why do African-Caribbean people adopt particular family structures? Do African-Caribbean people's decisions about partnering and parenting affect their or their children's chances in other spheres of life such as education or employment? Then we shall discover that what Modood called "modern individualism" of African-Caribbean people arose from a long term repression, economic lynching and discrimination: the adverse effect is low educational attainment. Even when few who are determined to succeed, when they acquired knowledge and skills that make them stand out from the crowd, employment opportunities are denied because of the colour of their skins[314].

Our starting point in uncovering the truth about this problem is Berthoud's research which argued that, the key feature of family life in the African-Caribbean community' is the very low rate of marriage. According to his findings it is true across all age groups; and if we really want to see the entire picture we must then focused more clearly on the late twenties[315] . He shows us the statistics when compared with White that Two-thirds of White men and women in that age group have lived with a partner; little more than one-third of African-Caribbean's have done so. Among those with a partner, three-quarters of Whites, but only half of African-Caribbeans, are in a formal marriage. Among those who have married, the proportion that have separated or divorced is twice as high for African-Caribbeans as it is for Whites (across all age-groups under sixty).

Berthoud works seem plausible but did not say anything as to what could have been the cause rather what he concentrated on is on three factors which he considered as behaviour and as a result of these three factors- low partnership rates, low marriage rates, and high separation rates occurred. He used some data to support his claim by saying that only 39 percent of African-Caribbean adults under the age of sixty are in a formal marriage, compared with 60 percent of White adults under sixty. He later admitted that most African-Caribbean's in the older half of that age ranges are married, or at least have been; that it is among younger people that marriage rates are so low. Again he has failed to point at the cause which implies that he was suggesting that this single parenthood is cultural which seems to be an intellectual high sight. What is interesting though is the admittance that, he was not too sure of the reason but can predict that among the young it could partly be an ageing effect and young people will eventually get married but

314   Alba, R., and Nee, V., (1997) Rethinking Assimilation Theory for a New Era of Immigration, International Migration Review 21: 826—74.

315   Wilson, W., (1987) The Truly Disadvantaged: The Inner City, The Underclass and Public Policy, University of Chicago Press

also partly a cohort effect. He went further to argue that the present generation of African-Caribbean young people are less likely to marry than their predecessors were[316]. He also demonstrated that most of those who migrated to this country as adults are married to (or live with) a man or woman of their own ethnic group. But among British-born African-Caribbean's, half of men with a partner live with a White woman; a third of women with a partner live with a White man. These mixed partnerships are much more common than is found, for example, among African-Americans, and they have attracted some interest, whereas worry about "miscegenation" has always been central

Figure 14

Marital status: Caribbean's compare with white

	Percentage	
	Caribbean	White
Ever had a partner(age 25-29	38	68
Is (or was) married to their partner (age25-29	51	73
Seperated or divorced from their Spouse (16-59	18	9

Source: Fourth National Survey of Ethnic Minorities (EMiB Table 2.5, 2.7, and 2.9

issue for some racists, many liberal commentators see cross-cultural relationships as a welcome sign of increasing mutual acceptance between the White and the Black communities. What he failed to do is give us one name of such commenter who saw this intermarriage as a good thing: because intermarriages and cohabitation of black men and White women has been the bone of contention and the much stronger reason for discrimination and repression against African-Caribbean people. There is no doubt that mixed marriages are widely accepted among African-Caribbean's more than among Whites, and much more than among Asians. Modood disagreed with him by arguing that intermarriages between black people and White people is not seen favourably by the white community and for some black people, though, there remains a suspicion that marrying into a White family is disloyal to one's ethnicity of origin, an opportunist move into white society[317]. What Modood was trying to imply was that black people marrying White was as a result of economic hardship and by so doing they could lift themselves out of poverty. That is why he called it an opportunist move into White society. That seems to be an incorrect assumption to make because marrying into White society is not opportunist push; it is a sign that black people have no colour bar just like other ethnic minorities have. It shows they have nothing against anyone and can interact and integrate into British society that is meant to be liberal.[318] Nevertheless, Modood, seems to contradict himself by saying that the high rate of mixed marriage among Caribbean men is not associated with their social standing, in either direction: mixed relationships are about equally common among those with high and low levels of education, and among those with good and bad employment experiences. That exactly confirm the liberal attitude of black people that by marrying White is not an

---

316   Der, M. C., (1996), "Economic Embeddedness and Social Capital of Immigrants: Iranians in Los Angeles," PhD dissertation, University of California Los Angeles.

317   Kaplan, D., (1998), The Spatial Structure of Urban Ethnic Economies, Urban Geography 19: 489—501

318   Modood, T., Beishon, G., and Virdee, N., (1994, & 1998) Suppression of the vulnerable black people, London: Zed book.

opportunist move; it shows that black are not "close up society" they are open and friendly. It shows that they are ready to integrate into the British society if given the opportunity to do so[319].

However, what is important is not the few points he did not highlight, what is breathtaking is his findings about African-Caribbean family formation and the methodology he used to discover that the number of mixed partnerships among African-Caribbeans, combined with the low rate of partnership and marriage means that very few African-Caribbean men and women are married to each other: which in a sense has obvious implications.

The reason being that a small proportion of African-Caribbean men and women are living with each other in nuclear families. He got to the truth, by removing the flesh from the bone so that he will achieve an impeccable result. He did so very well by focusing on women so as to have more detailed analysis of African-Caribbean family structures that will not be misleading. As we have seem in many occasions that most surveys do not ask respondents to record all the children of which they are the father or mother, but only the children living with them at the time that is what he did . What he found was that a large proportion of Caribbean children do not live with their father. All he can do is describe the families of the women and make inferences from that about the probable position of the men.

His result was that One-third of Caribbean women in their early twenties have children; about half of those in their late twenties; three-quarters of those in their early thirties. He used this to prove his point that the African-Caribbean women are slightly earlier into the child-rearing phase than White women, but he admitted that the two ethnic groups are broadly similar in their fertility rates. He went further to say that it is on the question of partnership that the two groups diverge most widely. He used statistics to prove his point by arguing that one in ten White women with children (and under the age of thirty-five) are single (never-married) mothers. In the case of blacks, no less than half of African-Caribbean mothers are single parents on this definition[320].

---

319   Ford, R., and Millar, J., (eds.), Private Lives and Public Responses: Lone Parenthood and Future Policy in the UK, London: Policy Studies Institute, pp. 22—41.

320   Kim I., (1981) The New Urban Immigrants, Princeton University Press.

Figure 15 table

Estimated proportion of mothers who remained single, by age and date, holding other characteristics constant

	Logistic regression estimates, expressed as cell Percentage	
	Caribbean	White
Age of mother at birth of first child		
20	66	11
25	48	7
30	31	5
Age of oldest child		
0	53	9
5	48	7
10	42	6
15	37	4
Date of mother's 20th birthday		
1975	27	1
1980	37	3
1985	48	7
1990	50	15

Source: Labour Force Survey (YCM, Tables 14 and 23). The shaded band indicates some characteristics of the standard case against which variations are tested: the woman was born or schooled in Britain; she has O levels, GCSE, or equivalent qualifications (i.e. basic secondary qualifications obtained usually at age 16); she reached the age of twenty in 1985; she was aged twenty-five at the birth of the first child; that child is now five.

However, he admitted that the patterns of single parenthood within each ethnic group are not easy to analyze, because all of the potential influences are inter-related. On that basis a multivariate logistic regression equation has to be used to estimate the probability of a mother remaining single, depending on the age at which she first had children, the age of her oldest child, the year she passed her twentieth birthday, whether she was a migrant or a non-migrant, and what her educational qualifications were[321]. The analysis can be used to show what happens if each of these characteristics is varied one at a time, holding the other four constant (Table 8.2). For both Whites and African-Caribbean's, women who had been young when their first child was born were much more likely to be single mothers at the time of their interview, in both groups, mothers who had started a family at twenty were about twice as likely to be in that state as those who had waited another ten years. But Caribbean women retained six times as high a risk as White women, whatever their age at first birth. The age of the oldest child can be seen as the number of years since the woman became a mother. Both groups of women were less likely to be single, the longer the period of their motherhood. This can be interpreted in terms of about half of White single mothers, and about one-third of African-Caribbean mothers, marrying (or forming a live-in partnership) later. Modood is not alone because Haskey finding seems to be in line with his. Haskey theorized that single motherhood is not necessarily a temporary stage prior to marriage because many African-Caribbean women have children single and stay single.

His estimates in the first two panels of the table are all based on a notional cohort of women whose twentieth birthday occurred in 1985. It is well known that there has been a substantial increase in the number of single parents over the years and he warn that we would expect such a change in social expectations to be reflected in a cohort effect. The third panel confirms assertion: women who reached the potential childbearing phase of their lives in the most recent period were much more likely to be a single parent than their predecessors. In absolute terms this trend seemed strongest for the African-Caribbean women: the increase from 27 percent to 59 percent over fifteen years represents one-third of all African-Caribbean women with children. But in relative terms, the increase was even stronger for Whites: the number of White single mothers multiplied more than ten-fold over a decade and half[322].

Even though Haskey just like modood did not go far enough to point out what could have the reason for this disease of singlehood, Dench, Song and Edward think the they have broken the code despite the fact that much has been written about single mothers of African-Caribbean origin. They claim that the practice of living independently of the children's father can be traced to West Indian social and economic traditions themselves, perhaps, a hangover from the days of slavery when husbands and wives might be sold to separate plantations.[323] What is striking about these findings, though, is that behaviour said to be derived from Caribbean cultural values is becoming more, not less, common over the years in Britain. Dench, Song and Edward were also criticized because of the "behaviour" they call culture which seems to mask the real issue which Haskey pointed out briefly without much detail; which has got some connection to repression of the slavery era. However they can take some comfort because their conclusion is supported by another result from the logistic regression equation: after controlling for the age and cohort effects shown in Table 8.2, the proportion of African-Caribbean mothers who were single was 48

321   Lieberson, S., (1980) A Piece of the Pie, Berkeley, CA: University of California Press.

322   Grieco, M., (1987) Keeping it in the Family: Social Networks and Employment Chance, London and New York: Tavistock.

323   Dench, L., Song, G., and Edward, A., (1996), Defining Ethnic Groups: Origin or Identity? Patterns of Prejudice, 32, 2: 56—63.

percent among those who had been born in Britain or had arrived as children; it fell to only 2.4 percent among women who had come to Britain at the age of sixteen or later. Thus it is the second generation which has adopted the "West Indian" tradition, rather than the migrants themselves. If their research has shown that migrants from African-Caribbean are likely to stay in a relationship implies that the second generation could equally do the same if the repression directed to their parents are minimized. What their research implies is that the second generation have not got the family role model they will look up to in order to fashion their own relationship in the future. On that ground they think that what they are seeing is ideal and go down the same road, on that ground single motherhood become cool to them. Clearly from what we can deduct from this is that this new wave of modern living, singleness, is not born out of culture but economic hardship and low educational attainment[324].

What is outstanding about this research is that they agreed that among white women with low educational qualification are more likely to be single and tend to have children younger than their better-educated counterparts. Rowlingson and Mckey agreed by stating that white women who have children at an early age are often single mothers.[325] So Table 8.3 distinguishes the two components of single motherhood — whether women had children, and whether those with children were single. Less than a third of women with degrees had children (at the "standard" age of thirty); four-fifths of women with no qualifications

Figure 16

Estimated proportion of mothers who remained single, by qualifications, holding other characteristics constant

	Degree of equivalent	A level or equivalent	OLevel or equivalent	Lower qualification	None
	Logistic regression estimates, expressed as cell percentage				
Caribbean					
% Women who had children	29	57	72	78	79
% mothers who were single	37	47	48	54	59
% women who were single mothers	11	27	34	42	46
White					
% women who had children	30	57	69	78	83
% mothers who were single	5	5	7	10	15
% women who were single mothers	2	3	5	8	13

Source: Labour Force Survey (YCM Table 15)

324   Portes, A., and Zhou, M., (1992) Gaining the Upper Hand: Old and New Perspectives in the Study of Ethnic Minorities, Ethnic and Racial Studies 15:
491—522.

325   Rowlingson, J., and Mckey, H., (1999) Young Caribbean Men and the Labour Market: A Comparison with Other Ethnic Groups, York: Joseph Rowntree Foundation.

were mothers. The strong and consistent effect of qualifications on the proportion of women who had children was almost identical for both Whites and African-Caribbeans. In both groups there was a parallel tendency for less-qualified women with children to have remained single. The relative effect was stronger among White women (a ratio of 3 to 1 between unqualified women and graduates); but education was still an important source of variation in the much higher rate of single parenthood among African-Caribbeans. Putting the two sets of findings together, the Modood, analysis suggests that nearly half of all unqualified (thirty-year-old) African-Caribbean women were single mothers, compared with just 2 percent of white women with degrees[326].

If we then impose the question, "what does the high rate of single parenthood among African-Caribbean women imply for the family positions of Caribbean men? We shall come to the conclusion that the frequency of mixed partnerships means that we cannot automatically assume that the non-resident fathers of African-Caribbean single mothers are necessarily of Caribbean origin too. Nevertheless, the fact that a very large proportion of young Caribbean women with relatively low educational qualifications are single parents suggests that young Caribbean men with relatively low qualifications are unlikely to be living in the standard partner-plus-children family relationship[327]. Qualitative evidence has suggested that some Caribbean couples have retained the "visiting partner" relationships that are common in the West Indies, and that this often involves the man in financial and other paternal responsibilities. Quantitative evidence, though, suggests this "active" non-resident

Figure 17

Frequency of contact between non-resident fathers and their children (as reported by lone mothers)

	White mothers	Black mothers
Formerly married or cohabiting		
Father sees children once a week or more	38	25
Less often	30	34
Never or Father's whereabouts unknown	32	41
Mother has never cohabited		
Father sees children once a week or more	19	8
Less often	17	23
Never, or father's whereabouts unknown	64	69

Source: Families and children survey, 1999, new analysis.

fathers are very uncommon. According to Modood, only 8 percent of black single mothers taking part in the Families and Children Survey reported that their children's father saw them at least once a week (Table 8.4). Two-thirds said that he never saw them, or that she did not know where he was. On this evidence, black single mothers really do raise their children on their own. His critics argued that by the

326   Daniel, W., (1968) Racial Discrimination in England, Harmondsworth: Penguin.
327   Bailey, T., and Waldinger, W., (1991) Primary, Secondary and Enclave Labour Markets: A Training Systems Approach, American Sociological Review 56:432—45.

time he conducted his research, probably, he forgot to carry out some work on why the prison population is mostly African-Caribbeans. In the sense that it would have given us a good indication on why most African-Caribbean women are single: most often do not know where the men are[328].

Because of this insurmountable repression against these innocent people, nearly two-thirds (63 percent) of young adult African-Caribbean men (aged 22 to 35) are "unattached" — that is, they have neither a live-in partner nor live-in children. The equivalent figure for White men is less than half (47 percent). As before, it is difficult to sort out the influences of a range of potentially overlapping influences on men's family status, and a logistic regression equation has been used to measure the effect of each, independently of all the others. The first panel of Table 8.5 shows the expected tendency for the proportion remaining unattached to fall as young men grew older, and illustrates the clear divergence between white men and African-Caribbean men by age.

The comparison between the cohorts of young men who entered adulthood at various periods over the past two decades is more important. For both white and African-Caribbean men, the proportion estimated to remain unattached at the age of thirty doubled in fifteen years. There appears to have been what amounts to a transformation in young men's family relationships. Most young men in the 1975 cohort lived with partners and children by the age of thirty. By the 1990 cohort, most White and black young men remained single. African-Caribbean's were running ahead of Whites throughout the period, but the trend was equally strong for both groups.

Among African-Caribbean men who had been born in Britain (or migrated as children) were more likely to remain unattached (60 percent) than those who had arrived age sixteen or more (43 percent).

Figure 18

8.5 Estimated Proportion of men who remained unattached, by age and cohort, holding other characteristics constant

	Logistic regression estimates, expressed as cell percentag	
	Caribbean	**White**
Age		
20	88	81
25	77	65
30	60	45
Date of 20th birthday		
1975	37	27
1980	48	35
1985	60	45
1990	70	55

Source: Labour Force Survey (YCM, Table 18 and 24).

328   Loury, G. C., 1998, Discrimination in the Post-Civil Rights Era: Beyond Market Interactions, Journal of Economic Perspectives 12: 117—26.

Wilson disagrees with the notion that unattached black men and women is cultural, that the problem has nothing to do with cultural way of life. Besides, single motherhood or fatherhood is not culture in itself therefore culture should not have been the reason behind it[329]. He came up with the supposition that the high proportion of young black men who remain unattached may be related to their poor employment prospects. This hypothesis, which has been very influential in the United States, suggests that black women are reluctant to marry (or live with) a man whose chances of getting or keeping a good job make him an unreliable source of income for themselves and their children[330]. Better to remain single (and claim social assistance if necessary). Young men's family position has therefore been analyzed by some of the factors which might make a difference to their employability. Comparison across educational qualifications is complicated by the fact that better qualified people tend to form partnerships later in their twenties, simply because they spend longer in the education system. So Table 8.6 shows how long it took men to get married or cohabit, in terms of the duration of the period since they completed their studies. For both White men and African-Caribbean men, those with lower than average levels of qualification took longer than others to form partnerships. The relationship was strongest for African-Caribbeans in the extreme, African-Caribbean man with no qualifications would expect to live without a partner for twenty years after leaving school.

Wilson also purported that African-Caribbean men living in regions with high levels of unemployment also have lower than average partnering rates (LFS, new analysis). The relationship is much weaker for White men. This provides further evidence of a link between African-Caribbean men's job prospects and their marriage prospects.

Figure 19

Estimated number of years following education before half of men had a partner, by educational qualifications

	Logistic regression estimates	
	Caribbean	**White**
Degree	12.8	8.2
Alevel	15.0	9.8
Olevel	16.4	11.2
Others	16.5	10.7
None	20.2	12.0

Source: Labour Force Survey(new analysis).

---

329   Peach, C., (1996) Does Britain have Ghettoes?", Transactions of the British Institute of Geographers 21, 1: 216—35.

330   Wilson 2000a, "Ethnic Employment Penalties in Britain," Journal of Ethnic and Migration Studies, 26, 3: 389—4 16.

Figure 20

Composition of families with children, where at least one parent was Caribbean

	Global percentage		
	Caribbean father	**White father**	Father not present
Caribbean mother	24	10	48
White mother	15		
Mother not present	3		

Note: Stepfathers and stepmothers are not included as though they were natural fathers and mothers. A small number of mixed African-Caribbean couples have been included as both Caribbean.

Source: Labour force Survey, 1992-95, new analysis.

The two most striking aspects of African-Caribbean family formation are the large number of men and women who live without a partner; and the high proportion of those, with a partner, whose partner is White. Both findings are summarized in Table 8.7, for families with children. Only a quarter of "African-Caribbean" children live with two black parents[331].

Modood seems to be shifting his stands from calling the single parenthood a modern way of living for African-Caribbean people to the champion of the mixed race between Black and White as a good thing because most commentators seem to welcome the increase in the number of mixed relationships, as an indicator of reducing cultural, social, and economic barriers between ethnic groups. The reason he gave was perhaps it could be a sign of declining racism within the White community. In his research he plausibly argued that some black people are not comfortable with the whole idea of mixed race[332]. However that seems to be his own personal opinion because his findings did not support that assertion. Having said that, he went on to say that for the fact that some black people were anxious about the trend, on the other hand, needs to be recognized and not swept under the carpet. Wilson's work seems to be in agreement with Modood here but differ in the sense that in his work there is little evidence that men and women in mixed marriages are any better off or worse off than those who have chosen partners within their own ethnic group. There are nevertheless some consequences of mixed relationships which need to be taken into account in the analysis of multicultural Britain.

The first, and obvious one, is that a significant proportion of the children of African-Caribbeans will be of mixed origin. The sample of babies born in 2000 selected for the Millennium Cohort Survey is the only

331   Berthoud, R., (1998a) The Incomes of Ethnic Minorities, Institute for Social and Economic Research, Report 98—1, Colchester: University of Essex.

332   Portes, A., and Bach, R., (1985) Latin Journey, Berkeley, CA: University of California Press.

source which records the ethnic group of both fathers and mothers, including those of children born to single mothers. Of the 625 babies with any black parentage:

53 percent had two black parents;
4 percent had one black parent and one of mixed origin;
29 percent had black and White parents
14 percent had one parent of mixed origin, and one White.

So mixed parentage means an increase in the number of members of the next generation who are in some way African-Caribbean, and a reduction in the number who are unambiguously African-Caribbean.

According to Modood, none of the quantitative surveys available in the past provided accurate information about people of mixed origin, though the 2001 Census offers a much more effective classification. In the meantime, it is rather assumed that people of mixed origin perceive themselves, and are perceived by others, to be black. It seems likely that they have a more complex identity than that, reluctant to throw over one half of their heritage[333].

From the point of view of African-Caribbean's as a community, though, the trend may lead either to the decline, or the increasing isolation, of blackness as an independent identity[334]. Here it seems that Modood and Wilson's theory have come to emerge together without a clear definition of their differences. However their critics disagree on the notion that mixed race would lead to increase in isolation among black people or loss of blackness as an independent identity. Because mixed race is a signal that black can integrate with the White society and it is a way of saying that racism is not their portion. But that is not how the so called early commentators think integration should be or the form it should take. Whereas early commentators were eager for minorities to be assimilated into the majority culture, the essence of multiculturalism is that Britain should learn to value the diversity of communities making their various contributions to national life and not by African-Caribbean's marrying White women which has caused trouble in the past and was responsible for the race tension in Britain today. He went further to argue that if African-Caribbean people continue in this current form race relation might become difficult and that could impoverish our country, Britain.

The other main feature of African-Caribbean family formation is the number of single mothers, on the one hand, and of unattached men, on the other. It was emphasized at the beginning of this chapter that the proportion of young people in "intermediate" family forms is much higher in "northern/Protestant" European countries than in "Southern/ Catholic", and has risen rapidly in Britain over the last quarter of a century. African-Caribbean's could therefore be considered to be very "Northern/Protestant"; or very modern. In this light, they are ahead of the trend (while South Asians are behind the trend). But the scarcity of co-resident partnerships during the child-rearing years is so far ahead of the national trend as to represent a real difference of social convention, rather than the kind of variation between groups which might be expected in any society. While the different convention is often explained in terms of the matriarchal family structures common in the West Indies, it is important to take account of the fact that

333   Coleman, D., and Salt, J., (1996) (eds.) Demographic Characteristics of Ethnic Minority Populations, London: HMSO.

334   Smith D., (1977) Racial Disadvantage in Britain, Harmondsworth: Pdiguin

African-Caribbean's are not converging on the European norm the evidence clearly points to an increase in the number of unpatented parents from generation to generation and from year to year.

Qualitative evidence suggests that African-Caribbean's' own views of these trends may be ambivalent. Beishon, and Virdee found three potentially conflicting points of view.

Some African-Caribbean's emphasised individualism the importance of individual choice, the value of commitments generated by the quality of relationships rather than custom, duty or marriage certificate, and independence. Marriage has come to be regarded as just a lifestyle option, which one may or may not wish to choose, depending on individual circumstances." Thus there is a theoretical and principled preference for the less committing family forms that can be labelled modern individualism.

On the other hand, African-Caribbeans said that "their own communities were more family-orientated than the White British, and instilled more discipline and respect for age than their White contemporaries. Indeed, there was unity among the minorities in their criticism of what they perceived as a lack of commitment to parenting amongst Whites. The critics called it a cultural standpoint, that is they way African-Caribbean see parenting among the Whites. They further to argue that even though White children are seen as lacking discipline, they turned out to be smarter than their peers. Despite this criticism, African-Caribbeans did not stop talking of White children as not having respect for their elders, and as being out of control." This apparently might be older-fashioned view which is not necessarily inconsistent with a preference for lone-parenthood, since it might be argued that a mother (and a grandmother) could exert a firmer discipline on children than a mother and father together. "Fathers were in practice dispensable; there was no particular role or responsibility that fathers performed which could not be performed in their absence by mothers."

Nevertheless "it was noticeable that the ideal of marriage and joint parenting between resident fathers and mothers still exerted a considerable appeal among the African-Caribbean's. For the majority, marriage is an ideal which unfortunately only some achieve mainly because, in the view of women, men lack commitment." On this latter view, single motherhood may be accepted by African-Caribbean women, but it is the men who should bear the responsibility for their position.

There is a large literature on the question of whether children brought up by one parent experience worse outcomes than those with two[335]. Kiernan, Land, and Lewis argue that having only one resident parent may be a disadvantage, but the primary mechanism may be the poverty experienced by most such families, rather than the lack of a father as such

---

335   Kiernan, L., (1998) Family resources Survey, London: Equal Opportunity Commisson.

Figure 21

Proportion of families with children who depend on Income Support				
			Cell Percentage	
		Couples with children	One-parent families	All families with children
White		9	63	22
Caribbeans		13	53	36
Source: Family Resources Survey 1994/5 and 1995/6, new analysis				

Whatever the overall conclusion, little of the research can be applied directly to African-Caribbean families, where single parenthood is now a conventional rather than a deviant family form.

There is little doubt, though, about the financial position of African-Caribbean one-parent families. It is often remarked that African-Caribbean lone parents are more likely to support themselves through work than their White equivalents. The Fourth National Survey reported that only 27 percent of White lone parents living in an independent household had any employment; the figure for African-Caribbean's was 42 percent[336]. The Family Resources Survey, analyzing lone parents regardless of their household position, recorded 37 percent of White lone parents and 43 percent of African-Caribbean lone parents to have any earnings. African-Caribbean's may be ahead of Whites on this measure, but still, more than half of African-Caribbean lone parents have no job. There is no evidence to suggest that many of them receive the substantial and regular maintenance payments which would be needed to float them and their children above the poverty line. As Table 8.8 shows, the majority of one-parent families whether white or African-Caribbean have to claim Income Support. What seems difficult to follow is the notion that it's difficult to avoid the conclusion that it is the number of lone parents in the African-Caribbean community, rather than high levels of unemployment, which confines more than a third of all families with children to the safety net: which seems to be a contradiction to the idea that almost, half of the African-Caribbean women are jobless. Even though Work and Pension Department (WPD) concurs that this may be regarded as unfair deduction. However, it does conclude that African-Caribbean people are liability on the social security system (which was never designed to shoulder the primary long-term responsibility for large numbers of families). And it is unfair on the mothers and children, who are obliged to accept the poverty and the sense of dependence with which Income Support is inevitably associated[337].

This analysis does conjure up a picture of prosperous African-Caribbean men as selfishly keeping their earnings to themselves. It is true that an exceptionally high proportion of young men of African-Caribbean

336   Modood, T., Berthoud, J., Lakey, J., Nazroo, P., Smith, S., Beishon, S., (1997) Ethnic Minorities in Britain: Diversity and Disadvantage, London: Policy Studies Institute.

337   Barrington, A., (1994) Marriage and Family Formation Among the White and Ethnic Minority Populations in Britain, Ethnic and Racial Studies 17, 13:
517—47.

114

origin are unattached. It is very ironic for anyone to suggest that African-Caribbean people (men) are selfishly keeping their earnings to themselves which implies they have deficiencies of mind and perversity of heart. On the other hand, the analysis in Table 8.6 suggested that many of these bachelors have limited educational qualifications and poor prospects in the labour market. If that is the case, were did they get the money which they are keeping selfishly for themselves? Moreover, marital status itself has an independent effect on men's employment rates: for both Whites and African-Caribbeans, a young man living on his own is about twice as likely to be unemployed as a young man who lives with a partner, holding other characteristics constant (YCM, p.10). So the low rate of partnership in the Caribbean community may create poverty among men as well as among women and children.

Here, I think we have to look at the role of race and ethnicity in the production of social mobility, through a focus on families and neighbourhoods. The present section focuses more closely on how these forces translate into social mobility outcomes, with additional attention to the critical area of education and ancestry (which we will call "pre-market forces"), and a new emphasis on the way that race and ethnicity are woven into the labour market. The fundamental points of this research taken as a whole are: (a) important social forces not usually considered in any detail by economists are at work in both arenas; (b) race and ethnicity channel and magnify these forces; and (c) the comparative study of the two countries places these forces in sharper relief.

From the perspective taken here, social mobility is the joint product of the human capital of individuals, combined with the social capital embedded in ethno-racially specific networks. This human and social capital is refracted through the social organization of work, within labour market and political systems that are structured in part by the social meaning of race. Only when all of these considerations are taken together can we have a truly rounded understanding of how groups are stratified and how individuals attain economic and social status.

The standard way of thinking about the influence of racial or ethnic categories in the labour market is the model originally introduced by Gary Becker. In this model, individuals have specific human capital attributes, and employers under conditions of a competitive, full-employment economy will hire on the basis of these attributes. The exception to this occurs when employers have a "taste" or "preference" for discrimination — that is, an essentially irrational aversion to members of certain groups. The existence of such discriminatory preferences, together with the assumption that labour markets are perfectly competitive allows Becker to deduce the implications of a racial discrimination for racial disparities in employment and wages[338].

For Becker, this preference for discrimination is likely to be under severe pressure from the force of a competitive market economy, since satisfying it will cause the employer, ceteris paribus, to hire individuals of a lower quality or a higher wage than they would otherwise. This will' tend to raise the employers' costs and prices and as a result to lower his profit margin. Over the long term, so this standard economic argument goes, we would expect discriminatory behaviour to be largely eliminated[339].

---

338   Smith P., and Prior, G., (1997) the Fourth National Survey of Ethnic Minorities: Technical Report, London: National Centre for Social Research.

339   Borjas, G., (1994) Long-run Convergence of Ethnic Skill Differentials: The Children and Grandchildren of the Great Migration," Industrial and Labor Relations Review 47: 553—73.

Becker's argument has been very fruitful and important in the history of economic research on this topic. But, it is certainly not beyond criticism because of his notion of "preference" His work sees discrimination not as an aberration at the edges of the market, but it is something closer to a fundamental fact about how labour markets is designed and function against the African-Caribbean people. In Becker's model, employers have complete information as to the inherent quality of applicants and zero transaction costs in searching for them, and make decisions on the basis of their preferences, not that of their existing labour force. In the real world, employers have incomplete information, frequently substantial search costs and often have to adapt themselves to the preferences of the individuals currently working for them. Furthermore, in Becker's model discrimination occurs primarily because employers have aversions to certain groups but in the real world (as Waldinger's paper reminds us) discriminatory behaviour is due as much to employers' preference for certain groups as it is due to any distaste they may harbour against others especially African-Caribbean people.

If the preceding description of the real world of the labour market is realistic, how do race and ethnicity fit in? On the one hand, given that employers have imperfect information, they will often be inclined to use racial and ethnic markers as proxies for individual qualities. That is, employers will often hire from particular groups because they believe that the average quality of those groups is higher, and avoid others that they believe are generally untrustworthy such as African-Caribbean people. This is especially likely to be the case where there are few formal qualifications that can attest for individual characteristics (as in the low-wage labour market).

Furthermore, consider what happens when we recognize the importance of search costs for employers. Where search costs are high employers will seek methods that reduce these costs while providing them with generally reliable employees. (This is particularly the case if employee turnover rates are also high, so that employers cannot amortize search costs over a long-term employment relationship.) One way to do this is for employers to rely on "network hiring" to avoid employing African-Caribbean people by using their existing labour pool as a source for the referral of prospective new employees. 'Where incumbent employees are embedded in strong ethnic or racial networks such as the Asians, they will tend to refer individuals from those networks while excluding African-Caribbean people regarded as outsiders. 'What is more, search costs aside employers may prefer an ethnically or racially homogenous workforce if they believe such homogeneity will be valued by their employees (thereby reducing the monetary wage they have to pay) or where such homogeneity reduces transaction costs on the shop floor[340]. Over time employees such as Asian and White will treat, and have been treating these arrangements as a form of "entitlement," hoarding opportunity for "their own kind" while excluding others.

Thus, the ethnic or racial "niche" in the labour market effectively shields the group from full competition while giving those individuals already placed within the niche powerful leverage over fellow group members (since the insider has an asset of value to co ethnics not yet in the niche). It follows that groups with strong niches will also have profound incentives for continuing group identity on the part of individuals, since it is that identity which qualifies individuals for employment in the niche. While this process is not designed with exclusion of outsiders as its objective, it can nonetheless be a very efficient exclusionary mechanism adopted by employers and other institutions in Britain[341].

---

340   Anwar, M., (1994) Young Muslims in Britain: Attitudes, Educational Needs and Policy Implications, Leicester: The Islamic Foundation

341   Light, I., (1972) Ethnic Enterprise in America, Berkeley, CA: University of California Press.

Furthermore, in the standard economic model employers they have no strong ethnic or racial identification, and the distinction between the sources of business finance, on the one hand, and of labour on the other, is sharp. But especially with immigrant communities as Heath and Robinson emphasize self-employment is a very common pattern. Faced with a labour market where their qualifications (which may be difficult to evaluate as they are often obtained in African-Caribbean Countries, even those obtained in this country) are undervalued, or where their grasp of the language is imperfect, or where they anticipate discrimination, these immigrants will often choose to work for themselves rather than sell their labour in the market (that notion raises the question about the Asian Immigrants who, some cannot speak English on why they have more opportunities than the African-Caribbean people?) What is more, self-employment may allow labour practices that would be difficult (or illegal) in the formal labour market. An owner of a business may employ his family with little or no compensation, and make him work very long hours that would be prohibitively expensive if he employed others to do the same job. While the hourly wage from such an arrangement may be low, the total compensation from such intensity of labour both economically and in terms of status amongst peers may be high, and this appears to be a common pattern in self-employment, what might be called "self-exploitation?"

In addition, the "ethnic entrepreneur" will tend to hire co ethnics and shun those from outside his group; for a number of reasons and one of those reasons are African-Caribbean people are not wanted. Secondly, since majority are not Muslims it is difficult for them to be employed by these ethnic entrepreneurs who are mainly profess the faith. On the one hand, employing co ethnics may give the Asia entrepreneurs additional social stand in his community and conversely there may be strong social stigma to hiring African-Caribbean people who are considered to be outsiders. Thirdly, the information that flows through ethnic networks may allow ethnic entrepreneurs greater confidence in their hires and the extent to which the employee is embedded within that network may cause shame if his work is of low quality. Finally, especially in immigrant communities, co ethnics may be willing to trade off lower wages for employment in an environment where they can speak their native language, and the shielded nature of the immigrant community may make it difficult for the immigrant employee to recognize the labour standards that prevail outside that community[342].

But the informal economy that characterizes the previous discussion is not the entire economy perhaps not even the predominant part of the economy. One important fact of the modern economy and of modern society more generally, is the increasing reliance on formal qualifications as a substitute for informal knowledge of this shift, is the reliance on educational qualifications as a signalling device for individual qualities? Where groups are immigrants, the first generation may in large numbers be absorbed into the informal economy, whose characteristics track closely with those described above. But there are strong incentives for subsequent generations to move out of that ethnically and racially encoded economic system into the formal system driven by educational qualifications, where networks and niches are less important but not in the case of African-Caribbean people.

Thus differences in educational attainments across ethnic and racial groups must be an important part of our analysis. Attainment of educational qualifications may also be a reflection of the impression of discrimination. Model, finds in this analysis bore the evidence that discrimination in employment is

---

342   Virdee, S., (1998) Ethnic Minority Families, London:Polity Studies Institute.

somewhat higher in Britain, while Modood finds that higher levels of ethnic minority young people value the attainment of educational qualifications than Whites. These two factors may be linked; the expectation of discrimination may lead minorities to compensate by getting higher qualifications than they would otherwise. The downside of this, as Heath suggests, could be a somewhat higher unemployment rate, as some percentage of ethnic minorities become "overqualified," or in another interpretation, increase their reserve wage.' This pattern was also found in the United States by Waldinger, who observed that American blacks sought relatively higher educational attainment to compensate for their exclusion from niche economies[343]. In any event, what is clear is that the educational attainment of ethnic minorities is partially a function of group norms and family structure, as suggested by research in the preceding section, but may also be a reflection of rational adjustments to the structure of the labour market and patterns of perceived or real exclusion therein.

A final factor in social mobility that research in this section address is the importance of timing. All groups do not enter the economy at the same time, and when they enter may be as important as the internal characteristics of the group or the generic structure of the economy. On the one hand, as Robinson emphasizes, where groups enter the economy is partially a function of the structure of opportunity upon their arrival. Pakistanis went into industrial occupations less because of any specific capacity or taste for such jobs, and more because the movement of Whites out of the low end of industry opened up a niche for them there. Afro-Caribbean were found in government employment in hospitals and transport because of persistent labour shortages that caused the government to actively recruit them for such jobs. Waldinger makes a similar point, observing that where groups place themselves in the labour queue is largely a function of where space is being evacuated it is there that niches form that subsequent waves of co ethnics filter[344]. Groups may acquire a cultural affinity for such labour after the fact, or employers may associate them as a "good fit" for such jobs, but the reasons for their placement in particular parts of the economy cannot simply be understood in terms of the group's specific cultural attributes. It is important, therefore, to distinguish where ethnic niches form because of deep cultural group characteristics, and where they form because of the accidents of timing.

Conclusion

It is important for us to recognize, however, that the flip side of opportunity is almost always exclusion. Where White and Asians communities hoard opportunity and distribute it to their co ethnics, individuals from excluded groups are denied those opportunities. It is an interesting irony that many writers from these dominant groups suggest, that a free-market economy that is supposedly driven by the rational, calculating behaviour of free and equal individuals creates such powerful incentives for group attachment and identity. And there are reasons to believe that groups whose structure is not as collectively oriented and institutionalized such as African-Caribbean people and African-Americans in the United States may be relatively disadvantaged by an economy that organizes at least some parts of the labour market on

343   Waldinger, R., (1996) Still the Promised City: African-Americans and New Immigrants, New York: Harvard University Press.

344   Fainstein N., and Fainstein, C., (1994), Urban Regimes and Black Citizens: The Economic and Social Impacts of Black Political Incorporation in US Cities, International Journal of Urban and Regional Research 20, 1: 22—37.

ethnic and racial lines. Under critical examination we have come to the conclusion that reorganization of the labour market in the 80s and years that followed, was just to exclude the African-Caribbean people, its effect in the community is hopelessness and underachieving. They become heavily dependent economically instead of being independent. They can hardly own any business and cannot build one because job opportunities that would enable them to become wealth creators are denied them. Because of that African-Caribbean families find it very hard to provide their children the necessities of life, and underachievement become rampant among the youth. If this economic embargo impose on them are lifted, if there is an equal plan field, the African-Caribbean children will be doing better in schools than their opponents.

Chapter Six

The work Moral Code and the new poor

Introduction

THE WELFARE TO work programme is not doing anything to reduce the mass unemployment among the African-Caribbean community rather it has helped in creating the new poor and mass unemployment among African-Caribbean people. When redundancy is coming African-Caribbean people are the first to go. In the welfare state, they become a liability to decent people and regarded as unreachable by the so called decent people. The Philosophy, that the blacks lack the skill to appreciate the advantages of working life is a social construct to demonise the black people. Except, of course, it is the welfare to work, the sole alternative that economic rules tolerate; while demeaning dependency of the African-Caribbean people as sin, the work ethic in its current version brings most relief to the moral conscience of the well-off. If the condition of 'unemployment', even long term unemployment, suggested a transient stage in a working life, 'redundancy' is more honest about the nature of contemporary job losses among African-Caribbean people. The term 'unemployment', until recently used commonly to denote people with no paid work, expressed the unspoken assumption of the 'normality' of employment. The present day streamlined, downsized, capital and knowledge intensive industry casts African-Caribbean people as a constraint on the rise of productivity. The welfare to work ethic goes underclass African-Caribbean people become Unreachable which means also beyond the reach of the welfare to work. Then the assumption is that African-Caribbean people purely and simply lack the competence to value the reward of working life because they make wrong choices, putting 'no work' above work. Whatever the excuses of the British people are: if poverty continues to exist and grow amidst growing affluence, the welfare to work must have been ineffective. These days, African-Caribbean people are no longer the rejects of consumer society, defeated in the all out competitive wars; they are the outright enemies of some people in the British Society. African-Caribbean People on welfare are the natural catchments area for criminal gangs, and keeping people on welfare means enlarging the pool from which the criminals are recruited. Linking poverty with criminality has another effect: it helps to banish the African-Caribbean people from the universe of moral obligations. However successfully consciences may be silenced by persistent bombardment with the news of moral depravity and criminal inclinations of the non-working African-

Caribbean people, the permanent residues of moral impulse must be given, time and again, an outlet. The welfare to work emerges from this exercise safe and sound, ready to be used again as a whip to chase the African-Caribbean people nearer home away from the shelter they seek (in vain) back into the welfare state. While, money spent on these kinds of people is money wasted. Unless, of course, it is the welfare to work, the sole variant that economic rules tolerate. For the entrepreneurism our society and the affluent sections of well off societies, the welfare to work ethic is a one-sided affair. Presently, it is instrumental in bringing the idea of 'dependency' into disrepute: while demeaning dependency of the African-Caribbean people as sin, the work ethic in its present version brings most relief and comfort to the moral conscience of those born with a silver spoon in their mouth.

Historical prespective.

Historically, the welfare state began in 1945. The 1940-50 periods does mark a particular point in the history of welfare state in Britain. But to begin the story here distorts the record. But 1945 period promotes the idea of welfare developments in this country as part of a collective train journey which began with Lloyed George and ended with Mr Attlee, Labour's 1945 Prime minister, who safely steering the train into a collective welfare state terminal. Before then welfare state exist on a temporary basis. In the 19th century for example, the Britain's welfare state was characterized by voluntary provision with mutual and friendly societies delivering a whole range of benefits. Local authorities and other voluntary organizations run the hospitals together with the national system of panel doctors which were financed from health insurance contributions; they were set by the state and collected through mutually owned societies. Even before then, in the 18th century, the welfare state was run independently of the state. In the mediaeval times many hospitals were run by the churches. Back then such places were communities where the elderly and the frail in particular were looked after. Parishes were the first administrative units in Britain which had a responsibility to their poor. The Elizabethan Poor Law enshrined this right with the practice of sturdy and less sturdy beggars being sent back to their parish of origin ostensibly for help. This system, although modified, remained largely intact until the offensive launched by the Utilitarian reformers. For them, no fiddling with facts was beyond the pale if it could discredit the old regime. The new Poor law of 1834 was the result of this campaign, and where the principle of "less eligibility" was enforced, help in the new system would only be offered if a person came into the "house", as the poor institute was known, a standard of living awaited them which was below that on which the poorest labourer could survive.

In 1906 the Liberal Government won a landslide victory, though it was not base on a programme of welfare reform but what they did was to keep quiet about it, afraid of discussing any reform, the only reform they introduced at that time was to protect the friendly societies and mutually-owned bodies operating the health scheme then. They also introduced means-tested old age pension for those over 70 or more. At that time the average life expectancy for men was 48 years. By 1911 National health and unemployment insurance was introduced. What the Liberals did was to advance the principle of the insurance to finance this new welfare because they were anxious not to raise income tax and alienate the bedrock of its support. So the Liberals decided to follow the Bismarck's lead that has even faced more resistance to a tax base welfare. By then the German government did not have the power to levy taxes on income and insurance principle, then became the crucial aspect of state welfare. This resistance in income tax was overcome by Lloyd George when he appeals to the senses of the trade union. This victory was followed with an Act of 1925 by Neville Chamberlain who added to the insurance base with the Widows', Orphans and Old Age Contributory Pensions Act. This period was still dominated by unemployment. It was the financial chaos resulting from botched attempts to provide income for the mass unemployed and at the same time maintain an insurance fund that prompted the trade unions and others to call for universal welfare. The use of a household based means-test for unemployment assistance gave ground for this campaign.

When the politicians saw that the universal welfare campaign is now ingrained into the philosophy of the voters. Inquiry was launched in 1941 to look for the best ways to achieve the welfare state. Beveridge seized the opportunity, rewrote the script, and then redesigned the contours of British welfare. The implementation of Beveridge philosophy was seen as part of winning the peace. The philosophy was "security" "from cradle to the grave" as a means of conquering Want, one of the five giants Beveridge declared should be slain by way of post-war reconstruction. In the 70s it seems the idea of full employment and universal welfare were out growing it usefulness and the mission for fresh idea was set in motion. 1979 reform blamed the foreigners for the woes of the economy and promised to deal with the offenders. One of the ways of punishing the foreigner is through privatization which means that economic niche would take place and employers would be free to choose whom they want and reject whomever their colour seems offensive. A section of the community was singled out for this economic lynching. Their security "from cradle to grave" was quickly dismantled. Their services are no longer required and their labour is no longer part of wealth creation in this 21st century. As a result of that African-Caribbean communities are deliberately excluded from the main British economy. Since stock market cheers when unemployment is high among African-Caribbean people and shivers when it is low, employers have no choice but to sack the economic rejects (African-Caribbean's) since their profitability do no depend on labour. When redundancy is coming African-Caribbean people are the first to go. When fired, these African-Caribbean people join the underclass which is made of teenage gang members, juvenile delinquents, school dropouts' drug addicts' looters and arsonists, pimps and criminals. In the welfare state, they become a liability to decent people and regarded as unreachable by the so called decent people. The Philosophy, that the blacks lack the skill to appreciate the advantages of working life is a social construct to demonise the black people. Except, of course, it is the work moral code, the sole alternative that economic rules tolerate; while demeaning dependency of the African-Caribbean people as sin, the work ethic in its current version brings most relief to the moral conscience of the well-off.

Attack on the jobless blacks

The teachers and architect of early nineteenth century of welfare to work programme knew full well what they were talking about. During that time, labour was the sole source of wealth; to produce more, and to involve more labour in the process of production, meant much the same thing[345]. There were growing ranks of businessmen and women eager to produce more, and there were growing ranks of paupers reluctant to work and produce on the entrepreneurs' terms. The welfare to work could, conceivably,

---

345   Bowden, W., (1925) Industrial Society in England towards the End of the Eighteenth Century. London: Macmillan, pp.274—5.

induce the two to meet. The idea of work as the road leading simultaneously towards a wealthy nation and out of individual poverty rang true.

Towards the end of the twentieth century, the work moral code comes once more to the top of public debate; it looms large in both the diagnoses of current ills and the prescriptions for their cure[346]. It is most prominent in the welfare to-work programmes, initiated in the USA but, since their inception (though regardless of their dubious results), enviously eyed by a growing number of politicians in other affluent countries (including Britain). As Handler and Hasenfeld point out about WIN (the cryptonim for the American welfare-to-work programme): on its inauguration and throughout its complicated history, the rhetoric's justifying WIN bore little relationship to its actual impact. All the available evidence indicates that the programme has had gloomy results. Work policies and programmes have persisted in various forms, despite the overwhelming historical evidence that they have generally failed to reduce the welfare rolls in any appreciable way or to improve the economic self-sufficiency of the African-Caribbean's [347]. The reasons for their survival cannot, therefore, reside in their helpful effects on the African-Caribbean's on welfare, but rather in their apparent utility to the White people.

The unwillingness or putative of the present-day welfare African-Caribbean's to join in the productive effort in no way arrests the growth of productivity. The present day corporations do not need more workers from African-Caribbean community to increase their profits, and if they do need more workers they can easily find them elsewhere such Eastern Europe or Asia, on better terms? Than those attainable locally, even if this leads to the further impoverishment of the African-Caribbean community. After all, according to the latest Human Development Report from the UN, 1.3 billion of the world population live currently on a dollar a day or less; by these standards, even the 100 million black people living below the poverty line in the affluent West, the homeland of the welfare to work, have a long way to go[348].

However, in the world of big corporation's progress means today first and foremost 'downsizing', as a way of keeping out black people while technological progress means replacement of living labour of African-Caribbean's with electronic software. Just how dishonest the condemnation of African-Caribbean people for their unwillingness to work and the upshot notion that they would earn their living easily if only they shook off their state of unconsciousness and their habits of dependency, now sounds, is demonstrated by the fashion in which the Stock Exchange, that unwittingly sincere spokesperson for corporate interests, reacts to fluctuation in employment.

It is not merely a question of the absence of any sign of Stock Exchange anxiety, let alone a panic reaction, when the rise of overall unemployment in a given country is accelerating; the Stock Exchange does react, and reacts enthusiastically, to the news that employment is not likely to rise[349]. The information that from June to July 1996 the number of new vacancies in the Britain fell and the percentage of people officially out of work thereby rose, was reported under the title, 'Employment data cheer Stock Market' (the footie gained 70 points in one day). The value of shares in the giant conglomerate AT&T rose dramatically on

346   Hammonds, T, (1966) The Town Labourer 1760 – 1832 (first published in 1917). London: Longman, p.307.

347   Woollacott, m., (1997) Behind the myth of the self—made man, Guardia,,, 17 May.

348   Ferge, k., and Miller.S (1987) (eds.) Dynamics of Deprivation. Aldershot: Gower, pp.309—1 0.

349   Richard S., (1990)The Corrosion of Character: The Personal Consequences of Work in the New Capitalism. New York: W.W. Norton & Co., pp.47—51.

the day its managers announced the cutting of 40,000 jobs an experience repeated virtually daily on all stock exchanges around the world[350]. Ford requested its British workers to take up voluntary redundant.

Settlers vs. Migrants

Robert Reich suggested that four categories of employees can be found presently in the labour market. There are, first, 'symbol manipulators', in-inventors, advertisers, promoters and merchandisers of ideas. Others, mostly educators of all fields and levels, are active in the reproduction of Employable labour (that is, labour as commodity, fit to be bought and consumed). The third category comprises people hired for 'personal services' (rendered mostly to other people in their capacity of consumers) a large contingent of sellers of products and prompters/breeders of the desire to buy them. Finally, the fourth category: 'routine labourers' attached to traditional assembly lines and their 'new and improved' versions in the form of automated electronic appliances like, for instance, check out points in supermarkets[351].

Individuals of that last category apparently face least difficulty when it comes to selling their labour. Their prospective buyers are not particularly fastidious. Since neither extraordinary and special skills, difficult to master nor particular acumen in dealing with customers in face to face interactions are required for the kind of jobs 'routine labourers' are expected to perform, they can move relatively easily from one employment to another throughout the whole spectrum of paid-for low-skill work. But for the same reason they are also eminently disposable: their jobs are chronically unstable. They may be replaced at any moment with no loss to their employers, they could be fired on the spot when business slows down, since there are many like them ready to take up jobs once business picks up again and so they have no bargaining power, no bargaining assets, no chance of winning in a struggle for better employment terms and conditions, were they are able and willing to fight.

The aspiration for struggle, and particularly an aspiration shared with others 'like them' and so likely to lead to a solitary action, is, however, hard to come by. All circumstances seem to conspire against it. Such jobs as may be had are frail, can vanish at any moment and surely would not last for long; today's mates would surely move on to other, often far-away places; people one meets today won't be here tomorrow or the day after. Investing in workers' solidarity and in collective resistance, with all the long term, risk fraught efforts they require, promises little gain but exorbitant and difficult to calculate costs[352]. If such conditions last for a long time with no alternatives in sight, the worldviews and attitudes of employees adjust accordingly. 'Make as much as you can of today, think not of tomorrow' and 'each man for himself, nothing is to be earned by standing together' become unnoticeably but persistently the unquestioned principle of prudent and effective life strategy.

---

350   Richard R., (1998) Achieving our Country. Harvard University Press, p.85.

351   Townsend, p., (1993) Poverty in Europe, in Z. Ferge and SM. Miller (eds) Dynamics of Deprivation. Aldershot: Gower, p.73.

352   Henry A., (2002) Global capitalism and the return of the garrison state, Arena Journal 19: 141—60.

Putting all that into consideration, the term 'routine labourers' seems to be partly misleading. The kind of work activities in which the employees of the fourth category are engaged may be as monotonous, uncreative and dull, and demand as few skills, as the old style routine jobs of a Ford-style factory but what sets them apart when it comes to the attitudes and conduct they bring about is their admittedly chameleon like, shifting, temporary, short term, periodic and often short-lived nature[353]. Their-jobs are routine but not their employment. 'Routine' suggests monotonous repetition of the same and so it conveys faithfully the kind of other-directed action in which they are engaged day in day out as long as they remain hired to do it. But the routine nature of what they do makes hiring itself their access to jobs everything but routine.

Even the most tedious, uninspired and dull and often demeaning work favours the growth of stable, solidly rooted and durable human bonds only if (and because) it is expected to last for a long time to come in practice, infinitely. The feeling that 'we are all in the same boat' and in all likelihood will remain in that boat whatever happens weathering storms together and together enjoying smooth sailing propels and fosters the search for the most satisfying or the least oppressive mode of cohabitation. Why bother, though, if one is pretty certain that with each successive clock-in one is likely to find oneself in a different company? With such certainty, all lasting associations, firm commitments and unbreakable friendships look suspiciously like recipes for frustration and broken hearts. If you come to like the company for which you work and inscribe into it your own plans for the future, you are bound to be hurt at the next round of 'outsourcing' or 'rationalization', or even well before that[354]. All in all, such fateful transformations summarily code named 'flexibility of the labour market' cast a dark shadow on the future chances of solidarity and long-term, let alone whole hearted and unconditional, commitment and loyalty to 'common causes'[355]

As Richard Sennett found out on his second visit to a New York bakery, twenty years after his first visit , 'the morale and motivation of Afro-American workers dropped sharply in the various squeeze plays of downsizing: the surviving workers waited for the next blow of the axe rather than exulting in competitive victory over those who were fired'[356]. Whether (already) damned or (temporarily) saved, they were nursing their grudges and succumbed to their fears much in the same manner and with good reasons:

In all forms of work, from sculpting to serving meals, African-Caribbean people identify with tasks which challenge them, tasks which are difficult. But in this flexible workplace, with its multilingual workers coming and going irregularly, radically different orders coming in each day, the machinery is the only real standard of order, and so has to be easy to anyone, no matter who, to operate difficulty is counterproductive in a flexible regime. By a terrible paradox, when we diminish difficulty and resistance, we create the very conditions for uncritical and indifferent activity on the part of the users.

---

353   Richard R., (1999) Philosophy and Social Hope. Penguin Books, p.203.

354   Klein, N., (2001) No Logo. London: Flamingo, pp.XVII—XVIII.

355   Castoriadis., (1997) Anthropology, Philosophy, Politics (trans. D.A. Curtis; lecture given in Lausanne in 1989), Thesis Eleven, 49: 103—4.

356   Himmelfarb, G., (1984) The Idea of Poverty: England in the Early Industrial Age. London: Faber & Faber, pp.25, 79 if, 193.

As long as they stay employed, the occasional, exchangeable, and eminently disposable 'African-carribbean labourers' are bodily inside the workplace, but their spirits hardly ever follow the bodies. Workplace is still a source of living, but not of life-meaning and certainly not a greenhouse of human bonds sufficiently solid and trustworthy enough to support and sustain ethical convictions and standards of moral practices. Inside the walls of 'flexible' plants, offices, workhouses and shops, the principle of 'work ethics' sound hollow. Thorstein Veblen's 'workmanship instinct', if it survived the advent of flexibility at all, needs to seek its fulfilment elsewhere. And consumer markets are all too ready and willing to supply alternative venues, Pride once sought in the professional skill may be now derived (at the right price) from shopping excellence from finding the best 'selling outlet' in the maze of a shopping mall and the best outfit on the trolley or the best gadget on the shelves.

African-carribean People described by Reich as the 'routine labourers' (read: occasional and volatile, disposable and easily replaceable, tenuously related to their jobs and workplaces) are in no position to demand, let alone to obtain, closer and more intimate ties with the company that employs them[357]. Relationship between African-Caribbean employees and their bosses are no more symmetrical, dependence is no longer reciprocal. The era of 'Fordist factories' of huge, bulky and heavy industrial plants with a mass of locally recruited African-Caribbean labourers, where the wealth and profits of the bosses depended on the consent and morale of their employees as much as the livelihood of the employees depended on benevolence of their bosses that era is over. Dependence is no longer mutual it is one sided. Whereas the African-Caribbean job-seekers remain as before 'tied to the ground', un-free to move and so dependent on mostly local workplaces for their living capitals may now move with no constraint, paying little attention to distances and the state boundaries erected on their way. Voices routinely answering routine questions of callers from Shoreditch or Wakefield, nowadays may come from Bombay or Calcutta[358].

The Capitalists and factory owners seeking workers are no longer bound to rely on local labour markets and so they see no reason why they should select their camping sites by any other criteria than maximization of profit and the profusion of undemanding, docile and trouble-free labour. People fit and eager to assume the roles of 'routine labourers', to accept any job on offer and for any, even the most miserable wages, can be found everywhere. There is no need to bear lightly the inconvenience (and high costs) of rising self confidence (and so rising demands) of the local labourers, emboldened by the sheer duration of their employment and empowered by the solidarity that was given enough (too much) time to grow strong and harden[359]. When confronted with nomadic capital, settled labour has little chance to slow down, let alone to arrest, the capital when it prefers to move elsewhere and so it has an even lesser chance to bid for its rights and fight for its ambitions.

But what have become of the other, non-routine categories of the 'gainfully employed'? At the other end of the employment spectrum and close to the top of the power pyramid circulate those to whom space matters little and distance is not a bother; people of many places but of no one place in particular[360]. They are as light, energetic and volatile as the increasingly global and extra territorial trade and finances

---

357   Gaskell, P., (1999) Artisans and Machinery. London: Frank Cass p.78.

358   McClelland, k., (1987) Time to work, time to live: some aspects of work and the re—formation of class in Britain, 1850—1880, in P. Joyce (ed.) The Historical Meanings of Work. Cambridge: Cambridge University Press, p.184.

359   Gough, I., (1979) the Political Economy of the Welfare State, London: Macmillan, p.l I.

360   Offe, C., (1984) Contradictions of the out of work donation, London: Hutchinson, pp. 152—3.

that assisted at their birth and sustains their nomadic existence. According to Jacques Attali, he described African-Caribbeans as people 'who do not own factories, lands, nor occupy administrative positions. Their wealth comes from a portable asset: their knowledge of the laws of the labyrinth'. They 'love to create, play and be on the move'. They live in a society 'of volatile values, carefree about the future, egoistic and hedonistic'. They 'take the innovation as good news, instability as value, insecurity as very important, hybridity as richness'. In varying degrees, they all master and practice the art of 'adaptable life': acceptance of disorientation, immunity to dizziness and adaptation to the state of wooziness, tolerance to the absence of journey and of direction and to indefinite duration of travel. Addressing presumably African-Caribbean people, the anonymous columnist of the Observer hiding under the penname 'Barefoot Doctor' counsels to do everything one does with grace[361]. Taking a hint from Lao Tse, the oriental prophet of detachment and tranquillity, he describes the life stance most likely to achieve that effect: "Flowing like water, you swiftly move along, never fighting the current, stopping long enough to become stagnant or clinging to the riverbank or rock the possessions, situations or people that pass through your life not even trying to hold on to your opinions or world view, but simply sticking lightly yet intelligently to whatever presents itself as you pass by and then graciously letting it go without grasping[362]".

With African-Caribbeans who follows such pattern, their battle is lost before it started. Not necessarily because of the adversary's formidable power and skills but due to their life attitude, their elusiveness, stout refusal to engage and to take commitment, their mastery of the Houdini like art of escape from the tightest cages and of breaking the most sophisticated locks.[363]

To be sure, the locks meant allegedly to arrest or at least to slow down the wanderer of the new global elite are not particularly elaborate and certainly not unbreakable; the cages in which the governments meant to enclose the capital bearers have not been equipped with many locks either. According to the 1995 report of the World Labour Organization published in Geneva, globalization has reduced economic autonomy of states[364]: mobility of capitals trimmed their influence on the rates of interest and exchange, flexibility of multinational companies eroded the chances of controlling the volume of geographical distribution of investments, and the global mobility of technical and specialist labour made progressive taxation of incomes and wealth, and so the maintenance of public services, more difficult.

From whatever side you look at it, the spectre of fragility and precariousness haunts all kinds of jobs. Categories of employment differ solely by the resources they offer or deny the African-caribbeans to resist, to respond to the new volatility of the employers and employments with a similar buoyancy and 'delicateness' of their services and shifting engagements.

No African-Caribbean is insured against loss of jobs. And no one is protected against what until recently was called 'long term unemployment', (*a category where the multitude of Afro-Caribbean youths clustered*) but what more often, and rightly, tends to be described as 'redundancy[365]'. If the condition of 'unemployment',

361   D.........t....d Bradshaw J., (1983) B.........d the Poor. Th. M.... T... i.. British Social Policy, Oxford: Basil Blackwell & Martin Robertson

362   Kochman, T., (1981) Classroom modalities: black and white communicative styles in the classroom. In N. Mercer (ed.), Language in school and community, London: Edward Arnod.

363   Titmuss, R., (1968) Commitment to welfare, London: Allen & Unwin, p.143.

364   Duclos, O., (1997) La cosmocratoie, nouvelle classe planetarium, Le Monde Diplomatique, August, pp1-15

365   Halimi, S., (1997), Allocation, equite, egalite, Le Monde Diplomatique, Agust, p.18.

even long term unemployment, suggested a temporary stage in a working life, 'redundancy' is more honest about the nature of contemporary job losses. It suggests a finality and irreversibility of the disaster. It is stinking of a one way road to the dumping site.

From 'unemployment' to 'redundancy'

The term 'unemployment', until lately used commonly to represent people with no paid work, expressed the unspoken assumption of the 'normality' of employment[366]. The prefix 'un' signalled an anomaly an odd, irregular and temporary phenomenon that called, as all anomalies do, for a remedial action and that was likely to be rectified once the call was heard and the action taken. Even at the time of economic slowdown or depression the vision of 'full employment' stood steadfastly at the horizon: once we disentangle ourselves from the present depression and credit crunch, as we surely will, there will be jobs aplenty and a wage packet for everyone[367].

Hardly any recovery from successive short period of depression managed to restore the volume of African-Caribbean employment to the pre-depression levels. However encouraging, the current GNP and GDP statistics were jobs continued to vanish and the numbers of African-Caribbean people seeking jobs in vain or even abandoning all hope and so stopping to try continued to grow gradually and cautiously at first, but relentlessly. Nevertheless, the idea of the economic 'way forward' veered and warped towards doing as much (and more) than before with less hired labour than before and less management that hiring labour requires. With each successive turn of economic cycle the promise which the concept of 'unemployment' contained was ever more blatantly betrayed, and hopes it aroused appeared ever less realistic. Persistently, enough experience accumulated to prompt a genuine 'paradigm shift': the replacement of the term 'unemployment' with a new word redundancy[368].

Unlike the old term, the new word holds no promise, however sloping or vague. There is no hint of 'abnormality', of deviation from the rule, a transient nature of the current misery and no suggestion of the absence of jobs being but a temporary irritant that will be in due course done away with. Unlike the 'unemployed', who are temporarily out of a job but are presumed to be 'employable' and are expected to return to the ranks of the producers once the conditions return to normal and 'are right' again the 'redundant' are superfluous, supernumerary, un-needed. Either they were born into a society that is 'full' (that is, does not need more people in order to produce things and services needed for its continuous existence), or have become unnecessary due to the credit crunch and technological progress (that is the new ability to satisfy growing demand for goods and services with lesser effort and the involvement of less staff). When redundancy is coming African-Caribbean people are the first to go[369]. These people declared 'redundant' are written on the debit, not the credit side of economic balance, as they cannot, neither now nor in foreseeable future, add to the wealth of society while adding to its costs 'public expenditures'. They are a 'drain on resources' and a 'problem' with no obvious solution; economic growth and rising prosperity of the 'economically active' part of the population is unlikely to create demand for their labour

366   Auletta, K., (1982), The Underclass, New York: Random House, p.xiii.

367   Gans, H., (1995), The War against the poor: The Underclass and Antipoverty Policy, New York: Basic Books, p.2.

368   Handler, J., and Hasenfeld Y. (1991), the Moral Construction of Poverty, London: Sage, pp.139, 196-7

369   Julian, C., (1996), Veers Le Choc social, Le Monde Diplomatique, September

and recall them to active service[370]. For all practical intents and purposes, the economy would be better off were they not present; short of that, they should stay excluded from economic activity.

Just imagine how vague, naive or dishonest, the idea of 'return to work' has become, testifies to the profound change taking place in the very understanding of 'prosperity' and of 'good' and 'bad' tendency in economic life: In an authoritative in depth analysis of the present state of large European corporations (under the title 'European companies gain from the pain' and symptomatic subtitle 'Cost cutting has led to profits, if not to jobs' see International Herald Tribune, 17 November 1997), Torn Buerkie rejoices in the 'positive developments' in the European economy:

The sharply improved picture indicated that Europe Inc. is beginning to reap the rewards of painful restructuring efforts of recent years[371]. Following the methods adopted by U.S. companies in the 1980s, many European firms have been shedding labour, closing or selling off what they consider nonessential businesses and streamlining management in a drive for greater profitability.

Profits indeed grow fast, the cause for the shareholders' rejoicing and the learned analysts' enthusiastic approval, despite the apparently less important 'side effects' of the economic success. 'This newly robust corporate health is unlikely to reduce unemployment soon', Buerkie admits. Indeed, just in the last six years the manufacturing workforce shrank by 17.9 per cent in Britain (*90% of that 17.9 were blacks*), by 17.6 per cent in Germany and 13.4 per cent in France. In the US, where the 'positive developments' started around a decade earlier, the manufacturing labour shrank by 'only' 6.1 per cent: but solely because the flesh had been cut earlier almost to the bone[372].

One wonders that according to the surveys of concerns, worries and fears of contemporary Europeans, joblessness already suffered or threatened occupies the uncontested topmost position. According to one such survey (by MORI) 85 per cent of Finns, 78 per cent of French and Swedes, 73 per cent of Germans and 72 per cent of Spaniards see unemployment as the most important problem of their countries[373]. Let us recall that the criteria set for entry to European monetary union were set with the securing of a 'healthy economy' in mind, and that a falling rate of unemployment does not figure among these criteria. As a matter of fact, the desperate attempts to reach what passes today for the standard of 'economic health' are widely seen as the major obstacle against doing anything really effective to raise employment levels through job creation.

The hypothesis of work as simultaneously the highest human duty, the condition of moral decency, the guarantee of law and order and the cure for the plague of poverty, chimed in once with the labour-intensive industry which clamoured for more working hands in order to increase its product. The present day streamlined, downsized, capital and knowledge intensive industry casts African-Caribbean people as a constraint on the rise of productivity. In direct defiance of the once canonical Smith/Ricardo/Marx labour theories of value, excess of labour is viewed as anathema, and any search for more profit on the capital invested focuses first on further possibilities to cut down the number of employees. 'Economic growth' and the rise of employment are, for all practical intents, at cross purposes; technological progress is

370   International Herald Tribune, (1997) November 17
371   Robert, R., (1991) The Work of Nations, New York: Vintage Books
372   John, V., (1997) Empire of burgers, Guardian 20 June.
373   Kapuscinski, R., (1997), Lapidarian 111, Warsaw: Czytelnik, pp.146

measured by the replacement and elimination of African-Caribbean workforce. Under such circumstances the commandments and blandishments of the work ethic sound increasingly hollow. They do not reflect any more the 'needs of industry' and can hardly be portrayed as the key to the 'wealth of the nation'. Their persistence, or rather their recent resuscitation in political discourse, can be explained only by some new functions which the welfare to work ethic is expected to perform in the post- industrial, consumer society of this 21st century[374].

As Ferge and Miller suggest the recent renaissance of welfare to work ethic propaganda serves the 'separation of the deserving and non-deserving African-Caribbean people, putting the blame on the last, and justifying thereby society's indifference to them', and hence 'the acceptance of poverty as an inevitable plague due to personal defects, and an ensuing insensibility towards the African-Caribbean people who are deprived'[375]. In other words, while no longer supplying the means to reduce poverty, the welfare to work ethic may yet help to reconcile society to the eternal presence of the poor, and allow society to live, more or less quietly and at peace with itself; in their presence.

The discovery of the 'underclass'

The term 'working class' belongs to the imagery of a society in which the tasks and functions of the better-off and the worse-off are divided different but complementary. 'Working class' evokes an image of a class of people who have a role to play in the life of a society, who make a useful contribution to that society as a whole and expect to be rewarded accordingly.

The term 'lower class' belongs to the imagery of social mobility of a society in which people are on the move and each position is but temporary and in principle open to change. 'Lower class' evokes an image of a African-Caribbean people who stand or are cast at the bottom of a ladder which they may yet climb, and so exit from their present inferiority.

The term 'underclass' belongs to the imagery of a society which is not all-embracing and comprehensive, which is smaller than the sum of its parts. 'Underclass' evokes an image of African-Caribbean people who are beyond classes and outside hierarchy, with neither chance nor need of re-admission; people without role, making no useful contribution to the lives of the rest, and in principle beyond redemption.

This is the inventory of people crowded together in the generic image of the underclass, described by Herbert J. Gans: this behavioural definition denominates African-Caribbean people who drop out of school, do not work, and, if they are young women, have babies without benefit of marriage and go on welfare[376]. The behavioural underclass also includes the homeless, beggars, and panhandlers, poor addicts to alcohol and drugs, and street criminals. Because the term is flexible, African-Caribbean people who live in 'the projects', illegal immigrants, and teenage gang members are often also assigned to the underclass.

374   Banfield, E., (1996) The Unheavenly City: The Nature and Future of our Urban Crisis, Boston: Little Brown, pp. 34-5

375   Finkielkraut, A., (1996), Humanite Perdue: Essai sur le XX siecle, Paris: Seuil.

376   Kempe, R., (2000) child abuse, London: Fontana/Open Books.

Indeed, the very flexibility of the behavioural definition is what lends itself to the term becoming a label that can be used to stigmatize African-Caribbean people, whatever their actual behaviour.

Whatever that can put those all together look sensible? What do African-caribbean people have in common with alcoholics, illegal immigrants and school dropouts? One trait that does mark them all is that others see no good reason for their existence and may imagine themselves to be much better off if they were not around. People get cast in the underclass because they are seen as totally useless - something the rest of us could do nicely without[377]. They are, indeed, stain on an otherwise pretty landscape, ugly and yet greedy weeds, which add nothing to the harmonious beauty of the garden but suck out a lot of plant feed. Everyone would gain if they vanished.

Since African-Caribbeans are all useless, hopeless and a waste of time, the dangers they carry dominate the perception of them. The dangers are as varied as their carriers. They range from outright violence, murder and robbery lurking in a dark street, through nuisance and embarrassment caused by the conscience disturbing sight of human misery, to the 'drain on common resources'. And where a danger is suspected, fear is quick to follow[378]. 'Underclass' relates to people who are visible and prominent mostly for being feared; who are feared.

Uselessness and danger belong to the ample family of W.B. Gallie's 'essentially contested concepts'; according to his theory when term is used as the criteria of designation, they therefore display the 'flexibility' which makes the resulting classifications so exquisitely fit to accommodate all the most sinister demons haunting a society, tormented by doubts about the durability of any usefulness, as well as by spreading feelings of fears[379]. The mental map of the world drawn with their help provides an infinitely vast playground form successive "moral panics". The obtained divisions can be stretched with little effort to absorb and domesticate new threats, while at the same time allowing self-indulgent terrors to focus on a target which is reassuring just for being concrete.

This is, arguably, one very important use which the worthlessness of the African-Caribbean people offer to a society in which no trade or profession can be any longer certain of its own long term usefulness; and an important service, which the dangerousness of the African-Caribbeans offer to a society shaken by anxieties too numerous for it to be able to say with any degree of confidence what there is to be afraid of, and what is to be done to tone down the fear[380].

It was not perhaps merely by accident that the discovery of the African-Caribbean underclass occurred at the time when the Cold War was grinding to a halt, fast losing much of its terror generating power; that the African-Caribbean underclass debate came into full swing and settled in the centre of public attention immediately the ' Empire' imploded and collapsed. The danger no longer threatens from neither outside; nor does it reside in the "outside internalized foreign powers" internal footholds and bridgeheads, the fifth

---

377   Jeffrey, J., (1998) Labour Formative Years, London: Lawrence & Wishart.
378   Neil M., Phil O., and Sam M., (1993) Tears of the Crocodile: From Rio to Reality in the Developing World London: Pluto Press.
379   Edward, B., (1994) The Economics of the Tropical Timber Trade London: Earthscan
380   Jim, V., and Heather S., (1990) The International Trade in Wastes: A Greenpeace Inventory Washington: Greenpeace

column implanted by the enemy from outside[381]. The political threat of a foreign- fomented and trained revolution is no longer real and is difficult to make credible. Having nowhere else to strike roots, danger must reside now inside society and grow out of local African-Caribbean community. One is tempted to say that were there no African-Caribbean underclass, it would have to be invented.

This does not mean, of course, that there are no beggars, drug-users and unwed mothers the kind of 'miserable' or 'repugnant' people regularly pointed to whenever the existence of an underclass is questioned. It does mean, though, that their presence in society does not in the slightest suffice to prove the existence of the underclass[382]. Putting them all into one category is a classificatory decision, not the verdict of facts; condensing them into one entity, charging them all, collectively, with hopelessness and with harbouring awesome dangers to the rest of society, is an exercise in value- choice and evaluation, not a description. Above all, while the idea of the African-Caribbean underclass rests on the presumption that society (the totality which holds inside everything that makes it viable) may be smaller than the sum of its parts, the underclass denoted by the idea is bigger than the sum of its parts: the act of inclusion adds a new quality which no part on its own would possess. In reality, "African-Caribbeans" and "Long term unemployed "are not the same creature. It takes a great deal of effort (though little thought) to make the first into the second.

The work ethic goes underclass

The word 'underclass' was first used by Gunnar Myrdal in 1963, to signal the dangers of de-industrialization, which as he feared was likely to make growing chunks of the population permanently unemployed and unemployable; not because of deficiencies or moral faults in the people who found themselves out of work, but purely and simply because of the lack of employment for all those who needed it and desired it[383]. This was not the result of the "new deal "programme failing to inspire, but of society's failure to guarantee life according to the welfare to work programme's principle. Members of African-Caribbean communities labelled the underclass, in Myrdal's sense, were victims of exclusion. Their new status was not the outcome of opting-out, as the exclusion was the product of economic logic, over which African-Caribbeans earmarked for exclusion had no control and no influence.

The theory of the underclass exploded into public attention much later, on 29 August 1977, via a cover story in Time magazine. And it did so carrying a quite different meaning: that of 'a large group of people who are more intractable, more socially alien and more hostile than almost anyone had imagined. They are the unreachable: the British underclass.' A long list followed this definition. It included juvenile delinquents, school dropouts, drug addicts, welfare mothers, looters, arsonists, violent criminals, unmarried neither,

381   Thomas C., (1991) Africa and the World Economy: Caught Between a Rock and a Hard Place in John, H., and Donald, R., eds, Africa in World Politics Boulder, Cob.: Westview Press,

382   Barbier, E., (1995) Elephant Ivory and Tropical Timber: The Role of Trade Interventions in Sustainable Management', Journal of Environment and Development pp.205.

383   Cheru, F., (1992) Structural Adjustment, Primary resource Trade and sustainable Development in Sub-Saharan Africa, World Development 20, 4

pimps, pushers, panhandlers; all the names of decent people's overt fear and all the covert burdens of decent people's consciences[384].

'Stubborn', 'Alien' and 'Hostile' as a result of all these, they are unreachable. No point in stretching out a helping hand, it would simply hang in the void. These African-Caribbean people were beyond cure; and they were beyond cure because they had chosen a life of disease.

Unreachable meant also beyond the reach of the welfare to work. Caution, blandishments, appeals to conscience would not pierce through the wall of voluntary alienation from everything which was dear to ordinary people. This was not just a question of refusal to work or of a preference for an idle and parasitic life, but of an open hostility to everything the welfare to work stood for against the innocent black people.

When Ken Auletta embark on a research, in 1981 to1982 a series of investigative tour into the 'underclass' world, reported in the New Yorker and later collected in a widely read and highly influential book, he was prompted, by his own admission, by the anxiety felt by most of his fellow-citizens: *I wondered: who are those people behind the bulging crime, welfare, and drug statistics and the all too visible rise in antisocial behaviour that afflicts most American cities? I quickly learned that among students of poverty there is little disagreement that a fairly distinct black and white underclass does exist; that this underclass generally feels excluded from society, rejects commonly accepted values, suffers from behavioural, as well as income deficiencies[385]. They don't just tend to be poor; to most Americans their behaviour seems aberrant.'*

Note the vocabulary, the syntax, the rhetoric of the discourse within which the image of the underclass is generated and sustained. Auletta's text is perhaps the best site to study it, because unlike most of his less scrupulous successors Auletta does not engage in simple 'underclass bashing'; on the contrary, he leans over backwards to retain and manifest his objectivity, and pities as much as condemns the negative heroes of his story.

However, we should not forget that 'bulging crime' and 'bulging welfare', as well as welfare and drug statistics, mentioned in one breath and set at the same level. Thus no argument, let alone proof, is needed to explain why they have found themselves in each other's neighbourhood and why they have all been classed, as instances of the same 'antisocial' behaviour. One need not take the risky step of pointing out explicitly that drug-pushing and being on welfare are similarly antisocial, are afflictions of the same order; the implicit suggestion to this effect (which would surely raise a few eyebrows if made explicit) has been achieved by a purely syntactic plot[386].

---

384   Udoh, V., (1994) ed. Environmental and Economic Dilemmas of Developing Countries: Africa in the 21st Century. Westport: Conn Praeger

385   Nafziger, E.W., and Auvinen, J., (1997) War, Hunger, and Displacement: An Econometric Investigation into the Sources of Humanitarian Emergencies, Working Paper No. 142, World Institute for Development Economics Research, United Nations University.

386   Pinstrup-Andersen P., Pandya-Lorch, R., and Rosegrant, M.W., (1999) World Food Prospects: Critical Issues for the Early Twenty-First Century, 2020 Vision Food Policy Report, Washington DC: International Food Policy Research Institute.

Having said that it is worth noting as well that the underclass rejects common values, because it feels excluded. The underclass is the active and acting, action generating, initiative taking side in a two sided relationship that has 'most British people' as the other protagonist; it is the behaviour of the African-Caribbean people alone, that comes under critical scrutiny and is declared abnormal. On the other hand it is 'most British people' who, of right, sit in judgment, but it is the actions of the African-Caribbean that are judged. If not for its antisocial deeds, the African-Caribbeans would not be brought to court. Most importantly, however, there would then be no need for the court's session, since there would be no case to ponder, no crime to punish or negligence to repair.

The rhetoric is followed by practices, from which it gets retrospective confirmation and draws the arguments it might have been short of when first used. The more ample and widespread such practices, the more self evident sound the suggestions which triggered them and the less chance there is of the rhetorical manoeuvre ever being spotted, let alone objected to. Nonetheless, most of Auletta's empirical material was drawn from the Wildcat Skills Training Centre, an institution established with the noble intention of rehabilitating and restoring to society the acknowledged members of the underclass. Who was eligible for admission? Four qualifications gave an equal right to be trained at the Centre. A candidate had to be a fairly recent prison convict or an ex-addict still undergoing treatment, a female on welfare, without children under the age of 6, or a youth between 17 and 20 who had dropped out of school[387]. Whoever set the rules of admission must have decided beforehand that these four 'types', so distinct to an untrained eye, suffered from the same kind of problem, or rather presented the same kind of problem and therefore needed the same kind of treatment. What started as the rule setters' decision, however, must have turned into the Wildcat Centre students' reality: for a considerable time they were put in each other's company, subjected to the same regime, and instructed daily as to the commonality of their fate. And being inside the Wildcat Centre supplied for the duration all the social definition they needed and could reasonably work for. Once more word had become flesh.

Auletta is at pains to remind his readers time and again that 'underclassness' is not a matter of poverty, or, at least, that it cannot be explained solely by poverty. He points out that of 25 million to 29 million Americans officially below the poverty line, only an 'estimated 9 million do not assimilate' and 'operate outside the generally accepted boundaries of society', set apart as they are 'by their "deviant" or antisocial behaviour'. The implicit suggestions are that the elimination of poverty, were it at all conceivable, and would not put an end to the underclass phenomenon. If one may be poor and yet 'operate within accepted boundaries', then factors other than poverty must be responsible for descending into the underclass. These factors were seen to be psychological and behavioural afflictions, made perhaps more frequent under conditions of poverty, but not determined by it[388].

According to this suggestion, descent into the underclass is a matter of choice deliberate or by default. It is a choice even if people fall into the underclass simply because they fail or neglect to do what is needed to extricate themselves from poverty. Not doing what is needed, in a country of free choosers,

---

387   Reardon, T., and Matlon, P., (1989) Seasonal food insecurity and vulnerability in drought-affected regions of Burkina Faso in D.E., Sahn (ed.) Seasonal Variation in Third World Agriculture: The Consequences for Food Security, Baltimore and London: Johns Hopkins University Press.

388   Sen, A., (1981) Poverty and Famines, Oxford: Oxford University Press.

134

is easily, without a second thought, interpreted as choosing something else instead in this case 'unsocial behaviour'. Falling into the 'underclass is an exercise in freedom. In a society of free consumers curbing one's freedom is impermissible; but so is, many would say, not curtailing the freedom of people who use their freedom to abridge other people's freedoms, by accosting, pestering, threatening, fun-spoiling, burdening consciences arid otherwise making other people's lives misrable.

Separating the 'problem of the underclass' from the 'issue of poverty' is like hitting several birds with one stone. Its most obvious effect is in a society famous for its love of litigation to deny the people assigned to the underclass the right to 'claim damages' by presenting themselves as victims of societal malfunction[389]. In whatever litigation may follow their case, the burden of proof will be shifted fairly and squarely onto the 'African-Caribbean underclasses. It is they who must take the first step and prove their goodwill and determination to be good. Whatever is to be done must be done in the first place by the under African-Caribbeans themselves (though of course there is no shortage of professional and self-appointed counsellors to advise them as to what it is exactly that they must do). If nothing happens and the spectre of the poverty refuses to go away, the explanation is simple; it is also clear who is to blame. If the rest of society has something to reproach itself for it is only for its insufficient determination to curtail the African-Caribbean iniquitous choices. More police, more prisons, ever more severe and frightening punishments seem then the most obvious means to repair the mistake

Perhaps more seminal yet is another effect: the abnormality of the African-Caribbean underclass phenomenon 'normalizes' the issue of poverty. It is the African-Caribbean underclass which is placed outside the accepted boundaries of society, but the African-Caribbeans constitutes, as we remember, only a fraction of the 'officially poor'. It is precisely because the African-Caribbean underclass is such a big and urgent problem that the bulk of people living in poverty are not a great issue that needs to be tackled urgently. Against the background of the uniformly ugly and repulsive landscape of the underprivileged, the 'merely poor' shine as temporarily unlucky but essentially decent people who unlike the African-Caribbeans will make all the right choices and eventually find their way back into the accepted boundaries of society. Just as falling into the underclass and staying there is a matter of choice, so the rehabilitation from the state of poverty is also a matter of choice the right choice this time. The tacit suggestion conveyed by the idea that the decline of the African-Caribbean person into the poverty is the outcome of choice is that another choice may accomplish the opposite and lift the Them from their social degradation[390].

A central and largely uncontested since unwritten rule of a consumer society is that being free to choose requires competence: skill and determination to use the power of choice. Freedom to choose does not mean that all choices are right there are good and bad choices, better and worse choices[391]. The kind of choice made is the evidence of competence or its lack, the African-Caribbean is the aggregate product of wrong individual choices; proof the choices of its incompetence members.

389   Swaminathan, M.S., (1996) Sustainable Nutrition Security for Africa: Lessons from India, San Francisco: The Hunger Project.

390   Maxwell, S., and Frankenberger, T., (1992) Household Food Security: Concepts, Indicators, Measurements, New York and Rome: UINICEF and IFAD.

391   Bryceson, D.F., (1999) Sub-Saharan Africa betwixt and between: rural livelihood practices and policies', Working Paper 43, Leiden: Afrika-Studiecentrum.

In his highly influential tract on the roots of present-day poverty, Lawrence C. Mead argued that incompetence as the paramount cause of the persistence of poverty amid affluence, and of the sordid failure of all successive state run policies meant to eliminate it. The African-Caribbean people purely and simply lack the competence to appreciate the advantages of working life; they make wrong choices, putting 'no work' above work. It is because of that incompetence, says Mead that the invocation of the work moral code falls on deaf ears and fails to influence the choices of the African-Caribbean people: the issue hinges on whether the needy can be responsible for themselves and, above all, on whether they have the competence to manage their lives Whatever outward causes one cites, a mystery in the heart of no work remains the passivity of the seriously excluded in seizing the opportunities that apparently exist for them. To explain no work, I see no avoiding some appeal to psychology or culture. Mostly, seriously disadvantaged African-Caribbean youths appear to avoid work, not because of their economic situation, but because of what they believe[392]. In the absence of prohibitive barriers to employment, the question of the personality of the black emerges as the key to understanding and overcoming poverty. Psychology is the last frontier in the search for the causes of low work effort. Why do the black not seize, the opportunities as assiduously as the culture assumes they will? Who exactly are they? The core of the culture of poverty seems to be inability to control one's life what psychologists call inefficacy.

The opportunities are there; are not all of us the walking proof of that? But opportunities must be also seen as such, and embraced, and that takes competence: some wits, some will and some effort. The African-Caribbeans obviously lack all three. This impairment of the blacks are, all things considered, good, reassuring news. We are responsible, offering the lack opportunities. The blacks are irresponsible, refusing to take them. Just like the medics who reluctantly throw in the towel when their patients consistently refuse to cooperate with the prescribed treatment, we all may as well give up our efforts to provide job opportunities in the face of the stubborn, reluctance of the black to work as 21st century slaves[393]. There are limits to what we can do. The teachings of the work moral code are available to anyone who will listen, and opportunities to work wait to be seized the rest is up to the Blacks themselves. They have no right to demand anything else from us.

If poverty continues to exist and grow amidst growing affluence, the work moral code must have been ineffective. But if we believe that it stays ineffective only because its commandments are not properly listened to and obeyed, then this failure to listen and obey can only be explained by either moral defectiveness or criminal intent on the part of those who fall out.

Let me reiterate it again: in the beginning, the work moral code was a highly effective means of filling up factories hungry for more labour. With labour turning fast into an obstacle to higher productivity, the work moral code still has a role to play, but this time as an effective means to ,wash clean all the hands and consciences inside the accepted boundaries of society of the guilt of abandoning a large number of their fellow citizens to permanent redundancy. Purity of hands and consciences is reached by the twin measure of the moral condemnation of the African-Caribbeans arid the moral absolution of the rest.

---

392   Bernstein, H., Crow, B., and Johnson, H., (1992) (eds.) Rural Livelihoods: Crises and Responses, Oxford: Oxford University Press for the Open University.

393   Onselen, V., (1996) The Seed is Mine: The Life of Kas Maine, a South African Sharecropper, 1894—1985, New York: Hill and Wang

To be black is criminal

Mead's pamphlet against the black people who 'have chosen' not to work for their living ends with an emphatic invocation: 'Social policy must resist passive poverty justly and firmly much as the West contained communism until sanity breaks in and the opposed system collapses of its own weight[394].' The metaphor is faultlessly chosen. One of the foremost services that the African-Caribbean renders to the present day affluent society is the sucking in of the fears and anxieties no longer drained by a potent enemy outside. The African-Caribbeans are the enemies inside the walls, destined to replace the external enemies as drugs crucial to collective sanity; a safety valve for collective tensions born of individual insecurity.

The African-Caribbeans are particularly well fit to play this role. Mead says repeatedly that what prods 'normal', decent Britons to form a united front against the welfare spongers, criminals and school dropouts, is what they perceive as the dire inconsistency of those they unite against: the African-Caribbean people offend all the cherished values of the majority while clinging to them and desiring the same joys of consumer life as other people boast to have earned[395]. In other words, what British society hold against the blacks in their midst is that its dreams and the model of life it desires are so uncannily similar to their own. And yet the similarity can hardly be seen as a matter of inconsistency. As Peter Townsend points out, it is the logic of a consumer society to mould its poor as unfulfilled consumers[396]. 'Consumer lifestyles are becoming increasingly inaccessible to those on the low incomes defined historically in terms of a fixed purchasing value of subsistence or basic needs'. However, it is precisely that inaccessibility of consumer lifestyles that the consumer society trains its members to experience as the most painful of deprivations.

Every type of social order produces some visions of the dangers which threaten its identity. But each society spawns visions made to its own measure to the measure of the kind of social order it struggles to achieve. On the whole, these visions tend to be mirror images of the society which spawns them, while images of threat tend to be self portraits of the society with minus signs[397]. Or, to put this in psychoanalytical terms, threats are projections of a society's own inner ambivalence about its ways and means, about the fashion in which it lives and perpetuates its living. A society unsure about the survival of its mode of being develops the mentality of a besieged fortress. The enemies who lay siege to its walls are its own, very own, 'inner demons': the suppressed, ambient fears which permeate its daily life, its 'normality', yet which, in order to make the daily reality endurable, must be squashed and squeezed out of the lived-through quotidianity and moulded into an alien body: into a tangible enemy whom one can fight, and fight again, and even hope to conquer.

In line with this universal rule, the danger which haunted the classic, order-building and order-obsessed modern state was that of the revolution. The enemies were the revolutionaries or, rather, the hot headed, harebrained, all too radical reformists, the subversive forces trying to replace the extant state managed

394   Scoones, I., (1998) Sustainable rural livelihoods: a framework for analysis Working Paper 72, University of Sussex: Institute of Development Studies.

395   Murray, C., (2000) Changing livelihoods: the Free State, 1990s African Studies 59(1): 115—42.

396   Townsend, P., (1989) intellectual development: birth to adulthood, New York: Academic Press.

397   Hartmann, B., and Boyce, J.K., (1983) a Quiet Violence: View from a Bangladesh Village, London: Zed Books.

order with another state managed order, with a counter order reversing each and any principle by which the present order lived or aimed to live.

The self image of social order has changed since those times and so the image of the threat the image of order with a minus sign has acquired a new shape. Whatever has been registered in recent years as rising criminality (a process, let us note, which happened to run parallel to the falling membership of the Communist or other radical parties of 'alternative order'), is not a product of malfunction or neglect, but the consumer society's own product, logically (if not legally) legitimate. What is more, it is also its inescapable product. The higher the consumer demand is (that is, the more effective the market seduction is), the more the consumer society is safe and prosperous. Yet, simultaneously, the wider and deeper the gap grows between those who desire and can satisfy their desires (those who have been seduced and proceed to act in the way the state of being seduced prompts them to act), and those who have been seduced and yet are unable to act in the way the seduced are expected to act. Market seduction is, simultaneously, the great equalizer and the great divider. To be effective, the enticement to consume, and to consume more, must be transmitted in all directions and addressed indiscriminately to everybody who will listen[398]. But more people can listen than can respond in the fashion which the seductive message was meant to elicit. Those who cannot act on the desires so induced are treated daily to the dazzling spectacle of those who can. Lavish consumption, they are told, is the sign of success, a highway leading straight to public applause and fame. They, also learn that possessing and consuming certain objects and practising certain lifestyles is the necessary condition of happiness; perhaps even of human dignity.

If consumption is the measure of a successful life, of happiness and even of human decency, then the lid has been taken off human desires; no amount of acquisitions and exciting sensations is likely ever to bring satisfaction in the way 'keeping up to the standards' once promised: there are no standards to keep up to[399]. The finishing line moves forward together with the runner, the goals keep forever a step or two ahead as one tries to reach them. Records keep being broken, and there seems to be no end to what a human may desire. Dazzled and baffled, people learn that in the newly privatized and thus 'liberated' companies which they remember as austere public institutions constantly famished for cash, the present managers draw salaries measured in millions, while those sacked from their managerial chairs are indemnified, again in millions of pounds, for their botched and sloppy work. From all places, through all communication channels, the message comes loud and clear: there are no standards except that of grabbing more, and no rules, except the imperative of 'playing one's cards right'.

The disarming, disempowering and suppressing of unfulfilled underclass is therefore an indispensable supplement to integration through seduction in a market led society of consumers. The impotent, indolent consumers (blacks) are to be kept outside the system. They are the waste product of the consumer society, a waste product which the capitalist system cannot stop spitting out without grinding to a halt and calling in the receivers.

Given the nature of the consumer society now in play, the misery of those left out of it, once treated as a collectively caused blight which needed to be dealt with by collective means, can be only redefined as an

398   Francis, E., (2000) Making a Living: Changing Livelihoods in Rural Africa, London: Rutledge.
399   Ellis, F., (2000) Rural Livelihoods and Diversity in Developing Countries, Oxford: Oxford University Press.

individual crime. The 'African-Caribbean classes' are thus redefined as classes of criminals[400]. And so the prison fully and truly deputize now for the fading welfare institutions, and in all probability will have to do this to a growing extent as welfare provisions continue to peter out.

The growing incidence of behaviour classified as criminal is not an obstacle on the road to a fully fledged and all embracing consumerist society. On the contrary, it is its natural accompaniment and prerequisite. This is so, admittedly, for a number of reasons, but the main reason among them is perhaps the fact that those left out of the global system, the unfulfilled consumers whose resources do not measure up to their desires, and who have therefore little or no chance of coming out of poverty by its official rules are the living incarnation of the 'inner demons' specific to consumer life. Their ghettoization and criminalization, the severity of the sufferings administered to them and the overall cruelty of the fate visited upon them, are metaphorically speaking the ways of exorcizing such inner demons and burning them out in an image. The criminalized margins serve as *soi-disant* tools of sanitation: the sewers into which the inevitable, but poisonous, effluvia of consumerist seduction are disposed, so that the people who manage to stay in the global economic system of consumerism need not worry about the state of their own health[401]. If this is, however, the prime stimulus of the present exuberance of what the great Norwegian criminologist, Nils Christie, called 'the prison industry', then the hope that the process can be slowed down, let alone halted or reversed in a thoroughly deregulated and privatized society animated and run by the consumer market, is to say the least slime.

Nowhere is the connection exposed more fully than in the Britain and United States, where the unqualified rule of the consumer market reached, in the years of Bush Blair free-for-all, further than in any other country. The years of deregulation and dismantling of welfare provisions were also the years of rising criminality, of a growing police force and prison population. They were the years in which an ever gorier and spectacularly cruel lot needed to be reserved for those declared criminal, in order to match the fast growing fears and anxieties, nervousness and uncertainty, anger and fury of the silent or not-so-silent majority of ostensibly successful consumers. The more powerful the 'inner demons' became; the more insatiable the desire of the majority grew to see the crime punished and justice done. The liberal Tony Blair won the parliamentary election promising to multiply the ranks of the police and build new and more secure prisons. Some observers (among them Peter Linebaugh of the University of Toledo, Ohio, the author of The London Hanged) believe that Blair owed his election to the widely publicized exclusion of a retarded black people who his education, education, education, failed them due to unemployment which endemic among African-Caribbean parents. Two years later Blair's opponents in the radical right sections of the Conservative Party swept the board in the local elections having convinced the electorate that Blair had not done enough to fight criminality and that they would do more. The second election of Blair was won in a campaign in which both candidates tried to out-shout and over take each other in their promises of a strong police force and no mercy for all those who 'offend society's values while clinging to them' who make a bid for the consumerist life without proper credentials and without contributing to the perpetuation of consumer society[402].

---

400   Christensen, G., (1991) Towards Food Security in the Horn of Africa, Working Paper No. 4, Oxford: Food Studies Group.

401   Jennifer, C., (1994) Africa, NGO, and the International Toxic Waste Trade', Journal of Environment and Development 3, 2.

402   John, V.,(1998) Black Gold Claims a High Price, Guardian Weekly, 15 Jan.

In 1972, just as the welfare era reached its summit and just before its fall began, the Supreme Court of the United States, mirroring the public mood of the time, ruled the death penalty to be arbitrary and capricious, and as such unfit to serve the cause of justice. Several other rulings later, the Court in 1988 permitted the execution of 16-year-olds, in 1989 the execution of the mentally retarded and, finally, in 1992 in the infamous case of Herrera vs. Collins it ruled that the accused may be innocent, but still could be executed if trials were properly conducted and constitutionally correct[403]. The recent Crime Bill passed by the Senate and the House of Representatives extends the number of offences punishable by death to 57 or even, according to certain interpretations. 70 With high publicity and a lot of fanfare, a federal state of the art execution chamber, with a death row planned to hold 120 convicts, was built at the US penitentiary in Terre Haute, Indiana. At the beginning of 1994, altogether 2,802 people were awaiting execution in American prisons. Of these, 1,102 were Afro-American, while 33 were sentenced to death when juveniles[404]. The overwhelming majority of death row inmates come, expectedly, from that huge and growing warehouse where the failures and the rejects of consumer society are stored. As Linebaugh suggests, the spectacle of execution is 'cynically used by politicians to terrorize a growing underclass' - In demanding the terrorization of the underclass, the silent American majority attempts to terrorize away its own inner terrors.

On that basis Herbert Gans argued that, 'the feelings harboured by the more fortunate classes about the African-Caribbean people are a mixture of fear, anger and disapproval, but fear may be the most important element in the mixture'. Indeed, the emotionally loaded mixture of sentiments may be motivationally and politically effective only in so far as the fear is intense and truly terrifying. The widely advertised defiance of the work ethic by the poor and their reluctance to share in the hard work of the decent majority is enough to cause widespread anger and disapproval. When, however, the image of the idle black people is overlaid with the alarming news of rising criminality and violence against the lives and property of the decent majority, disapproval is topped up by fear; none obedience to the work moral code becomes a fearful act, in addition to being morally odious and repulsive.

Poverty turns then from the subject matter of social policy into a problem for penology and criminal law. The blacks are no longer the rejects of consumer society, defeated in the all out competitive wars; they are the outright enemies of society[405]. There is but a tenuous and easily crossed line dividing the recipients of welfare from drug-pushers, robbers and murderers. People on welfare are the natural catchments area for criminal gangs, and keeping people on welfare means enlarging the pool from which the criminals are recruited.

Expulsion from the universe of moral obligations

Linking poverty with criminality has another effect: it helps to banish the African-Caribbean people from the universe of moral obligations. The substance of morality is the impulse of responsibility for the integrity

403   Clark, m., (2001) Culture and thought. A Psychological Introduction, New York: John Wiley.

404   Leach, M., and Robin, M., (1999) (eds.) the Lie of the Land: Challenging Received Wisdom on the African Environment. London: International African Institute.

405   Timberlake, L., (1985) Africa in Crisis. London: Earthscan

and well-being of other people who are weak, unfortunate and suffering; criminalization of African-Caribbean people tends to extinguish and take away that sudden urge. As actual or potential criminals, the African-Caribbean cease to be an ethical problem they are exempt from our moral responsibility. There is no more a moral question of defending the African-Caribbean people against the cruelty of their fate; instead, there is the ethical question of defending the right and proper lives of decent people against the assaults likely to be plotted in Mean Street 'ghettos no go areas[406]. As has been said before, since in the present day society the unemployed African-Caribbean people are no longer 'reserve army of labour', there is no economic sense in keeping them in good shape just in case they are called back to active service as producers.

This does not by itself mean, though, that there is no moral sense in providing them with conditions of dignified human existence. Their well-being may not be relevant to the struggle for productivity and profitability, but it is still crucially relevant to the moral 'sentiments and concerns owed to human beings as well as the self esteem of the human community[407]. Gans begins his book with a quotation from Thomas Paine: "*When it shall be said in Britain and the rest of the world, that African-Caribbean people are happy; neither ignorance nor distress is to be found among them; my jails are empty of prisoners, my streets of beggars; the aged are not in want, the taxes are not oppressive when these things can be said, then may that country boast of its constitution and its government[408]*".

In the early stages of modern history the work moral code had the distinct advantage of linking economic interests to the ethical concerns of the kind spelled out by Thomas Paine. Bringing the poor to the factory to work might have served the interests of the producers and merchandisers of goods (and these interests might even have supplied most vigour to the propaganda of the work ethic) but it also appealed to the moral sensitivity of the public, worried, disturbed and ashamed by the sight of human misery suffered by the unemployed. Given the seemingly insatiable thirst of emerging mass industry for an ever-growing supply of labour, moral concerns could seek a legitimate and realistic outlet in spreading the gospel of the work ethic. There was, one might say, a historically occasioned encounter between the interests of capital and the moral sentiments of society at large[409].

This assumption does no longer hold water; the ostensibly unchanged message of the work moral code has entered a new kind of relationship with public morality. It is no longer an outlet for moral sentiments; instead, it has become a powerful instrument of the late twentieth century version of 'adaphorization' the process whereby the ethical opprobrium is taken away from morally repugnant acts.

To 'adaphorize' an action is to declare it morally neutral or, rather, make it subject to assessment by others than moral criteria while being exempt from moral evaluation. The call to abide by the commandments

406   Felix E.,(2000) Third World Resource Base and Technology Transfer: Environmental Dilemmas of African Extractive Economy, in James, ed., Environmental and Economic Dilemmas, Oxford: Oxford University press.

407   Khanya, M., (2000) Guidelines for undertaking a regional/national Sustainable Rural Livelihoods study see www. khanya mrc.com.

408   Gens, P., (1990) the culture context of learning and thinking: an exploration in experimental anthropology, London: Tavistock.

409   Kracht, U., and Schulz, M., (1999) Food Security and Nutrition: The Global Challenge, New York: St Martin's Press. Strategies for overcoming hunger and malnutrition.

of the work ethic serves now as a test of eligibility for moral empathy. Most of those to whom the appeal is addressed are expected (bound) to fail this test, and once they fail they can be without compunction assumed to have put themselves, by their own choice, outside the realm of moral obligation. Society can now relinquish all further responsibility for their predicament without feeling guilty about abandoning its ethical duty[410].

The stifling of moral impulse can never be complete, and so the exile from the universe of moral obligations cannot be absolute. However successfully consciences may be silenced by persistent bombardment with the news of moral depravity and criminal inclinations of the non-working African-Caribbean people, the indissoluble residues of moral impulse must be given, time and again, an outlet. Such an outlet is provided by periodical 'carnivals of charity' massive but as a rule short lived explosions of pent up moral feelings triggered by lurid sights of particularly hideous sufferings and particularly devastating misery. As all carnivals, however, are meant to obliquely reinforce, not to undermine, the rules of calm temperament, the spectacles of mass charity render day-to-day equanimity and moral indifference more bearable; in the end, they fortify the beliefs which justify the ethical exile of the African-Caribbeans.

As Ryszard Kapuscinski, one of the most formidable chronographers of contemporary living, has recently explained, that effect is achieved by three interconnected expedients consistently applied by the media who preside over these "charity fairs[411]"

First, the news of a famine or another wave of uprooting and enforced homelessness comes as a rule coupled with the reminder that the same distant lands where the people 'as seen on TV' die of famine and disease are the birthplace of 'Africans'. It does not matter that all the 'Africans' together embrace no more than 10 per cent of the world population. They are assumed to demonstrate what needs to be proved that the sorry plight of the hungry and the homeless is their *sui generis* choice. Alternatives are available, but not taken as a result of lack of industry or resolve. The underlying message is that the African-Caribbeans themselves bear responsibility for their fate. They could, as the 'white' did, choose a life of work and thrift instead.

Second, such news is so scripted and edited as to reduce the problem of poverty and deprivation to the question of hunger alone[412]. This clever scheme has two effects: the real scale of poverty among African-Caribbean people is played down (800 million people are permanently undernourished, but something like 4 billion, two thirds of the world population, live in poverty), and the task ahead is limited to 'finding food for the hungry[413]. But, as Kapuscinski points out, such a presentation of the problem of poverty (as exemplified by a recent issue of The Economist analysing world poverty under the heading 'How to feed the world') 'terribly degrades, virtually denies full humanity to people whom we want, allegedly,

410   Smith, M., Pointing, J., and Maxwell, S. l., (1993) Household Food Security: Concepts and Definitions: An Annotated Bibliography, Development Bibliography 8, Brighton: Institute of Development Studies.

411   El Obeid, A., Johnson, S.R., Jensen, H.H., and Smith, L.C., (1999) Food Security: New Solutions for the Twenty-first Century, Iowa: Iowa State University Press.

412   Food and Agricultural Organization (FAQ) (1996a) World Food Summit: Synthesis of the Technical Background Documents, Rome: FAQ.

413   www.actionaid.org.uk

to help'[414]. The equation 'poverty equal to hunger' conceals many other complex aspects of poverty: 'horrible living and housing conditions, illness, illiteracy, aggression, falling apart families, weakening of social bonds, lack of future and non productiveness, low educational attainment among African-Caribbean youths'. These are afflictions which cannot be cured with high protein biscuits and powdered milk. Kapuscinski remembers wandering through African townships and villages and meeting children 'who begged him not of bread, water, chocolate or toys, but a ball pen, since they went to school and had nothing to write with.

Let us add that all associations between the horrid pictures of famine as presented by the media and the plight of the African-Caribbean people accused of violating the principles of the work moral code are carefully avoided. People are shown along with their hunger, but however much viewers strain their eyes they cannot see a single work tool, plot of arable land or head of cattle in the picture. It is as if there is no connection between the emptiness of the work ethic's promises in a world which needs no more labour, and the plight of these people, offered as an outlet for pent-up moral impulses. The work moral code emerges from this exercise unscathed, ready to be used again as a whip to chase the African-Caribbean people nearer home away from the shelter they seek (in vain) in the welfare state.

Third, spectacles of disasters, as presented by the media, supported and reinforce the ordinary, daily moral withdrawal in another way. Apart from unloading the accumulated supplies of moral sentiments, their long-term effect is that: the developed part of the world surrounds itself with a sanitary belt of uncommitment, erects a global Berlin Wall; all the information coming from 'Africa' is pictures of war, murders, drugs, looting, contagious diseases, refugees and hunger; that is, of something threatening Britain[415]. When they want to show the pictures of refugees they will show the face of black people while those their applications are considered and granted the leave to remain in UK are Asian. That is why the population of Pakistan as a country has overtaken the population of the entire African Continent.

Only rarely, and in a half voice, with no connection with the scenes of civil wars and massacres, do we hear of the murderous weapons used, and even less often are we reminded of what we know but prefer not to be told about: that all those weapons used to make African homelands into killing fields have been supplied by our arms factories, jealous of their order books and proud of their competitiveness that lifeblood of our own cherished prosperity. A synthetic image of self-inflicted brutality sediments itself into public consciousness; an image of 'mean streets' and 'no go areas' writ large, a magnified rendition of a gangland, an alien, sub-human world beyond morality and beyond salvation. Attempts to save that Africa from the worst consequences of its own brutality may only bring momentary effects and in the long run are bound to fail; all the lifelines thrown will be surely re-twisted into more nooses[416]..

---

414   Kapusciski, B. (1999) Food security: a conceptual basis in U. Kracht and M. Schulz (eds) Food Security and Nutrition: The Global Challenge, New York: St Martin's Press.

415   Bagchi, D.K., Blaikie, P., Cameron, J., Chattopadhyay, M., Gyawali, N., and Seddon, D., (1998) Conceptual and methodological challenges in the study of livelihood trajectories: case-studies in Eastern India and Western Nepal Journal of International Development 10: 453—68.

416   Food and Agricultural Organization (FAQ) (1996b) World Food Summit: Rome Declaration on World Food Security and World Food Summit Plan of Action, Rome: FAO.

And then the well-tried, trusty tool of adaphorization comes into its own: the sober, rational calculation of costs and effects. Money spent on these kinds of people is money wasted. Wasting money is one thing which, as everybody will readily agree, we cannot afford.

Neither the victims of famine as ethical subjects, nor our own stance towards them is a moral issue. Morality is for carnivals only those spectacular, instantaneous, yet short-lived, explosive condensations of pity and compassion. When it comes to our (the effluents') collective responsibility for the continuing misery of the Africans, economic calculation takes over, and the rules of free trade, competitiveness and productivity replace morality precepts. Where economy speaks, morality had better keep silent.

Unless, of course, it is the work moral code, the sole variant that economic rules tolerate. The work ethic is not an adversary of economy bent on profitability and competitiveness, but it is necessary and welcome supplement. For the affluent part of the world and the affluent sections of well off societies, the work ethic is a one-sided affair It spells out the duties of those who struggle with the task of survival; it says nothing about the duties of those 'who rose above mere survival and went on to more elevated, loftier concerns. In particular, it denies the dependency of the first upon the second, and so releases the second from responsibility for the first[417]..

Presently, the work moral code is instrumental in bringing the idea of 'dependency' into disrepute. Dependency is, increasingly, a dirty word. The welfare state is accused of cultivating dependency, of raising it to the level of self-perpetuating culture, and this is a crowning argument for dismantling it[418]. Moral responsibility is the first victim of this holy war against dependency, as dependency of the 'Other' is but a mirror image of one's own responsibility, the starting point of any moral relationship and the founding assumption of all moral action. While denigrating dependency of the African-Caribbean people as sin, the work ethic in its present rendition brings most relief to the moral scruples of the affluent.

Conclusion

In this chapter, we have understood that in the past, the term "unemployment meant something temporary. When a lot of people were unemployed or claiming benefit, the government trembles because it is a sign of bad economic management. But these days it is good news, when unemployment is high it means the economy is stable but when they go down the stock market shivers because it will induce inflation on the system.

When redundancy is coming black people are the first to go. The present day streamlining, downsizing, credit crunch, capital and knowledge intensive industry casts African-Caribbean people as a constraint on the rise of productivity. The white and Asians evoke their own image as people who have a role to play in the life of British society who make a useful contribution to the society who should be rewarded

---

417   Pollard, S., (1963) Factory discipline in the industrial revolution, The Economic History Review, second series, 16: 254—71.

418   Mill, J., (1998) Principles of Political Economy, vol. II, 4th (ed.) London: John W. Parker & Son, p.337.

accordingly. They are the only people that should hold permanent job, as for blacks; they should be hired and fired at will. When fired, these black people join the underclass which is made of teenage gang members, juvenile delinquents, school dropouts' drug addicts' looters and arsonists, pimps and criminals. In the welfare state, they become a burden to decent people and regarded as unreachable by the so called decent people. Whether they like it or not black community is not the place underclass exists, because underclass can equally be found among the white and Asia communities who sit in judgement against African-Caribbean people. Both white and black underclass feel excluded from the society in protest and reject the commonly accepted values, as a result suffer from behavioural and as well as income deficiencies. The truth is, black people are not refusing to extricate themselves from poverty rather what they are doing is rejecting the repression of the state simply because of the colour of their skin. The whole idea that the blacks lack the competence to appreciate the advantages of working life is a social construct to demonise the black people. They do not make wrong choices by putting "no work" above "work". Their choices are made for them and force it down their throat and when they resist this economic oppression they would be portrayed as lazy and incompetent, the oppressors make it sound as if there is no connection between the emptiness of the work ethic's promises in a world which needs no more labour, and the plight of these African-Caribbean people, offered as an outlet for bent moral impulses. The work moral code emerges from this exercise unscathed, ready to be used again as a whip to chase the African-Caribbean people nearer home away from the shelter they seek (in vain) in the welfare state. They assume that money spent on these kinds of people is money wasted. Unless, of course, it is the work moral code, the sole variant that economic rules tolerate. For the affluent part of the world and the affluent sections of well off societies, the work ethic is a one-sided affair. Presently, the work moral code is instrumental in bringing the idea of 'dependency' into disrepute. While denigrating dependency of the African-Caribbean people as sin, the work ethic in its present interpretation brings most relief to the moral conscience of the well-off.

Chapter Seven
Political Culture

Introduction

UP AND DOWN the country, economic lynching has become the order of the day. It is not a new phenomenal, it is as old as the history of black man in Britain: yet economic lynching is not less today than it had been in the last 400 years. Rather it is getting worse in this 21ˢᵗ century, because British white and Asian people have fashioned racism and discrimination as an instrument of social advancement and political opportunism. Politicians of all persuasions start using it to a indiscriminately; exploiting the situation for their own selfish ends. Prejudice, racism, and discrimination become the grid by which reputation is measured. To become a patriotic citizen of British nation state, you have to put on your armour of racism for the destruction of the African-Caribbean people, whose skin colour is deemed offensive. Criminalization of African-Caribbean people becomes the only criteria by which their success is judged. The more authorities criminalize them, the better chances they have in advancing their own political career. By this repression, the incentives of better jobs are removed and opportunity to earn a livelihood is denied. As a result of that African-Caribbean people find it difficult to compete in the labour market.

Figure 22

Male average (median) hourly pay, employees, 18 & over, Britain, 2004

Group	£ per hour
Pakistani/Bangladeshi	£10.95
Caribbean	£5.25
African	£4.50
White	£9.31
Indian	£12.50
Mixed/others	£7.60

Source: National Minimum wage[1], Low pay Commission Report 2005, table 4.6

This suppression is not as a result of theft, personal characteristics or incompetence of the Black people, no! It is on the basis of the colour of their skin. British man's prejudice made him believe that his reputation depend on the company he keeps, certainly, black man's company is not one of "coolest" to keep, even to employ them is seen as a bad omen because you have been contaminated and no longer pure. Even when some of them are not racist by nature his reputation and role required him to do so: because that is what the society expected from him. If he happened to go contrary to that expectation he would be seen as the enemy of the state. That is why, instead of teachers teaching the Black children what they should know.

Teachers deliberately put them in subnormal education because that is what the society expected from them. These children will leave school without a appropriate qualification or skill to equip them for life outside school. The state machinery, the police will be deployed to keep eyes on them and to lock them up when there is economic down turn. Whenever you hear politicians debating about the increase in crime what they mean is that there are too many Black people walking down on the street of London, since it is the only place blacks are located, lock them up and throw away the key so as to curb their numbers. Whenever and wherever a crime is committed an unfortunate African-Caribbean man goes down for it, not because the poor soul committed the crime, it is because his skin colour is black. His Blackness is the only evidence of his crime and prison will become his second home. If by mistake he was release to come out, he will find it very difficult to adjust to normal life outside prison. Before he knows what is happening, he is back again inside for life. That confirms what Rhany, an Indian Barrister said that whenever a black man is seen he can only be a "pipe or a criminal[419]"

Instead of state proving these children with "Education, Education, Education", the state handed them with "Prison, Prison, Prison", where they would be excluded and garnished their teeth for life. Typical example is Damien Henson, a 24 year old, serving life imprisonment. While the government, that failed this young man and petered out his life, who suppose to be serving the life sentence because it failed the Black people, on top of that Damien was made victim twice. Just because he is black, born in a broken home, brought up in care. As it is the state design to perpetually keep the black people at the bottom of economic ladder, broken homes become one of the many instrument of this social control so that African-Caribbean children will grow up without their father, as single mothers, black women have to

419   Rhany, M., (1779) the theory of social construct, Cambridge: MIT Press

[1] National Minimum wage, Low pay Commission Report 2005

work harder to put food on the table for their families. She left home 5am in the morning and come back home 12 'O'clock midnight, putting up more than 18 hour per day without much to show for it. Before she comes back home the children have gone to bed, before the children wake up she is getting ready for the next day hustle and she would hardly spend any time with her children. As she left the house she is thinking about the safety of her children while the children in the other hand, are worried about the health of their mother. They would go to school with divided attention due their family problem. The Teacher, without any concern with what the children are going through and not interested in finding out will place them on subnormal education where their future is destroyed even before it began. The state will be busy hunting for their fathers to send them back to Africa or Caribbean as a means of maintaining the culture of hopelessness among African-Caribbean people. The same rule is not applied to other ethnic minorities. If an Asian man has a child he will automatically be given British passport and right to remain indefinite. Their children will grow up with their fathers and mothers together while the African-Caribbean people will grow up not knowing who their fathers are.

This is a typical of black families in Britain today. Damien Hanson's mother is not an exception. The husband was captured, in state "hunting for Niggers", sent back to Jamaica, leaving Mrs Henson to carter for her children, while 50,000 Pakistanis were arriving in Britain every year with British passport and right to remain in UK indefinitely. Mrs Henson was left with a broken heart, unable to look after Damien, he was taken into care. As expected of Teachers, to criminalize Damien, he was placed under subnormal education. He left school at 14, without a single GCSE or skill to prepare him for life outside school. In September 1995, he was sentence for 12months imprisonment for a crime. The only evidence the police had against him was the colour of his skin for the fact that he left school without any qualification; skills nor job; there is no other suspect in his case. As far as the police are concern, the crime could not have been committed by any other person except Damien who is a school drop out. Evidence was planted by the police and he was taken away from the street. Garnishing his teeth among his kinsmen sent down the same root because the colour of their skins is irritating. In 2004, Damien was put away for life, on allegation that he killed a white Millionaire. The criminal Justice wants someone to go down for it quickly and Damien was chosen, "O!" poor Damien. Because the police do not want to be seen as doing nothing, this boy was taken away and locked up for the crime he did not commit:

> *Perceived humiliation of measure after measure,*
> *The new poor law, the restriction of the right of petition,*
> *The collective punishment African-Caribbean people,*
> *And the lynching of the innocent beyond the grave*[420].

The only evidence police had against him was, his is black, secondly he is a jail bird. The media pours fuel into fire by influence the case, making sure he goes down in life. This is the way "The Daily Times" put it, "A Burglar at 14, a Murderer at 24"

"A SERIAL offender obsessed by the rich and famous was found guilty yesterday of stabbing to death the City financier John Monckton in a bloody robbery at his £3 million home. Damien Hanson, 24, who went by the street names of "Omen" and "666" the number of the beast in Revelation, was also convicted of the attempted murder of Homeyra Monckton, 46, the wife of the senior Legal & General

---

420   Richardson, R., (1988) Death, Dissection and the Destitute, London: phoenix press.

bonds director. Hanson was facing a life sentence last night after a jury at the Old Bailey condemned him, having deliberated for more than 23 hours.

The court was told during the month-long trial that the Moncktons were targeted because of their wealth and with their traumatised younger daughter I, now 10, looking on through the banisters endured "every householder's worst nightmare".

Hanson, who was also convicted of robbery, and his childhood friend Effiot White, also 24, tricked their way into the couple's elegant home in Chelsea on the night of November 29 last 2003 when White pretended to be a postman with a parcel to deliver. White has already pleaded guilty to robbery but denies murder and attempted murder. He claimed in the witness box that he played no part in the violence and did not know that Hanson was armed.

The jury told the judge, Mr Justice Calvert-Smith, that they could make no further Progress in deliberating their verdicts on White and were sent home for the night Hanson betrayed no emotion when, unanimously found guilty of murder, he glanced fleetingly at his co-defendant as he left the dock. Sentencing was deferred until after Christmas.

He had maintained throughout the trial that he had not taken part in the robbery and had been visiting his sister in Brixton, South London, but the jury rejected his alibi. Hanson had accidentally stabbed White, a convicted drug dealer, in his frenzy and police traced White from a trail of blood that he left at the scene. Hanson was found guilty of the attempted murder of Mrs Monckton by a 11-1 majority and was convicted unanimously of the robbery charge. The life of the Iranian-born mother of two, who had been stabbed twice in the back by Hanson as he robbed her of costume jewellery worth £4,000, was saved by the courage of her daughter, who ran downstairs, past the body of her father, and dialled 999.

After fleeing the house, Hanson and White drove to Crystal Palace, South London, where they set fire to their clothing before heading to a takeaway. Hanson had been staying at a bail hostel in Streatham, South London, after having been released from prison three months earlier, half way through a 12-year sentence for attempted murder. While he was in Highpoint prison, Suffolk, Hanson had researched rich people such as the Duke of Westminster on a library computer.

When police searched his room they found a collection of articles on the rich and on diamonds and how to sell them. These included The Sunday Times Rich List, though the Moncktons were not on it. The court was told that after forcing their way into the house, White wrestled with Mr Monckton, grabbing him in a bearhug from behind, while Hanson, alone, attacked Mrs Menckton, stabbing her twice in the back.

After stripping her of the jewellery, Hanson knifed her husband in the side though, in doing so, he accidentally wounded White.

White and Hanson were born within three months of each other in West London. They met at Harwood School, Fulham, when they were 9, but were not said to be close friends[421].

---

421   Daily Times, (2005) December, Friday 16.

Figure 23

The Beginnings of A life of Crime

Sept 1995 Aged 14, Hanson gets 12 months conditional discharge for burglary	Aug 1997 Aged 16, robs youth of a Rolex watch, had 12in butcher's knife & gun.
Oct 1995 Stabs youth during £30 street robbery	April 1998 Sentenced for 12 years for attempted murder and conspiracy to rob.
June 1996 Attempted burglary in South London	August 2004 Released from jail on parole after serving six years.
August 1996 Sentenced to 18 months in Youth jail for unlawful wounding	Nov. 2004 Murders John Monckton
Feb 1997 Given four months for attempted burglary.	

The description of Hanson by the media was awful because they painted him as the devil incarnate. Simply, because Monckton was white, rich and famous. The media want to create an image of black people as murderers who are good at nothing but crime. But the crime committed against African-Caribbeans go unnoticed. What we are seeing here is that "to be black is to be a criminal[422]", as far as your colour is black that is an offence on its own. "To be black is to be a criminal" that was the notion that led to murder of Black war hero Christopher Alder by four white and Asian Officers and drag to his death. How disgraceful to treat a man who fought to defend the honour and integrity of our sovereign state (Britain). This is how Daily Mail reported it:

"Left to Die by Racist Police". "Neglected, a war hero who choked in custody". An appalling catalogue of neglect and indifference led to the death of a black war hero at the feet of laughing white and Asia police officers. According to Charlotte Gill, the Independent Police Complaints Commission found the men responsible of 'unwitting racism' against paratrooper Christopher Alder. But none will face new disciplinary hearings over the death of the 37 year old that was forced to choke to death on his own blood on a police cell floor. Three of the officers have been allowed to retire on ground of physical or mental ill health receiving packages worth up to £500,000. These murderers were so bold and confident to condemn the IPPC verdict. Despite the fact that they refused to co-operate with the IPPC's investigation, publicly explain what happened or show remorse for the death. This IPPC probe followed the broadcast of shocking CCTV footage of his dying gasps as the Asians and White officers looked on. The IPCC said that, because the Falklands War veteran was black, they had assumed drink or drugs despite that none of the African-Caribbean countries produces drug. The only places the drugs are produce are in Asia but black are more likely to go to prison on drug offences than those that produce and smuggle it. Mr Alder's skin colour had led to the officers adopting a 'negative racial stereotype' of him. The report continued:

- It was assumed at the hospital that he was suffering from the effects of alcohol or drugs and the effects of a head injury were not given sufficient weight.

---

422   Metro, (2006) March, Friday 31

- There was a willingness to believe he was unhurt, despite having been severely struck.
- There was willingness to attribute his problems to bad attitude rather than to injury.
- Officers were reluctant to touch or rouse him at the police station because he is black.
- Language such as coloured and 'of negroid appearance was used.
- There were monkey imitations directed at a white prisoner and also a reference to a hood with slits for eyeholes.

IPCC chairman Nick Hardwick said PC Matthew Barr, PC Neil Blakey, PC Nigel Dawson and Sergeant John Dunn were guilty of a 'most serious neglect of duty' to Mr Alder:

It is the most damning verdict on the police service since the Macpherson report into the death of Stephen Lawrence found evidence of 'institutional racism'. Mr Hardwick said. 'I believe the failure of the police officers concerned to assist Mr Alder effectively on the night he died was largely due to assumptions they made about him based on negative racial stereotypes. 'I cannot say for certain that Mr Alder Would have been treated more appropriately had he been white but, I do believe the fact he was black stacked the odds more heavily against, him.

'The banter and casual attitude displayed both before Mr Alder arrived, while he lay dying in the custody suite and before he was eventually removed was grossly insensitive in the extreme.'

On the night of April 1, 1998, father-of-two Mr Alder, from Hull, was punched during an. argument outside a nightclub in the city.

An ambulance and the police were called and Mr Alder was taken to hospital but he was hostile to medical staff, perhaps because of his injury, and they declined to treat him.

He was discharged into the hands of Humberside police who arrested him for breach of the peace and put him in a police van. By the time he arrived at Queen's Gardens station he was unconscious and his trousers were around his knees. He was left handcuffed on the floor.

The officers claim they thought he was 'putting on an act' as he lay dying. for 11 minutes.

Mr Hardwick said the way he was treated reflected 'stereotypical assumptions and attitudes based on Mr Alder's colour'. 'The duty to extend basic human concern and compassion to a man who was lying face down, half naked, incontinent and bleeding does not need to be established in a court of law. It should be self-evident.

The IPCC said that, in addition to the four men, PC Mark Ellerington was also involved in the death to a lesser extent.

An inquest has recorded everdict of unlawful killing. All the five officers were charged with manslaughter but acquitted in 2002 on the orders of the trial judge. They were also cleared by a police inquiry. But, despite the IPCC's criticism, none of the five will face further action as they have already been acquitted in a criminal trial and cleared by the internal police disciplinary process. But within the police they called for widespread reform and modernisation across all forces. It said constabularies needed to continue to heed the recommendations of the 1999 Lawrence inquiry by Lord McPherson in tackling racism.

The IPCC criticised the 'major failure of the police discipline system' in bringing the officers to account. Mr Hardwick even accused Gordon Clark, then Deputy Chief Constable of Humberside police, of deliberately Impeding the original disciplinary procedures.

Mr Alder's sister, Janet, renewed her call for a public inquiry in which everyone Involved in his death was required by law to give evidence. But Borne Secretary Charles Clarke has refused. This means the officers involved are unlikely to ever be forced to give evidence.

Janet said: 'It Is nearly eight years since my brother Christopher died the most horrific, Inhumane death, without respect, without dignity My family have suffered uncontrollably while these police officers have been retired off.' Chief Constable Tim Horns apologised to Mr Alder's family yesterday for 'our failure to treat Christopher with sufficient compassion and to the desired standard that night'.

In a statement Issued through the Police Federation, the five officers said they were 'deeply disappointed' by the IPCC report into his death and 'strongly dispute' its findings. Mr Alder's family are planning to take the case to the European Court of Human Rights in Strasbourg. A separate report by the Health-care Commission was critical that Mr Alder was discharged from hospital into police custody without being given a proper diagnosis. Eleven minutes elapse before the officers realise Mr Alder Is not 'putting on an act' but is choking.

The officers realise that Christopher Alder has just died on the floor of their police station A SERIES of investigations into Christopher Alder's death were riddled with mistakes and 'serious failings', the IPCC found. Gordon Clark, Deputy Chief Constable of Humberside at the time of the tragedy, declined to establish a tribunal into the actions of the five officers. Even when he was forced to do so by the Police Complaints Authority, the forerunner to the IPCC, he restricted its powers. Sean Price, Chief Constable of Cleveland, presided over the tribunal but was denied legal advice during the hearing. This placed him in an 'impossible position' and he now accepts that as a result he made errors in his handling of the tribunal, the report said. There were also 'significant failings' in the two police investigations into the tragedy.

West Yorkshire Police Investigated the circumstances of Mr Alder's death while Humberside police focused on Jason Paul who was involved in a fight with Mr Alder on the night he died. The report said Humberside was allowed to take too much of the initiative, despite its own officers being the subject of the investigation.

A civil jury later found that Mr Paul had been unlawfully arrested and charged to divert attention away from the part the police themselves played in Mr Alder's death.

The whole aftermath of the case represents 'a major failure of the police discipline system,' the IPCC argued.

The commission also requested said the Asian doctors who discharge a patient into police custody should provide a report confirming the fitness of the patient, and instructions for the custody officer. The NHS and the police must also develop joint national guidance on the management of patients who are aggressive and need medical treatment. Let us look at the ridiculous allegations mad against Henson: He was convicted on the ground that he pretended to be a postman on the night of 29 November 2004, with a parcel to deliver. What a feeble excuse to send an innocent black boy to his death when everyone knows that letters cannot be delivered at night. Even though Mr Monckton is not a foreigner but British, a millionaire and well read, common sense would have told him that post office in Britain does not deliver letters at night. Could it have been that Mr Monckton was expecting a letter from a private source at that of night? If that is the case, he must have known his killer and that person must have been someone born of the same social status with Mr Monckton's. It could have been another millionaire who he has got business dealings with but this time went wrong indeed. The police knew the person but thought it would be a political land mine to arrest the killer, instead, unfortunate black boy has to be framed and caged to divert attention, to avoid tooth for tart. Despite the fact that the police had no evidence against Henson, no forensic evidence nor CCTV footage linking him to crime, yet, he was convicted on planted evident and sentenced for life imprisonment.

Compare this with Christopher Alder's, a black war hero murdered by lynching police officers. The video footage show the police officers lynching Mr Alder to death and monkey noises heard on the background. This video evidence never mad it to the court so that it would not implicate the White and Asian officers that committed this crime against humanity. The lynching of Christopher Alder to death according to one Asian officer is another "nigger" taken out. Instead of punishing them, the men were rewarded with huge amount of money for carrying out the state operation of "taking out the niggers". NHS managers promoted the Asian Doctors who signed Mr Alder's death warrant and hand him over to the lynching police officers.

> Lo! The bending form of the black war hero,
> "His anxious careworn brow, he smites in anguish, solitary now:
> No rural cot, no lovely daughter's smile, no son's, to soothe him in the dread Bastille.
> No tender partner of his sorrows near, to cool his bosom with a falling tear;
> At thoughts of by-gone days he inlay mourns, and vainly on the wretched floor turns: no help is nigh,
> a dread and fearful gloom surrounds him with the horrors of his doom. A worse than felon's doom: for when his life returns to God!
> Then the bloody knife of Asian Doctors must to its work the body that was starved. Blacks of the British nation state! Ye, whose living head, wept, when he saw that Christopher was dead! Can ye unmoved with hearts as hard as Burke;
> Behold the lynching police thus do its work; See innocent war hero doomed by tyrant rule To be the may-sport of the wealthy fools; With hands unhallowed swearing the thread That binds the heart of Christopher to the lamented dead."

What we have witnessed here is unholy alliance between Asians who dominate the NHS and the police to peter out the innocent black people who have done them no wrong: Who there only crime is the colour of their skin. Who could have believe it that in this new era, Britain is still lynching black to their dead using state machineries such as the Police, NHS and Immigration.

Overview

Pakistan

OVERALL IN THE 2001 Census there were 642,000 people who said they were born in Pakistan, up a third on 1991 and representing roughly 1.56% of the British population.

London has seen the largest change in the numbers, yet - unlike for other nationalities - the capital does not dominate in terms of overall figures for Pakistan born. The capital's figures are only marginally bigger than those found in the West Midlands and Yorkshire.

And the local areas with the biggest Pakistan-born communities are all outside London, reflecting economic migration to the Midlands and northern towns.

figure 24

445,767 Pakistan-born people were living in Britain at the time of the Census, up from 234,000 in 1991.

106,655 Pakistan-born people in London make it the most popular region as a whole – but the community hubs are mostly outside the capital.

5 of the top population centres for Pakistan-born people are in the West Midlands and a further two are in Yorkshire.

19,073 Pakistan-born people in Bradford's university area comprise 30% of the local population.

Distribution of people born in Pakistan

Sort by: Nation/region	TOTAL NUMBERS			AS % OF ALL PEOPLE		
	1991	2001	+/- %	1991	2001	+/- %
Whole of Britain	468,164	642,767	36.98	0.43	1.5	0.13
East Midlands	18,727	11,950	36.93	0.22	0.29	0.07
East of England	13,424	17,948	33.70	0.27	0.33	0.06
London	50,637	66,655	49.33	0.67	0.93	0.26
North East	4,033	5,491	36.15	0.16	0.22	0.06
North West	34,653	46,559	34.36	0.52	0.69	0.17
Scotland	9,452	12,645	33.78	0.19	0.25	0.06
South East	20,940	28,413	35.69	0.28	0.36	0.08
South West	3,225	4,036	25.15	0.07	0.08	0.01
Wales	2,898	3,481	20.12	0.10	0.12	0.02
West Midlands	56,289	63,593	34.48	0.92	1.21	0.29
Yorks & Humber	49,886	59,996	33.66	0.93	1.21	0.28

Most popular areas

Area	Regions	TOTAL NUMBERS			AS % OF ALL PEOPLE		
		1991	2001	+/- %	1991	2001	+/- %
Bradford University	Yorks & Humber	10,236	12,073	17.95	19.21	20.80	1.59
Sparkbrook	West Midlands	9,351	11,791	26.09	16.26	18.59	2.33
Undercliffe	Yorks & Humber	4,954	6,667	34.58	9.97	13.35	3.38
Ladywood E	West Midlands	5,571	6,357	14.11	11.22	11.70	0.48
Fox Hollies	West Midlands	4,667	6,352	36.10	9.41	11.74	2.33
Nelson	North West	3,446	4,796	39.18	8.04	8.78	0.74

156

When we look at the statistics above what we could notice is that in average 50,000 are given permission to stay in Britain indefinitely every year. In a space of twenty years of coming to Britain their population have out grown the entire African continent compare to 400 years of black existence in Britain. So the question is how come such a disparity? How come within a period of 20 years when the Pakistanis started coming to Britain their population has grown pass that of all the countries in Africa including the Caribbean countries put together, despite that African-Caribbean people have been in Britain for over 400years? The answer will leave you in no doubt as why African- Caribbean youths are underachieving at school. The political culture of repression, economic exclusion, hardship, family breakdown etc contributed to this calamity facing the new generation of black kids. Almost 20,000 black boys have been to prison of which half are serving longer sentences from 5 years to life imprisonment. Life for crime they did not commit. Those who have got partners before their time are likely to remain single throughout their life when they come out from prison. Those who have got children are likely to separate from their children and ban from seeing them by their partner because he cannot be able to provide the needs of the family. They children will be emotional raked due to their family breakdown, compounded by the suppression of the society.

We all know that this type of repression, lynching, unemployment, family breakdown etc is that part of British culture, to keep them as economic slaves of the 21st century by portray black people in a bad light; which was racially motivated. On 26th January, 2006 (pg4 Metro), Sir Ian Blair, the Met Chief argued that the Media is Institutionally Racist[423]. Because the way they report murder cases, when it involves black victims are institutionally racist: For the reason that the African-Caribbean victims do not get coverage as white or Asia victims. "What this shows is that Homicides among black communities does not interest mainstream media. He went on to say "Almost nobody in police circles could understand why the Soham murders became the biggest story in Britain". He compared the killing of Tom Rhys Pryce, a white lawyer stab to death in North-West London and a Black man gun down in Lewisham on a racial motivated crime. The murder of Tom Rhys was on every front page of British news paper but the murder of black people only get a paragraph on page 97. His critics argued that, Sir Ian's comment was cynical because he was under pressure over the shoot to kill policy of the Police which lead to the death of A Brazilian man in Oval Tube station. Probably he was trying to see if he can win public support to hang on to his job. Some people agreed with him but argued that what media was doing is deciding who should get a high profile coverage that such prioritization is far from being a racist[424].

Father absence

Nationwide, approximately three-quarters of fathers live with their children and the children's mother, but nearly three-quarter of African-Caribbean fathers do not. This proportion has more than doubled in less than twenty years. There are 1.7 million lone parents in Britain today caring for around three million children. Nine out of ten of them are women[425]. The increase in the scale of father absence over the last two decades is associated with important shifts in its causes. In 1984 single (never married) women accounted for only one- quarter of lone mothers. In 1997 it was more than four in ten. Contrary

---

423   Metro, (2006) January 26
424   Guardian Newspaper, (2006) January 25
425   Lawrence, M., (2000) The new Politics of poverty: the Non-working Poor in Britain, London: Basic Books

to fevered media reports about the lifestyles of the rich and famous on the one hand or the so-called 'underclass' on the other, this change has not been due to a great increase in women making a deliberate choice for lone motherhood.

Indeed, over the last twenty years there has been little increase in the percentage of solely registered births. Rather, the reason is increasing levels of relationship breakdown, especially of cohabiting relationships among African-Caribbean people perpetuated by the state to reduce the number of African-Caribbean people in Britain on the basis of their colour[426].

Obviously one also needs to consider the frequency with which African-Caribbean children see non-resident fathers. Research suggests that for four in ten of these children this is at least once a week, and at least once a month for a further two in ten. This leaves four in ten that see their fathers less than once a month, including one in ten who never see their fathers at all. Other research suggests that in about forty per cent of all divorces, fathers lose effective contact with their children after two years. There is, therefore, no doubt that hundreds of thousands, if not millions, of children have little or no contact with their fathers.

None of this is intended as a criticism of the heroic role of lone parents, mostly lone mothers. But father absence does matter. Guy argued that the great majority did not choose to become lone parents, and would prefer to share the parenting of their children with a loving and helpful adult of the opposite sex. Moreover, because they know how hard it is to be a lone parent, they do not want their children to become lone parents themselves. And of course we must understand that father absence and lone parenthood are not one and the same issue. Many two-parent families are for various reasons 'under-fathered'. And, of course, there are children in care or living with grandparents that lack both father and mother. In short, what we need is an honest national change and move beyond old-fashioned debates about lone parenthood[427]. Nor should we be fixated with the issue of benefits. Of course, financial support is usually necessary where fathers are absent, but money provides care in just one dimension and cannot make up for the loss of the three-dimensional care represented by active and responsible fathers.

Fathers: unique and irreplaceable

Fathers are unique because they offer skills and instincts that are different from those provided by a mother. Fathers are irreplaceable because they offer holistic care that money, whether from the state or from a job, cannot make up for. The influence of a father is crucial to boys and girls as they grow from infancy through adolescence and into adulthood[428]. From a child's point of view a father is important because he takes responsibility for the family, attempts to answer their questions, shows kindness and compassion, and cares for them and their mother. As they grow older it will be their father who lays down, and enforces boundaries for them and sets an example of reliability and integrity. Their father will help them to find and face challenges in their lives and he will be there to give them time, encouragement

426   Streeter, R., (2001) Transforming charity: towards a results-Oriented Social Sector, New York: Hudson Institute.
427   Sunday Telegraph (2001) October 28
428   Liu, Y., (2003) Overtime work, insufficient sleep, and risk of non- fatal acute myocardial infarction in African-Caribbean men in Britain: Occupational and environmental medicine.

and praise, and help them pick themselves up if and when things go wrong. Eventually he will help them leave home to launch out on their own adult lives.

Black children from lone-parent families are more likely than their two-parent contemporaries to suffer from poor health, educational failure; involvement in criminal activity and other negative outcomes is supported by an enormous body of research. The controversy lies in explaining how family structure is linked to the life outcomes of the children concerned[429]. Clearly factors as diverse as the emotional trauma of divorce and the reduction in income associated with family breakdown all have a part to play. However, it is the specific phenomenon of father absence that many researchers have identified as particularly damaging to children, especially boys. Don Eberly, a senior social policy advisor in the Bush administration, has documented this research.' Though research into, and public awareness of, the consequences of father absence is more developed in the United States, the phenomenon has been documented by both Left' as well as Right in Britain.

Fatherhood is also important to a mother in supporting her and providing balance to the parenting of children. African-Caribbean Mothers and fathers need their emotional 'tanks' topped up through the care of their spouses as they give out emotionally to their children. It is not surprising those lone mothers, or those in tenuous relationships, suffer higher rates of depression than those in committed relationships. Children are heavily influenced by their observations of how their parents relate to each other[430]. Mothers and fathers, ideally expressing their commitment to each other in marriage, model an adult relationship for their children and give them confidence to embark on a similar relationship themselves. Research confirms the popular perception that depriving children of such a model negatively affects their chances of maintaining relationships in adulthood. Finally, we should not forget that fatherhood is good for African-Caribbean men! The experience of being a father and of developing fatherhood skills makes a profound contribution to the development of male identity. This is not some 'social construction' but simply what most men want and need. The procreation and nurture of small children, the knowledge of being loved by a child and the skills and self-discipline needed to bring up children generate and develop character in men. A father receives love and trust from his children that will provide him with emotional fulfilment, self-esteem and a sense of purpose[431]. Research shows that when African-Caribbean men are severed from their role as husbands and fathers they earn less, and are more prone to substance abuse and have increased mortality rates.

Promoting responsible fatherhood

What can be done to reconnect African-Caribbean's absent fathers to their families? And what can be done to help men develop their fatherhood skills? Back in 1999, under the direction of the family-minded Paul Boateng, then Minister of State at the Home Office, the Government began to ask the same questions. The outcome was the establishment of Fathers Direct, a Home Office-funded charity whose brief was 'to change the whole culture which surrounds fathers, which undervalues the real passion that many have for their children. Fathers Direct will tackle the invisibility of all the good fathering which goes on.

---

429   Robert, P., (2004) stressed parents failing teenagers, California: Simon and Schuster.
430   Power, G., (2002) under pressure: Are we getting the most from our MPs, London: Hansard society.
431   Policy Studies Institute/London School of Economics, (20002) Working in Britain: The Work Foundation.

But however well intentioned, setting up one small charity and a website does not change the whole culture. That can only happen when the message that fatherhood matters is embodied in a real way for real men and their families. This needs to start with pre-fatherhood education, school and community based programmes to teach boys and young men about the consequences and responsibilities of becoming a father; such programmes largely have a preventative approach, seeking to dissuade young men fathering children outside of a stable and solvent relationship. The next layer of support is the resourcing of fatherhood, equipping African-Caribbean men to fulfil their responsibilities as fathers by making available information, advice and moral support; this is especially relevant where fatherhood takes place in difficult circumstances. The third and most important tier of help should be support for the family relationships in which fatherhood is sustained; in particular, the relationship between parents, including an honest look at the effectiveness of marriage as an institution that locks fatherhood into families; and, where divorce or separation is unavoidable, efforts to maintain or re-establish the bond between father and child.

So where will this help come from and how will it be funded? The second question is the easier one to answer. Measures to prevent African-Caribbean father absence would cost the public purse much less than measures aimed at filling a father-sized gap with money. The real problem lies in imagining the structures that could deliver the multi-layered services required to support fatherhood in all its complexity. The solution lies in looking away from Whitehall and towards local communities. The last ten years have seen a flowering of family support services provided at a local level by a wide range of statutory and voluntary organisations. Clearly, these grassroots bodies have, thus far, made a stronger response to the growth of father absence programmes than has central government. But where the government can help is to bring some coordination to the system, so that central funds can be more effectively channelled to the grassroots as priorities switch from remedial to preventative action.

America's high-profile and bipartisan National Fatherhood Initiative provides an example of how national leadership can work with local innovation. A great strength of the NFI is that it is willing to take a risk on some very innovative programmes indeed. Melanie Phillips writes of the work of the Institute for Responsible Fatherhood and Family Revitalisation, a black-led organisation based in Washington, DC.' Instead of waiting for teenage 'deadbeat dads' to come to them, Institute workers go and find the dads by befriending the mothers of their children. They then work with the young men, who are often out of work, into drugs and involved with crime. There is no embarrassment about telling the men that they have a moral responsibility to their children and that they must leave behind junk food, drugs, drink and violence, but equally they are encouraged to 'forgive the past' so that they can make things right in the present. The Institute provides help with jobs, healthcare, education, budgeting and marriage counselling. Savings are matched dollar for dollar. in short, the programme tears up the 'non-judgementally' of conventional social work, but it works: 73 per cent of the dads find jobs, 87 per cent stay off drugs and almost all of them start being real fathers to their children again.

Dare we take such risks in Britain? The only certainties are that current policy is failing and that it will take a wide range of African-Caribbean grassroots organisations to deliver the right help in the varied and intensely personal situations where fatherhood is absent.

Children and fathers after divorce

Of course, there are causes of father absence that only the government can deal with. One of the most significant is the woeful record of the British courts in maintaining contact between African-Caribbean children and their fathers following divorce or separation. The fact that there are no official statistics on the outcome of the 110,000 access cases brought by non-resident parents every year is itself a cause for concern. But given that between 35 per cent and 50 per cent of African-Caribbean fathers lose contact with their children after separation or divorce, the fear is that there is a systemic failure of the courts to make or enforce the right decisions on access. The Government appears to share these fears. The formation of the Children and Family Court Advisory and Support Service (CAFCASS) would seem to be one response, as would the intention of the Lord Chancellor's Department to give the courts new powers to deal with parents who flout contact orders.

However, these measures do not address the real issue, which is that the family courts dispense legal process in the same way that the welfare state provides help to poor without regard to the personal relationships on which the care of vulnerable African-Caribbean people ultimately depends. The one-dimensional care provided by the family courts begins with the Children Act, which stipulates 'the best interests of the child' as the starting point for court decision on access. This fails to recognise the entitlement of every child, to have regular contact with both their parents. In other words priority of consideration should be given to joint custody an (facilitating a joint commitment by the mother and father to the future care of their children. This is the basis of the family court system in other countries such as Sweden and it is a fundamental first step in remedying the deficiencies of the British system.

Of course, there are individual cases where shared parenting is neither possible nor desirable, for instance, where there is a history of violence, abuse, drug addiction, threat of abduction or mental illness. Depending on circumstances, complete denial of access may be required, or some form of restricted or supervised access. However, to needlessly deny a child contact with a parent should itself be regarded as a form of child abuse.

Other important reforms would flow from that understanding. Divorce or separation is often accompanied by feelings of betrayal and anger. That much is understandable. What is not is that, against such a background, the future of a child should be decided within an adversarial system of law. The courts should first encourage, and if necessary require, separating couples to attend counselling sessions. These would stress the importance of maintaining contact between the child and both parents and then prepare each parent for a process of arbitration with the purpose of agreeing parenting arrangements with minimum recourse to lawyers and courtrooms.

However, the scope for mediation does not limit the need for reform. The relational approach to family justice is even more important where non-adversarial means fail to keep cases from the courtroom. The decisions of the court should be enforced without delay. The parent with custody (usually the mother) must not be allowed to use denial of access as a weapon against the other parent.

Equally the non-resident parent (usually the father) must not be allowed to use legal procedures to bully the other parent into concessions. Clearly, the courts need new powers to guarantee enforcement, but the courts must also be able to use them effectively. This is unlikely when the hearings in an ongoing custody battle are presided over by a succession of different judges. This lack of continuity plays into the hands of parents who use delaying tactics to flout access orders or legal technicalities to harass the other parent. In theory, continuity should be provided by the family court welfare officers, who advise the judge on each case. However, as child access cases become increasingly difficult due to complicating factors such as drug abuse, violence and the sheer mess of fractured family relationships, the system is coming under strain. Speaking to frontline staff, it does not take long to establish a picture of excessive caseloads, low wages and high rates of sick leave.

All this only begins to describe the flaws in a system that struggles to dispense the law, let alone the care and attention that justice requires in family situations of such extreme sensitivity. It is clear that mere tinkering with structures, as seen in the botched formation of CAFCASS, is grossly inadequate. The entire system needs to be rebuilt around a child's need for a mum and a dad. A new 'Family Service' is required that could act with the full legal authority of the courts, but in a completely different mode focused on mediation first and then, if that fails, the effective and speedy implementation of access orders. One judge needs to take responsibility for each case from beginning to end, and judges should be assisted by properly resourced case co-ordinators who would bring in mediation specialists and other support staff as appropriate. Volunteers should also be involved, who in providing a friendly ear and unbiased advice outside of official proceedings could transform parental attitudes.

Of course, there would be costs in setting up such a system. But there would be savings too both directly in terms of legal aid and court costs, and indirectly in terms of averting damage done to children deprived of their fathers. This is an analysis that should be extended to the welfare state as a whole. Can we afford to continue giving care in one dimension? Whether it is legal process or cash benefits, what the state provides cannot substitute for the three-dimensional relationships which sustain us all. What we need is not a welfare state, but a welfare society that works with the grain of humanity; not against it. Until that is done African-Caribbean youth will continue to underachieve educationally.

Conclusion

Instead of state proving these children with "Education, Education, Education", the state handed them with "Prison, Prison, Prison", where they would be excluded and garnished their teeth for life. As it is the state design to perpetually keep the African-caribbean people at the bottom of economic ladder, broken homes become one of the many instrument of this social control so that African-Caribbean children will grow up without their father, as single mothers, black women have to work harder to put food on the table for their families. If an Asian man has a child he will automatically be given British passport and right to remain indefinite. Their children will grow up with their fathers and mothers together while the African-Caribbean people will grow up not knowing who their fathers are. This is a typical of black families in Britain today. Damien Hanson's mother is not an exception.

"To be black is to be a criminal" that was the notion that led to murder of Black war hero Christopher Alder by four white and Asian Officers and drag to his death. "He was left to Die by Racist Police". An appalling catalogue of neglect and indifference led to the death of this African-Caribbean war hero at the feet of laughing white and Asia police officers. According to Charlotte Gill, the Independent

Police Complaints Commission concluded that the men were responsible for 'unwitting racism' against paratrooper Christopher Alder. Because on the day he died Officers were reluctant to touch or rouse him at the police station because he is black.

West Yorkshire Police Investigated the circumstances of Mr Alder's death while Humberside police focused on Jason Paul who was involved in a fight with Mr Alder on the night he died. The video footage show the police officers lynching Mr Alder to death and monkey noises heard on the background. NHS managers promoted, Instead of dismissing the Asian Doctors who signed Mr Alder's death warrant and hand him over to the lynching police officers.

Nationwide, approximately three-quarters of fathers live with their children and the children's mother, but nearly three-quarter of African-Caribbean fathers do not. There are 1.7 million lone parents in Britain today caring for around three million children 75 are black. Rather, the reason given is increasing levels of relationship breakdown, especially of cohabiting relationships among African-Caribbean people. This brake down in relationships among African-Caribbean people is perpetuated by the state to reduce the number of African-Caribbean people in Britain on the basis of their colour. Obviously one also needs to consider the frequency with which African-Caribbean children see non-resident fathers. Other research suggests that in about forty per cent of divorces, fathers lose effective contact with their children after two years.

Black children from lone-parent families are more likely than their two-parent contemporaries to suffer from poor health, educational failure; involvement in criminal activity and other negative outcomes. This has been supported by an enormous body of research. There is no doubt that family structure is linked to the life outcomes of children. Fatherhood is also important to a mother in supporting her and providing balance to the parenting of children. Mothers and fathers need their emotional 'tanks' topped up through the care of their spouses as they give out emotionally to their children. Finally, we should not forget that fatherhood is good for African-Caribbean men! The procreation and nurture of small children, the knowledge of being loved by a child and the skills and self-discipline needed to bring up children generate and develop character in men.

What can be done to reconnect African-Caribbean's absent fathers to their families? This needs to start with pre-fatherhood education, school and community based programmes to teach boys and young men about the consequences and responsibilities of becoming a father; such programmes largely have a preventative approach, seeking to dissuade young men fathering children outside of a stable and solvent relationship. Measures to prevent African-Caribbean father absence would cost the public purse much less than measures aimed at filling a father-sized gap with money.

One of the most significant is the woeful record of the British courts in maintaining contact between children and fathers following separation.

Bibliography

Abbot, S.,(1971) The Prevention of Racial Discrimination in Britain, London: Oxford University Press.

Alba, R., and Nee, V., (1997) Rethinking Assimilation Theory for a New Era of Immigration, International Migration Review 21: 826—74.

Anthias, F., and Yuvai D., (1992) Racialized Boundaries: Race, Nation, Gender, Colour and Class and the Anti-racist Struggle, London: Routledge.

Antonovsky, A., (1990) Towards a refinement of the "marginal man" concept, Social Forces, 35(1): 57-62.

Anwar, M., (1994) Young Muslims in Britain: Attitudes, Educational Needs and Policy Implications, Leicester: The Islamic Foundation

Auletta, K., (1982), The Underclass, New York: Random House, p.xiii.

Angus, M., (2005) Exclusion and discrimination against the Minority: Metro newspaper

Abbot, C., (1998) Education and culture, Oxford: Oxford University Press.

Abbot, M., (1999) Race Relations, London: Tavistock.

Alexander, P., and Halpern, R., (2000) (eds.) Radicalizing Class, Classifying Race:

Antony, M., (1999) The theory of segregation, New York: Harper Collin.

Amaobi, C., (1996) African Liberation Day, Published by AAP Press pages 13-15

Back, L., (1999) New Ethnicities and Urban Culture: Race and Multi-culture in Young Lives, London: UCL Press.

Bagchi, D.K., Blaikie, P., Cameron, J., Chattopadhyay, M., Gyawali, N., and Seddon, D., (1998) Conceptual and methodological challenges in the study of livelihood trajectories: case-studies in Eastern India and Western Nepal Journal of International Development 10: 453—68.

Bagley, C., (1970) "Social Structure and Prejudice in Five English Boroughs", London: Institute of Race Relations.

Bailey, T., and Waldinger, W., (1991) Primary, Secondary and Enclave Labour Markets: A Training Systems Approach, American Sociological Review 56:432—45.

Barbier, E., (1995) Elephant Ivory and Tropical Timber: The Role of Trade Interventions in Sustainable Management', Journal of Environment and Development pp.205.

Barker, M., (1979) Racism the New Inheritors, Radical Philosophy, vol.21, 1979

Barton, M., (1987) Racial Theories. Cambridge: Cambridge University Press.

Barton, M., (1992) The Idea of Race, London: Tavistock.

Barton, M., (20002) Race Relation, London: Tavistock

Benhabib, S., (1992) 'Models of Public Space: Hannah Arendt, the Liberal Tradition, and Jurgen Habermas', in C., Calhoun (ed.), Habermas and the Public Sphere. Cambridge, MA: MIT Press.

Benson, S., (1990) Ambiguous Ethnicity, Cambridge: Cambridge University Press.

Berkin, C., (1980) Women War and Revolution, New York: Holmes and Meier,

Bernstein, H., Crow, B., and Johnson, H., (1992) (eds.) Rural Livelihoods: Crises and Responses, Oxford: Oxford University Press for the Open University.

Berthoud, R., (1998a) The Incomes of Ethnic Minorities, Institute for Social and Economic Research, Report 98—1,
Colchester: University of Essex.

Besson, G., and Brereton, B., (1992) (eds.), the Book of Trinida for Trinidad: Paila Publishing.

Blair, M., (1992) Racism and Education, Milton Keynes: Open University Press.

Blake,J., Family Structure in Jamaica: the Social Context of Reproduction, New York: Free Press of Olencoe, 1961

Bonnett, A., (2000) White Identities: Historical and International Perspectives. Hemel Hempstead: Prentice Hall.

Borjas, G., (1994) Long-run Convergence of Ethnic Skill Differentials: The Children and Grandchildren of the Great Migration," Industrial and Labor Relations Review 47: 553—73, Boston: Northeastern University Press.

Bousquet, B., and Douglas, C., (1991) West Indian Women at War: British Race in World War 2 London: Lawrence and Wisharl.

Bowden, W., (1925) Industrial Society in England towards the End of the Eighteenth Century. London: Macmillan, pp.274—5.

Brake, M., (1986) Comparative Youth Culture, London: Routledge.

Braud, A., (1985) No Magic Bullet: A Social History of Venereal Disease in the United States since 1880, New York and Oxford: Oxford University Press.

Brown, A., (2001) Mixed Feelings: The Complex Lives of Mixed-race Britons, London: The Woman's Press.

Bryant, C., (1997) Citizenship, National Identity and the Accommodation of Difference: Reflections on the German, French, Dutch and British cases, New Community, vol.23, no2.

Bryceson, D.F., (1999) Sub-Saharan Africa betwixt and between: rural livelihood practices and policies', Working Paper 43, Leiden: Africa-Study Centre.

Bryophyte, J., and Smart, C., (1990) (eds.), Women in Law: Expiration's in Law, Family and Sexuality, London and Boston: Rutledge and Kegan Paul.

Buckley, N., (1999) Slaves in Red Coats: The Relish West India Reagents, 1795—1815, London and New Haven: Yale University Press.

Butler, T., and Savage, M., (1996) "Social Change and the Middle Classes", London: University College London Press.

Barton, M., (1967a) Race Relations, London: Tavistock.

Barton, M., (1967b) Race Relations, London: Tavistock.

Back, L., (1996) New Ethnicities and Urban Culture. London: UCL Press.

Back, L., and Solomos, J., (2000) (eds) Theories of Race and Racism: A Reader. London and New York: Routledge.

Bagley, C., (1970) Social structure and prejudice in five English Boroughs, London: Institute of Race Relations.

Banfield, E., (1996) The Unheavenly City: The Nature and Future of our Urban Crisis, Boston: Little Brown, pp. 34-5

Banks, N., (1995) Mixed up Kid, Social Work Today 24(3): 12-13

Barton, M., (1972) Promoting Racial Harmony, Cambridge: Cambridge University Press.

Barrington, A., (1994) Marriage and Family Formation Among the White and Ethnic Minority Populations in Britain, Ethnic and Racial Studies 17, 13:

Bhabha, H., (1997) Minority Culture and Creative Anxiet. From British Council (2003) Reinventing Britain web site.

Billings, M., (1978) "Fascists", London: Academic press

Black People's News Service, page 8, Issue February, 1970 and page 4 Issue September, 1970. Published by The Black Panther Movement, London.

BLACK VOICE, (1970) Issue August-September 1970. Page 4. BUFP Manifesto 26tb July, 1970. Popular Paper Of Black Unity And Freedom Party, London

Blake, J., (1961) Family Structure in Jamaica: The Social Context of Reproduction, New York: Free Press of Olendoe.

Booker, C., (1980) These Striking Time, Daily Telegraph, 27 January

Boyer, C., (1983) Dreaming the Rational City. Cambridge, MA: MIT Press.

Brereton, B., (1979) Race Rations in Colonial Trinidad, 7870-7900, London and New York: Cambridge University Press, 1979.

Brown-miller, S., (1995) Against Our Will: Men, Women and Rape, London: Secker and Warburg, 1975

Bryan, P., (1991) The Jamaica Peopl6 1880-1902 London and Basingstoke: Macmillan, 1991.

Butler, J., (1999) Gender Trouble: Feminism and the Subversion of Identity. London: Routledge.

Camegie, J., (1973) Some Aspects of Jamaica & liticr, 7918—l938jamaica: Institute of Jamaica, 1973.

Carey, P., (2001) 30 Days in Sydney: A Wildly Distorted Account. London: Bloomsbury.

Carter, B., (2000) Realism and Racism: Concepts of Race in Sociological Research. London: Routledge.

Chambers, T.,(1992) New migrants, London: Churchill.

Chapman, R., and Rutherford, J., (1988), Male Order: Unwrapping Masculinity, London: Lawrence and Wishart.

Charles, M., (2004) After the Cosmopolitan. London: Routledge.

Cheru, F., (1992) Structural Adjustment, Primary resource Trade and sustainable Development in Sub-Saharan Africa, World Development 20, 4

Christensen, G., (1991) Towards Food Security in the Horn of Africa, Working Paper No. 4, Oxford: Food Studies Group.

Christopher, J., (1988). The British empire at Zenith, London: Croon Helm.

Cipriani, A., (1993) Twenty-Five Years After: The British West Indies Regiment in the Great War, London: Caviar Press

Clothier, N., (1987) Block Valour: The South African Native Labour Contingent and the sinking of the "Mend?,
Pieterniariizburg: University of Nagal Press.

Cobley, k., (1990) Class and Consciousness: The Black Eet Bourgeoisie in South Africa, New York: Greenwood Press,

Cockjacklyn, N., (1992) Women and War in South Africa, London: Open Letters, 1992.

Colby, K., 2001) Class and Consciousness: The Black Bourgeoisie in South Africa, 1924—7950, New York: Greenwood Press, 1990.

Coleman, D., and Salt, J., (1996) (eds.) Demographic Characteristics of Ethnic Minority Populations, London: HMSO.

Conquest, R., (1977) "Socialism's", Defeat is not Enough: Daily Telegraph, 25 June.

Constantine, S., (1990) (ed), Emirates and Empire: British Settlement in the DDminio,,s between the Wars, Manchester and New York: Manchester University Press.

Costello, J., (2000)Love, Exclusion and ethnic minority position, London: Pan Books.

Crompton, R., (1997) "Economic Restructuring and Social Exclusion", London: University College London Press.

Cross, M., and Hanuman, D., (1999) Labour in the Caribbean, London: Oxford university press

Cundall, F., (1995) Jamaica's Part in the Great War 7914- 7918, London: Institute of Jamaica.

Cundall, F., (1998) Political and Social Disturbances in the West Indies: A Brief Account and Bibliography Kingston, Jamaica: Institute of Jamaica.

Calhoun, C., (ed.) (1992) Habermas and the Public Sphere. Cambridge, MA: MIT Press.

Calley, M., (2000) God's People: West Indian Pentecostal Sects in England, London: Oxford University Press.

Campbell, M., (1990) The Maroons of Jamaica, New Jersey: Africa World Press.

Castoriadis., (1997) Anthropology, Philosophy, Politics (trans. D.A. Curtis; lecture given in Lausanne in 1989)

Clark, K., (1989) Prejudice and Your Child, Boston, MA: Beacon Press.

Clark, m., (2001) Culture and thought. A Psychological Introduction, New York: John Wiley.

Clayton, A., (1988) France, Soldiers and Africa. London: Brassey's, 1988.

Cliff, K., (2002) patriotic politics and economic dispensation, Cambridge mass: Harvard University.

Cohen, A., (1993) Multi-Cultural Education, Cambridge: Harper & Row.

Cohen, P., (2002) 'Psychoanalysis and Racism: Reading the Other Scene', in D.T. Goldberg and J. Solomos (eds.), A Companion to Racial and Ethnic Studies. Oxford: Blackweil.

Cohen, S., (1990) The Indian Army: its Contribution to the Development of a Nation, Delhi Oxford University Press.

Collins, P., (2000) Black Feminist Thought, Cambridge, MA:Unwin Hyman
Conference Report by The High Commissions of Jamaica, Trinidad And Tobago, Guyana, Barbados, Commissioners For The Eastern Caribbean Government And Central Committee of Police Federation of England And Wales, 28" November, 1970. Held At The Commonwealth Institute, London. Published by Laurence London, Jamaican High Commissioner, 48 Grosvenor Street, London W1X OBJ

Conly, C., (1976) on the possibility of Action beyond Ideology, Social Praxis, vol.1, no.4.

Cowry, A., and Thompson, A., (1990) eds, The African—Caribbean Connection:

Curtin, P., (1985) The Role of Idols in a Tropical Colony 183 0-1865, Cambridge, Mass: Harvard University Press.

Daily Times, (2005) December, Friday 16.

Daniel, W., (1968) Race Discrimination and Prejudice, Harmonds: Penguin.

Daniel, W., (1968) Racial Discrimination in England, Harmondsworth: Penguin.

Daniel, W., (1970) Race discrimination and exclusion, London: Institute for Race Relation.

Daniel, W., (2001) Racial Discrimination in England, Harmondsworth: Penguin.

Dashiki Annual Report 1972/73. Published by The Dashiki Council, London. March, 1993.

Davis, M., (2000) Magical Urbanism: Latinos Reinvent the US Big City. London:

Deacon, A., and Bradshaw, J., (1983) Reserved the Poor: The Means Test in British Social Policy. Oxford: Basil Blackwell & Martin Robertson

Deakin, N., (2001) "Ethnic Minorities in Britain", Cambridge: Cambridge University Press.

Demuth, C., (1978) 'Sus' A Report On The Vagrancy Act 1824 Published by Runnymede Trust

Der, M. C., (1996), "Economic Embeddedness and Social Capital of Immigrants: Iranians in Los Angeles," PhD dissertation, University of California Los Angeles.

Desmond, P., (1996) Democracy and Difference: Changing Boundaries of the Political. Princeton: Princeton University Press.

Dixon, N., (1976) On the school of Military Incompetence, London: Jonathan Cape.

Dominic, L., (1995b) 'Conclusion', in S. Pile and M. Keith (eds.), Geographies of Resistance. London: Routledge.

Dopey, R., (1990) The Encyclopaedia of Military History, London and Sydney: Jane's Publishing

Dow, C., (1992) Record Service of members of the Trinidad Merchant and Planters' Contingent, 1915— 1918, Trinidad:Government publication.

Drew, D. and Demack, S. (1998) "A League Apart: Statistics in the Study of "Race" and Education", Milton Keynes: Open University Press.

Dupuch, E., (1982) A Salute to Friend and Foe Nassau, Bahamas: Tribune.

Dalal, F., (2002) Race, Colour and the Process of Racialization: New Perspectives from Analysis, Psychoanalysis, and Sociology. Hove: Brunner-Routiedge.

Daniel, B., (1968) Racial Minorities, Cambridge: Cambridge University Press. Pp. 107 also see Abbott, 1971:173—93 or Race, 1970, 9: 397—417.

Daniel, W., (1968) Racial Discrimination in England, Harmondsworth: Penguin.

David, B., (1966) "The Problem of Slavery in Western Culture", Harmondsworth: Penguin.

Dawkins, R., (1976) The Selfish Gene, Oxford: Oxford University Press.

Deakin, N., (2000) Colour, Citizenship and British Society, London: Panther.

Dench, L., Song, G., and Edward, A., (1996), Defining Ethnic Groups: Origin or Identity? Patterns of Prejudice, 32, 2: 56—63.

DeWitt, E., (1978) India and World War 11, New Delhi: Manohar Publications.

Dhaya, B., (1999) "Arab Migrant Community", Oxford: Oxford University Press.

Dimmitt, M., (1970) Experience of Black children in our Society, Oxford: Oxford University Press.

Donald, S., (1975) Cultural Bases of Racism and Group Aggression, Devon: Two Rider Press.

Duclos, O., (1997) La cosmocratoie, nouvelle classe planetarium, Le Monde Diplomatique, August, pp1-15

Dummett, A., (2000) "Tackling Racism: From Legislation to Integration", Basingstoke: Macmillan.

Durojaiye, A., (1979) Patterns of Frienship Choice in an Ethnically Mixed Junior School: Race, 13(2): 189-200.

Economist (2001) Primary Colours, 17 March.

Edward, B., (1994) The Economics of the Tropical Timber Trade London: Earthscan

Edward, R., (1976) Socio-biology, "the New Synthesis, New York: Harvard University.

Eisner, G., (1961) Jamaica, 1830— 7930: A Study in Economic Growth, London: University of Manchester Press.

Eisner, G., (1961) Jamica: A Study in Economic Growth1830— 7930, London: University of Manchester Press.

El Obeid, A., Johnson, S.R., Jensen, H.H., and Smith, L.C., (1999) Food Security: New Solutions for the Twenty-first Century, Iowa: Iowa State University Press.

Emmanuel, P., (1978) Crown Colony Politics in Grenada 7917-7957, Barbados: ISEI1 (Occasional papers no. 7.)

Estain, P., (1987) Women and War, New York: Basic Books.

Etittan, A., and Maynard, M., (1989) Sexism, Racism and Oppression, Oxford: Basil Blackwell

Etom, H., (2002) Racism: the New currency, Oxford: Oxford University Press.

Egbuna, O., (1979) "The Contradictions of Black Power", Race Today, August and September, pp.266-8, 298-9.

Eisenstein, Z., (1996) Hatreds: Racialized and Sexualized Conflicts in the Twenty First Century. New York: Routledge.

Ellis, F., (2000) Rural Livelihoods and Diversity in Developing Countries, Oxford: Oxford University Press.

Emmanuel, P., (1978) Crown Colony Politics in Grenada 7917-7957, Barbados: ISEI1 (Occasional papers no. 7.)

Evans, P., (1999) "Attitudes of young Immigrants", London: Runny-made Trust.

Eysenck, J., (1971) Race, Intelligence and Education, Kent: Temple Smith.

Fanon, F., (1997) The Wretched of the Earth, Harmondsworth: Penguin Books.

Fanon, F., (2000) Black Skin White Masks, London: Mac Gibbon and Kee.

Felix E.,(2000) Third World Resource Base and Technology Transfer: Environmental Dilemmas of African Extractive Economy, in James, ed., Environmental and Economic Dilemmas, Oxford: Oxford University press.

Ferge, k., and Miller.S (1987) (eds.) Dynamics of Deprivation. Aldershot: Gower, pp.309—10.

Field, F., (1991) Black Britons, London: Oxford University Press.

Finkielkraut, A., (1996), Humanite Perdue: Essai sur le XX siecle, Paris: Seuil.

Fitzgerald, M., (1998) "Race and Criminal Justice System", London: Routledge.

Food and Agricultural Organization (FAQ) (1996a) World Food Summit: Synthesis of the Technical Background Documents, Rome: FAQ.

Foster, P., (1991) Case Still not Proven: a Reply to Wright, C., "British Educational Research Journal", Vol.17, no.2.

Foster, P., (1992) Teacher Attitudes and Afro-Caribbean Educational Attainment, Oxford Review of Education, Vol.18, no.3.

Francis, E., (2000) Making a Living: Changing Livelihoods in Rural Africa, London: Rutledge.

Fainstein N., and Fainstein, C., (1994), Urban Regimes and Black Citizens: The Economic and Social Impacts of Black Political Incorporation in US Cities, International Journal of Urban and Regional Research 20, 1: 22—37.

Food and Agricultural Organization (FAQ) (1996b) World Food Summit: Rome Declaration on World Food Security and World Food Summit Plan of Action, Rome: FAO.

Foot, P., (1969) Immigration and Race in British Politics, London: Penguin.

Ford, R., and Millar, J., (eds.), Private Lives and Public Responses: Lone Parenthood and Future Policy in the UK, London: Policy Studies Institute, pp. 22—41.

Forman, E., (1977) The Anatomy of Human Destructiveness, London: Penguin.

Frayer, P., (1999) "Staying in power", London: Hodder and Stroughton.

Foot, P., (1969) The rise of Enoch Powell, Harmondsworth: Penguin.   84—128

Gans, H., (1995), The War against the poor: The Underclass and Antipoverty Policy, New York: Basic Books, p.2

Gaskell, P., (1999) Artisans and Machinery. London: Frank Cass p.78.

Gillborn, D., (1995) Racism and Antiracism in Real Schools, Milton Keynes: Open University Press.

Gillborn, D., (1995) Racism and Antiracism in Real Schools, Milton Keynes: Open University Press.

Gillborn, D., (1998) Racism and the Politics of Qualitative Research: Learning from Controversy and Critique in Connolly,

P., and Troyna, N., (eds) Researching Racism in Education, Buckingham: Open University Press.

Gillborn, D., and Mirza, H., (2000) Educational Inquality: Mapping Race, Class and Gender, London: OFSTED.

Gilroy, P., (1993a) the Black Atlantic: Modernity and Double Consciousness.

Glasgow Media Group, (1997) "Race", Migration and Media, Glasgow: GMG

Gough, I., (1979) The Political Economy of the Welfare State, London: Macmillan, p.l I.

Grieco, M., (1987) Keeping it in the Family: Social Networks and Employment Chance, London and New York: Tavistock.

Gurburg, L.(2000) Ethnic minority in Britain, London: Macmillan.

Green, D., (2000) Institutional Racism and the Police, "Institute of Study of Civil Society", London: Cambridge University Press.

Ghose, A., (1971) Editor, Tricontinental Outpost, Voice Of The Grassroots. Newsletter Issues 12 And 15, London 30" October.

Ghose, A., (1971) Editor, Tricontinental Outpost, Voice Of The Grassroots. Newsletter Issues 19 And 22, London 30" December.

Geddes, A., (1996) "The Politics of Immigration and Race", Manchester: Baseline.

Gens, P., (1990) The culture context of learning and thinking: an exploration in experimental anthropology, London: Tavistock.

Gilroy, P., (1993) "Small Acts", London: Serpent's Tail.

Goffman, E., (1974) Frame Analysis: An Essay on the Organization of Experience.

Goldberg, S., (1977) The Inevitability of Patriarchy, London: Temple Smith.

Greeley, A., (1998) Why Can't they be like us?, New York: Harvard University Press.

Guardian Newspaper, (2006) January 25

Habermas, J., (1991) The Structural Transformation of the Public Sphere: An Inquiry into a Category of Bourgeois Society (Thomas Burger, trans.). Cambridge, MA: MIT Press.

Halimi, S., (1997), Allocation, equite, egalite, Le Monde Diplomatique, Agust, p.18.

Halsey, A., (1995) "Change in British Society" 4th (ed), Oxford University Press, Oxford.

Handler, J., and Hasenfeld Y. (1991), The Moral Construction of Poverty, London: Sage, pp.139, 196-7

Health, A., Mills, C., and Roberts, J (1992) "Towards Meritocracy? Recent evidence on an Old Problem", in Crouch, C., (ed.) Social Research and Social Reform, Oxford: Oxford University Press.

Henes, V., (1993b) Small Acts: Thoughts on the Politics of Black Cultures. London: Serpent's Tail.

Herman, B., (1970), Secretary. General Letter Addressed to 'Dear Brothers And Sisters' on BLACK HOUSE, Racial Adjustment Action Society Headed Paper, pages 1,2 and 3.95-101 Holloway Road, London N7 2lst May

Heron, L., (2000) (ed) Truth, Dare or Promise, Black youth growing up in the Fifties, London:Virago.

Hesse, B., (1993) Black to Front and Black Again: Racialization Through Contested Times and Spaces, in M., Keith and S., Pile (eds.), Place and the Politics of Identity. London: Routledge.

Himmelfarb, G., (1984) The Idea of Poverty: England in the Early Industrial Age. London: Faber & Faber, pp.25, 79 if, 193.

Hines, V., (1970) Conversation With Michael Abdual Malik (Michael X) Recording At

Hines, V., (1972) The Black man and the future, London: Zulu Publication.
Historical and Cultural Perspectives; Bridgetown: Dept. of History, UWI and the NCI.

Humphrey, D., (1971) Because they are Black, Harmondsworth: Penguin.

Jacobson, M., (1998) Whiteness of a Different Color: European Immigrants and the Alchemy of Race. Cambridge, MA: Harvard University Press

Hakim, C., (1998) Issues of Racism at Work, London: Athlone.

Hall, S., (1996) The Question of Cultural Identity, London: Sage, pp1-17

Halsey, A., and Ridge, J., (1980) Family, Class and Education in Modern Britain, Oxford: Oxford University Press.

Hammersley, M., (1997) "Constructing Educational Inequality", Lewes: Falmer.

Hammond, T., (1960) The Town Labourer 1760 - 1832 (first published in 1917), London: Longrnan, p.307.

Haralambos, M., and Holborn, M., (2000) Sociology, 5th edn. London: Collins.

Hartmann, B., and Boyce, J.K., (1983) a Quiet Violence: View from a Bangladesh Village, London: Zed Books.

Haskey, J., (1998) The Ethnic Minority Populations Resident in Private Households, estimates by county and Metropolitan Districts of England and Wales: Population Trends, 63 (Spring): 22-25.

Haugaard, J., (2000) Research and policy on transracial Discrimination: Adoption Quarterly, 3(4): 35-41.

Haykin, P., (2000) Black Minority in Britain, London: Oxford University Press.

Heath, A., and Clifford, P., (1996) "Class inequalities and Educational reform in Twentieth Century Britain", London: Longman

Henry A., (2002) Global capitalism and the return of the garrison state, Arena Journal 19: 141—60.

Hines, V., (1972) Britain, The Black Man And The Future, Mangrove Court Report, London: Published by Zulu Publications, London.

Hochschild, A., (1999) King Leopold's Chost, A Story of Greed, Terror and Heroism in Colonial Africa; London: Macmillan.

Holmes, R., (2001) How Young Children Percieve Race, Thousand Oaks, CA: Sage.

Home Office (2000) Code of Practice on Reporting and Recording Racist Incidents, London: Home Office.

Humphrey, D., (20000) Because They are Black, Harmondsworth: Penguin

International Herald Tribune, (1997) November 17

Jeffrey, J., (1998) Labour Formative Years, London: Lawrence & Wishart.

Jennifer, C., (1994) Africa, NGO, and the International Toxic Waste Trade', Journal of Environment and Development 3, 2.

John, V., (1997) Empire of burgers, Guardian 20 June.

John, V.,(1998) Black Gold Claims a High Price, Guardian Weekly, 15 Jan.

Jahoda, K., (1964) How long should this go on?London: Cambridge University Press.

James, W., (1993) Migration, Racism and Identity Formation: the Caribbean Experience in Britain, London: Verso.

Jim, V., and Heather S., (1990) The International Trade in Wastes: A Greenpeace Inventory Washington: Greenpeace

Jordan, W., (2001) Black Over White: British Attitudes towards the Negro, Harmondsworth: Penguin.

Julian, C., (1996), Veers Le Choc social, Le Monde Diplomatique, September.

Kaplan, D., (1998), The Spatial Structure of Urban Ethnic Economies, Urban Geography 19: 489—501

Kapuscinski, R., (1997), Lapidarian 111, Warsaw: Czytelnik, pp.146

Karn, V., (1998) Race and Ethnicity in Housing: A Diversity of Experience, London: Routledge.

Keith, M., (1999) Rights and Wrongs: Youth, Community and Narratives of Racial Violence', in Cohen, P., (ed.), New
Ethnicities, Old racisms. London: Zed Books.

Kempe, R., (2000) child abuse, London: Fontana/Open Books.

Khanya, M., (2000) Guidelines for undertaking a regional/national Sustainable Rural Livelihoods study see www.khanya-mrc.co.za.

Kiernan, I.., (1998) Family resources Survey, London: Equal Opportunity Commisson.

Kim I., (1981) The New Urban Immigrants, Princeton University Press.

Klein, G., (1993) Education towards Race Equality, London: Cassell.

Klcin, N., (2001) No Logo. London: Flamingo, pp.XVII—XVIII.

Kracht, U., and Schulz, M., (1999) Food Security and Nutrition: The Global Challenge, New York: St Martin's Press. Strategies for
overcoming hunger and malnutrition.

Kapusciski, B. (1999) Food security: a conceptual basis in U. Kracht and M. Schulz (eds) Food Security and Nutrition· The Global Challenge, New York: St Martin's Press.

Karl, C., (1987) 'Recent Marxist Theories of Nationalism and the Issue of Racism'. British Journal of Sociology, XXXVIII, 1: 24—43.

Katz, I., (1996) The construction of Racial Identity in Children of Mixed Parentage: London Jessica Kingslcy.

Keith, M., (1993) Race, Riots and Policing: Lore and Disorder in a Multi-Racist Society. London: UCL Press.

Kochman, T., (1981) Classroom modalities: black and white communicative styles in the classroom. In N.
Mercer (ed.), Language in school and community, London: Edward Arnod.

Kymlicka, W., (1995) Multicultural Citizenship: A Liberal Theory of Minority Rights. Oxford: Clarendon Press.

Kymlika, W., (2000) Nation Building and Minority Rights: Comparing West and East, Journal of Ethnic and Migration Studies, vol.26, no.2.

Lawrence, M., (1980) Throwing a Naked Light on Political and Natural Gas, Daily Telegraph, 20 February.

Lawrence, M., (2000) The new Politics of poverty: the Non-working Poor in Britain, London: Basic Books

Leach, M., and Robin, M., (1999) (eds.) The Lie of the Land: Challenging Received Wisdom on the African Environment. London: International African Institute.

Lieberson, S., (1980) A Piece of the Pie, Berkeley, CA: University of California Press.

Little, K., (1997) African-Caribbeans in Britian, London: Routledge and Kegan Paul.

Liu, Y., (2003) Overtime work, insufficient sleep, and risk of non- fatal acute myocardial infarction in African-Caribbean men in Britain: Occupational and environmental medicine London: University of Minnesota Press.

Law, I., (1996) Racism, Ethnicity and Social Policy, London: Prentice Hall.

Lawrence, D., (1969) How prejudiced are we?, Race Today, October, 174-5

Lawrence, D., (1990) How Prejudiced are we? Race Today, October: 174-5

Lewis, G., and Phoenix, A., (2004) '"Race", "Ethnicity" and Identity', in K. Woodward (ed.), Questioning Identity. London: Routledge.

Light, I., (1972) Ethnic Enterprise in America, Berkeley, CA: University of California Press.

Litlewood, P., (1999) " Social Exclusion", Social Science teacher, Vol.29, no. 1

Liverpool Currier (1918) quoted in Peter Fryers

Loury, G. C., 1998, Discrimination in the Post-Civil Rights Era: Beyond Market Interactions, Journal of Economic Perspectives 12: 117—26.

MacMaster, N., (2001) Racism in Europe, London Palgrave Macmillan.

Malik, K., (1996) The Meaning of Race. London: Routledge.

Mamuwa, T., (2001) The effect of prejudice on Ethinic Minorities, New York: Sage

Marsh, K., (1994) Ethnic Minorities and the Labour Market, London, Tailstock.

Mason, P., (2002) "A Role for the Institution?", London: Oxford University Press.

Maxwell, S., and Frankenberger, T., (1992) Household Food Security: Concepts, Indicators, Measurements, New York and
Rome: UINICEF and IFAD.

McClelland, k., (1987) Time to work, time to live: some aspects of work and the re—formation of class in Britain, 1850—1880, in

MacDonald, R., (1997) "The Underclass and Social Exclusion", London: Routledge.

Macey, D., (2000) Frantz Fanon: A Life. London: Gretna Books.

Manchester Guardian

Mandy, T., (2005) Guardian news paper pp4.

Mark, M., (2005) Metro, Tuesday 25 October 2005, p2

Martin, B.,(2000) Between Camps: Nations, Culture and the Allure of Race. London: Allen Lane.

Mayor, B., (1992) Racism and Education, London: Sage.

Micheal, C., (2000) The sharing of Global Cake, Auckland, NZ: Heinemann.

Miles, R., (1993) Racism After Race relation, London: Routledge.

Milner, D., (1993) "Children and Race Ten Years On", London: Ward Lock Education.

Modood, T., (1997a) Ethnic Minorities in Britain, London: Policy Studies InstituteOFSTED, (1999) Raising the Attainment of Minority Ethnic Pupils, London: OFSTED

Modood, T., (1997b) Ethnic Minorities in Britain: Diversity and Disadvantage London: Policy Studies Institute.

Modood, T., and Werbner, P., (1997c) the Politics of Multi Culturalism in New Europe, London: Zed Book.

Modood, T., Beishon, G., and Virdee, N., (1994, & 1998) Suppression of the vulnerable black people, London: Zed book.

Mohammad, A., (1998) "The Role of Government in Britain's Racial Crisis", London: Sheed and Ward.

Mole, O., (1996) Untold hardship of Vulnerable black Children, London: Cambridge University press.

Morris, L., (2001) "Rights and Controls in the Management of Migration: the Case of Germany", Socialogical Review, vol.48,no.2.

Morrison, M., (2000) Inspecting Schools for Racial Equality, Stoke on Trent: Trentham.

Mullahs, P., (2000) Second generation African Youth: Identity and Ethnicity: New Community, 12:310-320

Murry, C., (1984) "Losing Ground", New York: Basic

Mynott, E., (2000) The Asylum Debate, Runnymade Bulletin, no.322.

Nafziger, E.W., and Auvinen, J., (1997) War, Hunger, and Displacement: An Econometric Investigation into the Sources of

Humanitarian Emergencies, Working Paper No. 142, World Institute for Development Economics Research, United Nations University.

Narayan, R., (1976) GRASSROOTS Newspaper Volume 4. No. 8 SeptemberOct0ber, Cricklewood To Leeds -The Cross-Country Legal Conspiracy, London.

National Minimum wage, Low pay Commission Report 2005

Nazroo, J., (1997) The Mental Health of Ethnic Minorities, London: Policy Studies Institute. New Society, 27 May 1971

Neil M., Phil O., and Sam M., (1993) Tears of the Crocodile: From Rio to Reality in the Developing World London: Pluto Press.

Nuttall, D., (1998) Differential School Effectiveness, "International Journal of Educational Research", vol.13.

Oliver, E., (2001) Social Change in Twentieth Century Europe, Milton Keynes and Philadelphia: Open University Press

Onselen, V., (1996) The Seed is Mine: The Life of Kas Maine, a South African Sharecropper, 1894—1985, New York: Hill and Wang

Owen, D., (2001) "Minority Ethnic Participation and Achievements in Education, Training and the Labour Market",
Department for Education and Employment, London: HMSO.

Offor, C., (1984) Contradictions of the out of work donation, London: Hutchinson, pp. 152—3.

Ogilvy, B., (1990) Staff attitudes and perceptions in multi-cultural nursery school: British Juornals of Developmental Psychology, 10:85-97

Paul, K., (1997) Whitewashing Britain, London: Cornell University Press.

Peach, C., (1996) Does Britain have Ghettoes?", Transactions of the British Institute of Geographers 21, 1: 216—35.

Peach, C., (1999) the force of West Indian Island Identities in Britain, London: Allen and Unwin.

Pinstrup-Andersen P., Pandya-Lorch, R., and Rosegrant, M.W., (1999) World Food Prospects: Critical Issues for the Early Twenty-First Century, 2020 Vision Food Policy Report, Washington DC: International Food Policy Research Institute.

Policy Studies Institute/London School of Economics, (20002) Working in Britain: The Work Foundation.

Pollard, S., (1963) Factory discipline in the industrial revolution, The Economic History Review, second series, 16: 254—71.

Portes, A., and Zhou, M., (1992) Gaining the Upper Hand: Old and New Perspectives in the Study of Ethnic Minorities, Ethnic and Racial Studies 15:

Powell, E., (1968) Freedom And Reality, London: Arrow Books.

Power, G., (2002) under pressure: Are we getting the most from our MPs, London: Hansard society.

Prime Minister's Strategy Unit Ethnic Minorities and the Labour Market, March 2003.

Osgerby, B., (1998) Youth in Britain Since 1945, Oxford: Blackwell.

Pacione, M., (1997) "Britain's Cities: Geographies of Division in Urban Britain", London: Zulu

Parekh, B., (1996) united Colour of Equality, New Statesman, 13 December.

Parker, D., (1994) "Encounters Across the Counter: Black People in Britain", New Community, vol.20, no4.

Peter, G., (1990) There Ain't No Black in the Union Jack, London: Hutchinson.

Peterson, P., (1992) the Urban Underclass and the Poverty Paradox, Washington, DC: Brookings Institution.

Peterson, W., (2001) Race and Inquality in Education, Milton Keynes: Open University Press.

Phizacklea, A., (1990) Labour and Racism, Oxford: Oxford University Press

Pierson, J., and Hallam, S., (2001) Ability Grouping in Education, London: Chapman.

Pilkington, A., (1993) Race and Ethnicity, Milton Keynes: Open University

Pollock, S., Breckenridge, C., and Chakrabarty, D., (2000) 'Cosmopolitanisms'. Public Culture, 12 (3): 577—91.

Portes, A., and Bach, R., (1985) Latin Journey, Berkeley, CA: University of California Press.

Powell, W., and Smith-Doerr, L., (1994) Networks and Economic Life, in N., Smelser and R.., Swedberg (eds.), The Handbook of Economic Sociology, Princeton University Press and New York: Russell Sage Foundation, pp. 368—402.

Race (1974) Towards Racial Justice, London Today Magazine. Volume 6 pp. 167-173

Race Today Collective. New Perspective On The Asian Struggle, Part 2. Race Grassroots Black Community News: Volume 4 No.3, page3 - 'What Is the BLF', 29 September, 1975. Published by The Black Liberation Front.

Ratcliffe, P., (1999) Housing Inequality and "Race": some Critical Reflections on the Concept of "Social Exclusion, Ethnic and Racial Studies, vol.22, no.1.

Rattansi, A., (2000) "Changing the Subject?" in Donald, A. and Rattansi, A. (eds) "Race, Culture and Difference, London: Sage.

Rattansi, A., (2003) 'Who's British? Prospect and the New Assimilationism', in Runnymede Trust (ed.), Cohesion, Community and Citizenship. London: Runnymede Trust.

Ray, W., (1970) Poverty and Exclusion of Young Caribbean's: Guardian,24 July

Reshuffle, M., (1989) Ethnic minority children in British Schools, Brighton: Harvester Press. Revolutionary Party, London.

Rex, J., (1971) Race, Community and conflict: a study of Sparkbrook, London: Oxford University Press.

Rex, J., (2000) Discrimination a scar in our conscience, London: zenith Books.

Rhany, M., (1779) the theory of social construct, Cambridge: MIT Press

Richard R., (1999) Philosophy and Social Hope. Penguin Books, p.203.

Richardson, R., (1988) Death, Dissection and the Destitute, London: phoenix press.

Robert, P., (2004) stressed parents failing teenagers, California: Simon and Schuster.

Robert, R., (1991) The Work of Nations, New York: Vintage Books

Robins, D., (1992) Tarnished Vision: Crime and Conflict in the Inner City. Glossary page 131. Published by Oxford University Press.

Robinson, V., (1998) Transients, Settlers and Refugees, Oxford: Clarendon.

Rory, R., (1998) 'Justice as a Larger Loyalty', in P. Cheah and B. Robbins (eds.),

Rowthorn, B., (2003) 'A Question of Responsibility'. Open Democracy www. opendemocracy.net/ debateSIartic40964SS

Race, (1976) Today Magazine Volume 8. No. 10. Pages 195-207. October 1976. Published by Race Today Collective, London.

Ramdin, R., (1997) The Making of Black working Class in Britain, Aldershot: Wildwood House.

Rampton, A., (1981) West Indian Children in Our Schools, London: HMSO Cmnd. 8273.

Ratliffe, P., (1996) Geographical Spread, Spatial Concentration and Internal Migration, London: HMSO.

Reardon, T., and Matlon, P., (1989) Seasonal food insecurity and vulnerability in drought-affected regions of Burkina Faso in D.E.,

Sahn (ed.) Seasonal Variation in Third World Agriculture: The Consequences for Food Security, Baltimore and London: Johns Hopkins University Press.

Rex, J., and Mason, D., (1986) (eds.) Theories of Race and Ethnic Relations. Cambridge: Cambridge University Press.

Richard R., (1998) Achieving our Country. Harvard University Press, p.85.

Richard S., (1990)The Corrosion of Character: The Personal Consequences of Work in the New Capitalism. New York:
W.W. Norton & Co., pp.47—51.

Rose, J., (1972) Colour and Race: a report on British Race Relations, London: Oxford University Press.

Rose, N., (1999) Powers of Freedom: Re framing Political Thought. Cambridge:

Rose, S., (1976) Scientific Racism and IQ, in Nicholas Rose (ed.) "The Political Economy of Science", London: Macmillan.

Rose, E., (1969) Colour and Citizenship: a report on British Race Relations, London: Oxford University Press.

Rowlingson, J., and Mckey, H., (1999) Young Caribbean Men and the Labour Market: A Comparison with Other Ethnic Groups, York: Joseph Rowntree Foundation.

Scoones, I., (1998) Sustainable rural livelihoods: a framework for analysis Working Paper 72, University of Sussex: Institute of Development Studies.

Sen, A., (1981) Poverty and Famines, Oxford: Oxford University Press.

Skellington, K., (1992) Racism and Anti Racism, London: Sage.

Smith D., (1977) Racial Disadvantage in Britain, Harmondsworth: Pdiguin

Smith P., and Prior, G., (1997) the Fourth National Survey of Ethnic Minorities: Technical Report, London: National Centre for Social Research.

Smith, M., Pointing, J., and Maxwell, S. l., (1993) Household Food Security: Concepts and Definitions: An Annotated Bibliography, Development Bibliography 8, Brighton: Institute of Development Studies.

Solomos, J., (1999) Ethnic and Racial Studies Today, London: Routledge.

Solomos, J., (2001) Racism and Migration in Western Europe", Oxford, Berg.

Stewart, R., (2001) Collin English Dictionary, Glasgow: Omnia Books Limited.

Stroude, L., (1986) Profile: Courtney Laws. 'SELF-HELP NEWS' No 10. Pages. Published by The National Federation Of Self-Kelp Organisations (UK), London

Stwart, A., (2000) "Social Inclusion: An Introduction", London: Macmillan. Sunday Telegraph (2001) October 28

Swaminathan, M.S., (1986) Sustainable Nutrition Security for Africa: Lessons from India, San Francisco: The Hunger Project.

Swann, M., (1995) Education for All: A Review of Research into the Education of Pupils of West Indian Origin, Windsor: NFER Nelson.

Sagger, S., (1992) the Dog that didn't Bark, Manchester: Manchester University Press.

Scarman, L., (1981) The scarman Report: The Brixton Disorders, London: HMSO.

Stephen, S., (1996) Children and the Politics of Culture, Princeton: Princeton University Press.

Streeter, R., (2001) Transforming charity: towards a results-Oriented Social Sector, New York: Hudson Institute.

Swann, M., (1985) Education for All, London: HMSO Comnd. 9453.

Taylor, P., (1992) The Politics of Race and Immigration in Britain, Developments in Politics, vol.4.

Taylor, S., (1992) The Politics of Race and Immigration in Britain, Developments in Politics, vol.4. The Black House 27 July.

Today Magazine, Vol. 11 No. 4. pages 104-105, November December, 1979, London.

Tomlinson, S., (2000) Ethnic Minority and Education: New Disadvantages, in Cox, T., (ed.) Combating Educational Disadvantage, London: Falmer.

Townsend, p., (1993) Poverty in Europe, in Z. Ferge and SM. Miller (eds) Dynamics of Deprivation. Aldershot: Gower, p.73.

Thomas C., (1991) Africa and the World Economy: Caught Between a Rock and a Hard Place in John, H., and Donald, R., eds, Africa in World Politics Boulder, Cob.: Westview Press,

Timberlake, L., (1985) Africa in Crisis. London: Earthscan

Titmuss, R., (1968) Commitment to welfare, London: Allen & Unwin, p.143.

Tomlinson, S., (2000) Ethnic Minorities and Education: New disadvantages, London: Falmer.

Townend, P., (1992) Inequality in Health, Harmondsworth: Penguin

Townsend, P., (1989) intellectual development: birth to adulthood, New York: Academic Press.

Troyna, B., (1984) "Fact or Artefact? The Eductional Underachievement of Black Pupils", British Journal of Sociology of Education, vol.5, no.2.

Troyna, B., (1990) Beyond Reasonable Doubt? Researching "Race" in Educational settings, Oxford Review of Education, vol.21,no4.

Troyna, B., and Williams, J., (1986) Racism, Education and the State, London: Croom Helm

Udoh, V., (1994) ed. Environmental and Economic Dilemmas of Developing Countries: Africa in the 21st Century. Westport: Conn Praeger

Virdee, S., (1998) Ethnic Minority Families, London:Polity Studies Institute.

Van, T., (1991) Racism and the Press, London: Routledge.

Vines, V.,(1995a) 'Ethnic Entrepreneurs and Street Rebels; Looking Inside the Inner City', in S., Pile and N., Thrift (eds.), Mapping the Subject. London: Routledge

Waldinger, R., (1996) Still the Promised City: African-Americans and New Immigrants, New York: Harvard University Press.

Walvin, C., (2000) Black Caricature: the Root of Racialism, London: Hutchinson.

Ward, R., (1971) Exclusion in the means of plenty, London: Pluto Press.

Werbner, P., (1992) "The Dialectics of Cultural Hybridity", London: Zed.

Who is Educating who (1997)? "The black educational movement and struggle for power", Race Today magazine, Volume 7. No 8. pp. 182

Wood, W., (1999) Keep the faith baby, London: The Bible Reading fellowship pp.10-16. www.BBC.co.uk

Walker, M., (1978) "The National front", New York: Fontana

Walvin, J., (1998) "Black Caricature: the roots of Racialism", London Hutchinson

Wilson 2000a, "Ethnic Employment Penalties in Britain," Journal of Ethnic and Migration Studies, 26, 3: 389—4 16.

Wilson, W., (1987) The Truly Disadvantaged: The Inner City, The Underclass and Public Policy, University of Chicago Press

Ward, R., (1971) Coloured families in council houses: progress and prospect in Manchester: Council for community relations

Wood, W., (1994) Keep the Faith Baby, pages 10-16. published by The Bible Reading Fellowship, 1994

Woodward, K., (1997) Identity and Difference, Oxford: Oxford University Press.

Woollacott, m., (1997) Behind the myth of the self—made man, Guardia,,, 17 May.

www.actionaid.org.uk

www.statistics.gov.uk

Young, H., (2001a) Labour's Law of Ethnic Punishment Shames us all, The Guardian, 8 may.

Young, H., (2001b) The Right to be British, The Guardian, 12 November.

Printed in the United States
by Baker & Taylor Publisher Services